CW00406383

‘UP THE CLARETS!’

The story of Burnley Football Club

'UP THE CLARETS!'

The Story of Burnley Football Club

DAVID WISEMAN

ROBERT HALE : LONDON

First published in Great Britain 1973

ISBN 0 7091 4310 9

Robert Hale & Company
63 Old Brompton Road
London S.W.7

Dedicated to

my grandad who encouraged me to support Burnley,
my father who first took me to watch Burnley,
my mother who put up with Burnley night and day,
my wife who so patiently supports a Burnley supporter,
and Rebecca who will one day be another Burnley fan!

PRINTED IN GREAT BRITAIN BY
BRISTOL TYPESETTING CO. LTD.
BARTON MANOR - ST. PHILIPS
BRISTOL

CONTENTS

ACKNOWLEDGEMENTS

In compiling the history of Burnley F.C., I wish to acknowledge my indebtedness to various people. In particular, I would like to thank my good friend and fellow Burnley fan, Brian Hobbs of 8, Chantry Road, Thornbury, Bristol, for his help in compiling the chapter on statistics; Mr Richard Caul, the Burnley Borough Librarian, for his enthusiasm and constant encouragement; Mr Ross Burton, head of the Burnley Central Reference Library, for his help in gathering material; the *Burnley Express* for their help in supplying several photographs; my wife Margaret, and Mrs Beryl Gartside for typing the manuscript; and various fellow Burnley supporters for kindly loaning their cherished material. Finally, I wish to express my appreciation to Mr G. Chesterfield of Messrs Robert Hale and Co. for his advice and guidance during the production of this book.

ILLUSTRATIONS

FOREWORD

Burnley Football Club is all things to all people who follow the game of soccer. To the Claret and Blue fan, it's his Saturday afternoon and Tuesday evening rendezvous, where he can let off steam by bawling, swearing, hurling insults or singing praises at players, referees even managers, according to the state of the game.

To the rest of the country it is a little town team that has achieved a considerable amount of success and figured quite a lot in the news, one way or another.

To me, it was and still is, a part of my life, because even though I left Turf Moor in unfortunate circumstances a decade ago, the memories of great moments, and sad ones, still pulsate strongly in my veins. In a flash I can turn the clock back to almost any moment during my thirteen-year stint there, and relive vividly the sights and sounds and smells of oil and sweat. Incidents are as clear now as the day they happened. It's possible even to recall the volume of noise, or lack of it, made by the fans on certain occasions.

But this isn't by any means an extraordinary gift. Any footballer is capable of reproducing, either as a mental picture or as a description, incidents in which he was involved years and years ago. But delving into one's store of memories has a drawback. Inevitably recollections of the good times, the tremendous matches, the outstanding goals, and the great players, cloud everything else. No one wants to turn the clock back to a mood of sadness or bitterness, to periods of frustrations and miserable performances, to times when one's faith was shaken in either club or player.

And it is here that the Rev David Wiesman scores. '*Up the Clarets!*' is a history book, written by a man devoted to Burnley Football Club, who has methodically recorded the struggling and mediocre times as well as the glorious days, from the birth of the club to the present. How many hours, weeks and months did he spend in Burnley Library, searching for every minute scrap of news and fact written about the Clarets since the formation of the club in the 1880s? His is a family steeped in Turf Moor soccer. Three generations have supported Burnley through hail and rain, and as long as the Turf remains a green field, it would be difficult to imagine a match there without a Wiseman in the crowd.

This book will be of interest to everyone between the ages of nine and ninety—at least one section will captivate each generation—that period in time which each fan remembers best.

A few may recall the earliest days, others the Bob Kelly era; for some it will be the immediate post-war Alan Brown side, whilst the not too old will relive the Harry Potts managerial successes, and the youngsters of course, will read starry-eyed of Jimmy Adamson's triumphant return to the First Division. Some big city clubs have achieved more, but certainly no side with similar resources has accomplished as much.

Burnley Football Club was my life for thirteen years, the town has been my home for over twenty, and there exists a bond which time will never sever. There must be many soccer lovers, not only in East Lancashire, but throughout the British Isles who feel passionately for this little town team, and it is they, and I, who are eternally grateful that David Wiseman's devotion was so powerful that it compelled him to write this book and present us with an almost kick for kick account of the Clarets' history.

Burnley — JIMMY MCILROY

INTRODUCTION

Burnley Football Club, for the last 90 years, has been as much a part of the local East Lancashire scene as the mill chimneys, the cobbled streets and gas lamps, that all went to create the Lancashire 'image'. But now the chimneys are coming down, the cobbled streets are being re-laid, and the old 'gormless' gas lamp is a curiosity piece at Towneley Hall. Burnley is now very much an old town with a new face, new fly-over roads, new shopping precincts, new houses, new industries. And as modern as anywhere else in Burnley, is Turf Moor, the home of Burnley Football Club.

This is the story of that football club, so long a part of the local scene, so often perhaps taken for granted, but so regularly putting the name of Burnley in newspaper headlines and on television screens all over the country.

I can't remember when I first went to Turf Moor, or the first game I saw, but it was some time during the 1946–47 season, when Burnley won promotion, reached Wembley, and I was seven! Those first years in the late forties, stood on the terraces of Turf Moor, will be forever linked in my memories with dinners of tripe or black puddings before the match, and teas of cheese and onion pie at my grandparents' home on Hollingreave Road in Burnley. My grandad had watched Burnley when they wore green jerseys, my father worshipped at the feet of Bob Kelly, and I was to grow up spellbound by Jimmy 'Mac'.

With modern stands, floodlights, development associations, and even greater things to come, we don't lack many things at Burnley these days, but what I have always wanted to see is a book to record for everyone, the history of what is a most remarkable club. I have waited long enough, for well over twenty years, so I decided that I'd better do something about it.

This is the result.

Burnley — David Wiseman

ONE

IN THE BEGINNING . . .

In *The History of the Lancashire Football Association*, written in 1928, it says, 'If ever a team were called on to start at the very bottom, it was the Burnley Football Club'. Well, the writer of that statement ought to know, because he was Mr Charles E. Sutcliffe, at one time or another, a Burnley player, League referee, Burnley F.C. director, and President of the Football League.

This then, is the story of Burnley Football Club, and we start where they began—'at the very bottom'.

The earliest mention of football in Burnley occurs in a magistrates' order of 1751, that the constable, churchwardens, and overseers should prosecute those 'idle persons' who practise on Sundays 'football, leaping, quoits, bowls, hunting, tippling in ale-houses, swearing and cursing', and so 'profane the Sabbath and absent themselves from Divine Service'. The game, if it can be so called when no rules were observed, was undoubtedly played in Burnley long before 1751, and though Sabbatarians condemned it as a Sunday game, there was no objection to it as a week-day sport until the increased number of houses and windows made 'playing in the streets' a very undesirable practice. Actually, the first match recorded in the local press was played in March 1876 between teams of half-timers working at Lowerhouse Mill; it doubtless resembled those of the mid-nineteenth century when village played village with teams of 20, 30 or even 100 on each side, in which the best runners formed the forward lines.

But where did the Football Club come from? The Football Club was really the offspring of the marriage of the Association Code, as played by the leading amateur clubs of the age, Old Etonians, Wanderers, Royal Engineers, and the like, and the Industrial Revolution, upon which towns like Burnley, Blackburn, Bolton and Accrington had been built.

In the 1870's King Cotton reigned in Lancashire. Smoky towns filled with thousands of back-to-back houses were to be found scattered all over North-East and South-East Lancashire. Around that time a serious decline in agricultural prosperity coincided with the great industrial boom in the North and the Midlands. Thousands of workers poured into the Lancashire towns like Burnley and Nelson. Many of these workers had their recreations like rugby and cricket, and because of this influx, many sports and social clubs began to spring up, especially in the well-attended Sunday Schools.

During those early years, rugby was very popular in and around Burnley; one of the leading teams at the time was Burnley Rovers, who played on Calder Vale. But in the late seventies, it is said that the club ceased to exist, and a meeting was called under the auspices of the Y.M.C.A., with the curate of St Peter's, the Rev M. W. Hill, presiding. It was decided to form a club under the title of the Y.M.C.A., but the name was soon changed once again to the Rovers. Some members of the original Burnley Rovers helped to forward the movement, and after much discussion, it was decided to adhere to the rugby code.

On May 18, 1882, Burnley Rovers Football Club, which had till then played rugby, held a special meeting at the Bull Hotel, with Mr A. Birley presiding. The Secretary, Mr G. C. Waddington, read a report showing that the club had 90 members. Mr Harry Bradshaw moved the recommendation of the Committee 'that the club in future play under Association Rules'. Mr Barratt seconded, and the following officers were appointed; President, Mr C. J. Massey (who had been a prominent player with the earlier Burnley Rovers rugby team); Vice-Presidents, Mr J. G. Broxup, Mr Monkman, Mr J. H. Whittaker, Mr A. Greenwood; Treasurer, Mr Baron; Secretary, Mr G. C. Waddington; Committee, Mr H. Bradshaw, Mr J. W. Harling, Mr T. Midgeley, Mr A. Birley, Mr W. Brown, Mr C. J. Hargreaves, Mr E. Halstead, Mr W. Hawcridge, Mr J. Stansfield and Mr A. Sutcliffe.

On August 10, 1882, a practice match between the newly formed Burnley Football Club (they had dropped the term 'Rovers'), and another local team, Burnley Wanderers, resulted in a 4–0 victory for the Calder Vale team. They also played a series of evening trial games 'to enable them to select the best possible elevens for the coming season'. To begin with, there was very little change in the players who had played rugby the previous season, and who were now learning the new game. Men like Harry Bradshaw, Fergie Slater, J. W. Holden, C. E. Sutcliffe and W. Brown were among those who one season played rugby, and the next were trying their hand, or rather their feet, at soccer.

In the *Burnley Express* of September 30, 1882, there is a report of a game played on the previous Saturday. 'On Saturday last, both the first and the second teams of Burnley and Brierfield had a trial of strength, and in both cases, victory was declared for Burnley;

the first team beating Brierfield by two goals to none, and the second obtaining a signal victory over Brierfield by ten goals (five of which were scored by W. Brown and two by A. Sutcliffe) to nil.' The following Saturday, Read beat Burnley by seven goals to three, and Burnley's team read: Goal, Birley; backs, Hargreaves and Marsland; half-backs, Walton and Waddington; centre, French and Brown; left-wing, Turner and Barlow; right-wing, Midgeley (captain) and Harling.

Of course, it would be more like a story from the *Wizard* or *Champion* to read that Burnley began winning games easily, right from the start. They didn't! One old player at Burnley said long ago: 'Goals were so easily scored against us, we were thankful records were not kept!' In those early days, Burnley wore amber and black shirts, and some local people christened them 'The Hornets'. We should remember that there was very little organisation in those first years, and the majority of Burnley's games in that first 1882–83 season were local friendlies against teams like Read, Great Harwood, Clitheroe and Kirkham.

But in the *Burnley Express* of October 14, 1882, we reach an early milestone in the club's history, the first real competitive match, a Lancashire Cup game.

'Today, the Burnley Football Club play their first competition for the Lancashire Challenge Cup at Calder Vale. Whilst wishing them every success in their endeavour to introduce good football into Burnley, we may say that we think there is the foundation of a good strong team in the town, and if the players will only try to become more acquainted with each other's capabilities, and study more the science of the game, we feel convinced that success will ultimately attend their efforts and place them in the front ranks of Lancashire football players. May the field be a large one, and may our local football players work shoulder to shoulder and lower the colours of the Astley Bridge team.'

Four days later, the paper summarily reported: 'Burnley v Astley Bridge. On Saturday afternoon last, these two clubs met on the ground of the former at Calder Vale to contest in the first round for the Lancashire Challenge Cup. Astley Bridge had it all their own way throughout, and won the game eight goals to none. A large company assembled to witness the match. This is the first year the Burnley club has played Association rules. Team: Goal, H. Walton; full-backs, S. Hargreaves and A. Birley; half-backs, J. Crabtree and G. Waddington; centres, W. Brown and S. Barlow; right-wing, T. Midgeley (captain) and F. Slater; left-wing, J. Marsland and T. French'. One only needs to compare that team with the previous one three weeks earlier, to realise how players were switched and swapped around . . . Birley from goal to full-back, Walton from half-back to goalkeeper, and Marsland from full-back to left-wing!

Another red-letter day in the club's story took place the following Saturday, when the first ever match took place between Burnley and Blackburn Rovers (Oct 21, 1882). The Rovers even at that time were a well established team, and so, of course, it was only their *second* team that they sent to Burnley!

'A match played between two teams of Burnley and Blackburn Rovers took place at Calder Vale on Saturday last. The Rovers had the game in their hands throughout, and won by ten goals to none. In justice to the Burnley players, it must be stated that this is their first season of playing association rules, and consequently they are not as well up as might be desired. Nevertheless they played very creditably, especially Chase (goal) and Brown (centre).' The team was goal, Chase; backs, Birley and Hargreaves; half-backs, Waddington, Cross and Marsland; right, Eastwood and Crabtree; left, French and Slater; centre, Brown.

Soon after the Blackburn game, Burnley met Read in a return game, and it seems they made determined efforts to improve and strengthen their team. They obviously succeeded, because Burnley came out winners by five goals to one. However, Burnley's pre-match tactics aroused much local feeling, as can be sensed by the following letter to the editor of the *Burnley Express*.

> 'Dear Sir, The Committee of the Read Cricket and Football Club beg to call the attention of the Burnley Football Club with regard to the publication of the match on Calder Vale on Saturday, October 28th, as they procured the services of Messrs W. H. Moorhouse and T. Bury (Darwen), Lathom (Blackburn), Clegg (Enfield), and Waddington (Accrington) and never advised us. When we aranged the match it was for Burnley and not North-East Lancashire, and in future, should any arrangements be made, we shall thank them to play as per agreement, and publish it accordingly.
>
> J. Walmsley (Assistant Secretary)'

It was obvious that already the pressures of wanting to have a successful team were causing Burnley to look elsewhere for players, other than fielding 'the locals'. Little did they realise what they were beginning! A prophetic note was struck in the Burnley v Haslingden match report of February 1883: 'A word of commendation is certainly due to all the players who were in grand form, more especially Smith and Crabtree, who have the making of two good young players, if they will only practise, and who on Saturday, played very creditably'. Young Crabtree, thirteen years later, turned out to be the captain of England!

It was soon after the Haslingden game that the Football Club moved to Turf Moor, for on February 17, 1883, Burnley played for the first time on Turf Moor against Rawtenstall. But once again,

Burnley failed to rise to the occasion, and were humbled in front of their own supporters, losing 6–3.

All this time, many other association football clubs were springing up locally . . . Burnley Olympic, Union Star, United Rangers, Brierfield Rovers, Burnley Ramblers, Burnley Wanderers, Burnley Ebenezer Rangers, St Stephen's, and several other church teams too. And so it was that in 1883, thirteen local teams competed for Dr Dean's Cup. Dr Dean was the medical officer for Burnley, and he donated the cup to be competed for by local teams . . . the gate money to be given to the proposed new Burnley Hospital. Burnley Football Club were one of the thirteen local teams, and they played a match, 'Probables v Improbables' in order to pick a team to compete. (Believe it or not, the 'Improbables' won 8–3!). The team they chose beat another Burnley team, Pentridge Rovers 3–0, and eventually won through to the Final.

In that first Final of the Hospital Cup (for that was what this competition grew to be called, becoming eventually one of the largest money-raising and talent-producing competitions in the country), Burnley beat Burnley Ramblers 2–1. The winning team was: R. B. Chase; S. Hargreaves and J. Marsland; H. Culpan, G. C. Waddington and T. Cross; J. Eastwood, A. Birley, W. Brown, T. Midgeley (captain) and R. Horsfield. The 'gate' came to £30 15s 6d—the largest sum ever raised at a football match in Burnley.

And so Burnley's first season as a football club came to a close. In it they played 25 games, won 11, drew 1 and lost 13. In reviewing the season, 'Hawkeye' in the *Express* said 'Burnley Football Club should not have to play against other Burnley teams—the cricket club don't! They should play foreigners' . . . by whom we presume, 'Hawkeye' meant teams like Blackburn Rovers, Liverpool and Preston.

In 1883, the game of association football was quite different from the game we recognise today as soccer. Some of the old-timers would be truly bewildered to run onto Turf Moor today and see stands, terraces, and floodlighting, and it would take them more than a season to appreciate the changes in rules since their time.

The players themselves looked different, with moustaches the order of the day. They wore long trousers or knicker-bockers—even as late as 1904, an F.A. rule insisted that shorts should be long enough to cover the knees. They wore tight jerseys, and on their heads, caps, often with a tassel.

Besides the players, three other people were involved in the game, two umpires and a referee. Each club appointed its own umpire, often the club secretary, to officiate in games, and their duties were to control the game, one umpire in each half of the field. Players appealed to the umpire nearest the incident for his opinion, and the only time the referee was involved was when umpires disagreed on a decision. In effect, the referee was there to decide between the two umpires, rather than the two teams.

The pitch looked quite different too . . . football pitches were usually much larger than they are today. The laws of the game instructed that the maximum length of the pitch could be 200 yards, whilst the maximum breadth was 100 yards. There was no penalty area, cross-bars were just beginning to take over from the tapes that had stretched between the goal-posts, and no goal nets.

Players, officials, pitches, and the rules too, were quite different from what we take for granted today. It was only in 1882 that the two-handed throw-in was introduced—previously the one-handed throw had been allowed. If a foul-throw occurred, a free-kick was awarded, instead of another throw-in. Players could not score direct from corner-kicks, and had to stand only six yards away from the ball for free-kicks, instead of the present ten yards. There were no such things as penalty-kicks, because there were no penalty areas. Previous to 1890 when the penalty-kick was introduced, it was left to the referee to decide whether to allow a goal *against* an offending player. The goalkeeper was allowed to handle the ball anywhere in his own half—indeed the only reason for having the *half-way line* was to limit the goalkeeper's freedom of handling the ball. 'The Committee does not consider a goalkeeper to be in defence of his own goal when he is in his opponent's half of the field, therefore a goalkeeper is prohibited from using his hands in his opponent's half'.

If Burnley had caused a stir by utilising players from outside their town boundaries in 1882–83, the following season was to see the club hitting the national sporting headlines in their attempts, lawful and otherwise, to improve their team. Interest in the game was growing at such a rate, and competition becoming so fierce, that most clubs were making every effort to improve their team by fielding better players. In 1883, Welsh, Irish and Scots were pouring into England, and particularly the North, to find work. Adverts in the Glasgow papers drew attention to jobs in Darwen, Bolton, Burnley, Blackburn and Preston.

In the summer of 1883, Daniel Friel, a Vale of Leven player, who had assisted Accrington, was persuaded to come to Burnley and coach the Burnley players. Later in the season, Burnley enlisted Jack 'Tich' Young of Bolton, Harper of Halliwell, and Jack Gair from Hearts. Daniel Friel accepted a tempting offer to stay at Burnley—as much as he had earned at Accrington during the winter months, all the year round, and ten shillings a week extra during the football season. Many Scottish players were being 'imported' by other Lancashire clubs, and so Burnley began to look more and more to the North for talent.

The poaching of players caused great unrest north of the border, and in later years, Burnley scouts used to tell of those early days when it was a risky thing to go to Scotland searching for players. Many was the time that scouts had unsigned notes slipped underneath their hotel bedroom door, warning them to 'get out of town, or else . . .!' On one occasion a member of the Burnley committee had to take refuge in a Dumbarton public house from a crowd of 500 men and women who had assembled 'to guard their own'. In the end he was made to promise never to return to Dumbarton. It was said that Mr E. Mitchell, Mr G. Armistead and Mr Harry Bradshaw, members of the Burnley Football Club committee, had always either just been to Scotland, or were just going there. Wages of course were small, though jobs were found for many of the imported players.

'The Scots crowded every football team in Lancashire, and in one particular case, only a single Englishman was included in the team, and he was said to have felt lonely', wrote one observer of the times. That team was Burnley, and the 'lonely Englishman' was Leonard Metcalfe. Instead of Lancashire 'locals' like Wigglesworth, Hargreaves and Sutcliffe, Burnley were now playing players like Bryce, Harper, Gair, Friel, Shiel, Beattie, McCrae and McNee. All these men were being paid to play for Burnley, though for the majority of them, it was only something like a half-crown a game.

In 1883–84, Burnley decided against joining the English Football Association. Soon afterwards, a rule was passed banning clubs from playing teams outside the Association, especially those who fielded professionals. Burnley stuck to their guns, and found themselves outlawed by the country! Most clubs, even the local teams like Blackburn Rovers and Darwen, cancelled their fixtures with Burnley. Burnley were even mentioned in one national newspaper as a 'notorious club'.

But other Lancashire teams weren't quite so honest it seems, and they remained in the Association whilst still playing professionals. Accrington were expelled, having been found guilty of giving an inducement to one Beresford, 'formerly of Stavely, now of Church' to join them. After a drawn cup-tie at Preston in January 1884, Upton Park protested against Preston, about the inclusion of undisguised professionals in the Preston side. Preston were thrown out of the competition, but William Sudell, a cotton manufacturer and a man of influence, who had founded the North End club, spoke up in true Northern bluntness. Professionalism, he said, was known to be common. Moreover, he protested, it was in no way harmful to the game. As the season drew on, several other Lancashire clubs were suspended. At the rate things were going, soon there would once again be only the traditionally amateur teams like the Old Etonians and the Royal Engineers playing football, and doubts were even cast as to whether men were being paid to join the Royal Engineers in order just to play football!

A typical Burnley team that played through that controversial 1883–84 season looked like: Wigglesworth; J. Gair and Whitehead; Harper, Birley and Waddington; Bryce and Walton; Ronaldson and W. Gair; Friel. Once again the club made a rapid exit from the Lancashire Challenge Cup, being beaten at Turf Moor, 4–1 by South Shore. The number of clubs in the Hospital Cup increased to 26, but Burnley beat Trinity in the Final to capture Dr Dean's trophy for the second season running. The purely local eleven that won the Hospital Cup read: J. Wigglesworth; S. Hargreaves and L. Metcalfe; H. Culpan, J. W. Harling and T. Cross; F. Towler, C. Fulton, A. Birley, H. Walton and T. Midgeley.

But though Burnley was the town's premier club, their reputation was challenged most of all by their greatest rivals at the time, nearby Padiham, known locally as 'The Pads'. The first time the two teams met in 1883–84, Burnley were thrashed to the tune of nine goals to one. When the clubs met again at Turf Moor in March 1884, over 12,000 people turned up to see the game, to create the earliest ground record attendance. Once again, Padiham won, this time 4–2, and so established themselves beyond doubt as the leading football club in the district, much to the chagrin of the Burnley team and their followers. Altogether that season, Burnley played 37 games, won 19 drew 5, lost 11, whilst two games were unfinished.

On October 10, 1884, Mr Sudell of Preston, convened a meeting of Lancashire representatives at Bolton. Because Burnley had such an interest in the outcome of the meeting, the Turf Moor club hired a horse and trap and went round all the little clubs in remote places to persuade them to go to Bolton. Their efforts were successful, for practically all the football clubs in Lancashire, except Blackburn Rovers and Blackburn Olympic, attended the meeting. Messrs Leech, Bradshaw and Tillotson represented Burnley at the Bolton assembly. Later there was a meeting at Blackburn, and then a third meeting of the 'rebels' took place at Manchester on October 30, 1884, at which it was proposed to form a break-away union to be known as the British Football Association. Support for the proposed B.F.A. came from 28 clubs (including Burnley); indeed all of them, with the exception of Sunderland and Aston Villa, were from Lancashire. The threat of such action was sufficient to make the F.A. act, and in 1885, it was agreed that professionals should be allowed to compete in all Cup competitions, County and Inter-Association matches, provided they comply with certain provisions.

This new rule, however, came too late for Burnley to field their full Scottish team in the Lancashire Cup, so they had to play their second team, as the first team was ineligible. Once again, they lost interest in the competition at the first hurdle, losing away to Bradshaw (Bolton) 2–1.

To add to the confused position regarding amateur/professional and Scottish/English players, in December 1884, the Scottish Association published a list of outlawed Scottish players, who had broken the law with regard to professionalism and moved South. Nine Burnley first team players were named. In an effort to improve relationships, Burnley invited three Scottish teams to Turf Moor in 1884. The Cowlairs drew 2–2 with Burnley; Kilmarnock beat the Lancashire team 3–2, whilst Burnley avenged themselves 4–0 against Glasgow Northern. In the Hospital Cup, Burnley, to make things more competitive for the other Burnley organisations, entered their Reserve team. And lost!

But, *the* big game of the 1884–85 season took place at Padiham on December 13, 1884, when the local rivals, clashed head-on once again. This time it was Burnley who came out on top, victors by 4–0. Joy amongst the Burnley supporters, and in the town's papers was inexpressible, and the following 'funeral card' was published in the local press the following week.

R.I.P.

Lament of the Padiham Footballites on Burnley winning by four to nothing Dec. 13th, 1884

Alas for Padiham players
Renown has from them gone.
The Burnley lads have thrashed them
By four clear goals to none.
For several years, the former
A good and well trained band
In summer or in winter,
Have held the upper hand.

But now alas no longer
Can Padiham claim the name
Of being the best hands at
Our national winter game
The Scottish Burnley players
Have shown them how to play
Tho' Padihamites were saying
Four to one on I'll lay.

The game was well contested
And each man he did try
To score against his opponents
And oft at goal did shy
But 'twas only at the last half
After all was said and done
That Padihamites discovered
They'd lost by four to none.

Then from the team's supporters
There rose a mighty shout
Which could be heard at Burnley
Or somewhere thereabout.
In an hour from the finish
'Twas impossible to roam
And find a Padihamite.
Each had journeyed to his home.

Whilst one of the earliest and one of the best of all local football writers, 'On The Ball', who wrote in Lancashire dialect for the *Burnley and East Lancashire Mid-Weekly Gazette*, wrote in his usual droll style, 'Eh ye Pads—you don't know how I and others have thirsted since March last, for an opportunity of turning the tables round against you'.

During that 1884–85 season, Burnley played a total of 64 games, winning 36, drawing 10, and losing 18.

Two of the games that 1884–85 season were when Burnley met Blackburn Rovers for the first time since October 1882. (Remember, Burnley had been 'outlawed' from playing against Association teams like Blackburn). Both games were at Burnley, the Rovers winning the first 4–2, but Burnley gaining ample revenge in the return game, winning 5–1. (Considering that Blackburn won the F.A. Cup for the second successive time that season, this 5–1 win was quite a famous victory for the Brun-side club.) And when Blackburn won the F.A. Cup for the third consecutive season in 1885–86, they played three 'friendlies' against Burnley, and didn't win one of them; two draws and a 2–0 victory for Burnley being the result of their clashes. But let us tell the full story . . . the Rovers didn't always play their best players when they met Burnley.

The probable reason for this was that Burnley (and indeed every other Lancashire football team) were very much the poor relations of Blackburn Rovers in the 1880's.

Blackburn Rovers were formed seven years before Burnley, and they were playing in F.A. Cup Finals before Burnley even began to play football in 1882. In the mid-eighties, they were playing all the country's leading teams, Queens Park, West Bromwich Albion, Aston Villa and the like; fixtures with local teams like Padiham, Darwen and Burnley only helped to fill in vacant Saturdays. So because of this, it wasn't always the Rovers' star players who came to Turf Moor. Burnley weren't the only team to be slighted in this fashion. On one occasion Darwen, on seeing the Rovers team full of reserves run onto the field, calmly walked off, and made their own reserves get changed to play the match! The following report of the Burnley v Blackburn Rovers game played at Turf Moor in October 1885, describes the casual attitude of the Rovers' team to local derbies with Burnley. 'Considerably after the time announced for the commencement of the match, only six of the Rovers had put in an appearance. Eventually, three more players showed themselves, and after the contest had commenced, a tenth man joined the ranks of the visitors, and this was the number that contended the game'. The game in question resulted in a 1–1 draw. On another occasion, after Burnley had beaten a weakened Blackburn team in 1886, the *Burnley Gazette* said 'If they do it again, let them play Burnley Wanderers!'

Another drawback to Blackburn fielding their reserve team, was that when Burnley did win, they didn't get much credit for the feat. 'As I said before, the Rovers played their full strength team, whilst Burnley on the other hand were without the assistance of McLintock in goal, and Friel in the centre. The *Manchester Courier*, in a report of the match, no doubt sent in from Blackburn, says the Rovers had hard lines. Had not Burnley hard lines on more than one occasion? The fact is that the team who exhibited the best play, won the match. Then why not say so? When a team holding the position of Blackburn Rovers is beaten on merit, there is every reason that the team which inflicts the defeat should have every credit for so doing, but I find that this is not always the case'. (Burnley 2 Blackburn Rovers 0, *Burnley Gazette*, December 1885).

About that time, the young football club at Turf Moor reached another milestone in their history. They competed in the F.A. Cup for the first time ever. Even this occasion was marred by the continuing amateur-professional battle, for Burnley were told that they could not play the Scottish players they had imported into the side. If they did play, and as a result won, the team would not be allowed to go forward to the subsequent round. After much negotiation to try and overcome this ruling, Burnley turned out their entire reserve eleven rather than resign from the competition. The outcome was disastrous, for against a team from nearby Darwen—Darwen Old Wanderers—Burnley went down 11–0. (This first venture into the F.A. Cup is still the club's heaviest defeat.) Because of the same restrictions on players, the club also scratched from the Lancashire Cup.

When the first team *did* play in the regular colours of blue and white stripes, it usually looked like this: McLintock; Lang and Sugg; Keenan, Beattie and Abrahams; McNee, McCrae, Friel, Kennedy and Wood. And because they were now settled at Turf Moor, the team began to play under the nickname 'The Moorites'.

The playing record during 1885–86 read:

P 58 W 37 D 8 L 13 goals for 162, goals against 84

Perhaps the outstanding occasion in 1886, not only for the football club, but for the whole of Burnley, was the visit of Prince Albert, son of Queen Victoria, who came to the town to open the new Victoria Hospital in October. This hospital had been built very much from the subscriptions and donations of local people, and football, through events like the Hospital Cup, had played no small part in raising the necessary money.

And so it was fitting that when Prince Albert came to Burnley, part of his programme was a visit to Turf Moor, to watch the Burnley v Bolton Wanderers game that afternoon. This game had been arranged between the two teams, with all the proceeds going to the Victoria Hospital. Special prices were in force that day—entrance to the ground was sixpence, the grandstand was the unbelievable sum of five shillings, and if you wanted a seat next to the Royal Party, they were available at a guinea each. Despite these new prices, a great crowd of 9,000 people packed into Turf Moor that afternoon. Burnley wore new caps for the occasion, and the Royal Party after watching the first half, left at half-time, with the score 3–1 in Bolton's favour. The final result was 4–3 for Bolton. It is believed that this was the first recorded occasion on which any member of the Royal Family graced a football match, and for many years afterwards, Burnley were nicknamed 'The Royalites'. Incidentally, the 9,000 people paid £215, and after expenses had been deducted (and accusations and suspicions of 'fiddling the books' had been made in the local press!), £62 was given by the club towards the new hospital.

The regular team in those days now turned out like: McConnell; Lang and Bury; Abrahams, Sugg and Keenan; Gallocher, McCrae, Friel, McFetteridge and Waugh. In the October of 1887, Burnley met their old rivals Darwen Old Wanderers in the F.A. Cup. The Turf Moor team gained their revenge for the earlier 11–0 trouncing by winning this time 4–0, but the F.A. ordered the game to be replayed because Frank Sugg had not been registered a month.

Not for the first time, Burnley took matters into their own hands, and defied the authorities; they ignored the F.A. order, and Darwen eventually scratched from the competition. The following January, the President of the club, Mr Massey, paid all expenses for a southern tour in which Burnley drew with the famed Corinthians

2–2, and beat Cambridge University 2–1. On top of these club successes, Burnley's captain, Keenan, was chosen as reserve right-half for the England team to play Wales.

The success of the team was judged not by how many games had been won, but by the comparative goal averages of the teams. During 1887–88, the Burnley team more than held their own, playing 59, winning 30, drawing 10 and losing 19. In doing so, they scored 135 against 86 goals.

But with the coming of professionalism, finance was becoming more important with every football season. It was becoming increasingly necessary for clubs to play their games on more business-like lines, rather than the earlier friendly atmosphere. Clubs had to find money to pay their players, and in 1888, even when fixtures were arranged, no one was certain their opponents would turn up. When they did, it was nothing for games to be delayed an hour or so, because of the team's late arrival. The time was ripe for some further organisation within the football world.

TWO

FAME AND SHAME

THE FOOTBALL LEAGUE was founded in 1888 on the suggestion of William McGregor, a bearded Scot, who settled in the Midlands, and became an influential official of Aston Villa. Because it was becoming more and more difficult to organise and complete friendly fixtures through conflicting Cup-ties, it was proposed to organise a football union. The outcome was a meeting held at Anderton's Hotel in Fleet Street, on the eve of the F.A. Cup Final of 1888 (when West Brom were playing Preston North End). The League was formed, and the original teams were Accrington, Aston Villa, Blackburn Rovers, Bolton Wanderers, Burnley, Derby County, Everton, Notts County, Preston North End, Stoke, West Bromwich Albion, and Wolverhampton Wanderers (half from the Midlands, half from Lancashire).

Once it was founded, the Football League went ahead with continuing success. Firm fixture lists, fairly punctual starts, and local rivalries assured the success of the new venture, especially after the first few games when points began to be awarded, and then in later years, when promotion and relegation arrived.

1888–89

Burnley's first League game on September 8, 1888, was away to Preston North End. Preston won 5–2, and went on to win the League Championship without losing a game. The week after they had lost their first League game, Burnley recorded their first ever League victory. The game itself proved to be one of the finest performances ever by a Burnley team, for playing away at Bolton, and at one time 3–0 down, the 'Moorites' came back to win 4–3. It was another month before Burnley won again, this time at Turf Moor, and this first home victory was also against Bolton Wanderers, 4–1.

That first League team that represented Burnley was a blend of youth and experience: Kay; Bury and Lang; Abrahams, Friel and Keenan; Hibbert, Brady, Poland, Gallocher and Yates. Some of that team, like Sandy Lang, Danny Friel and Jack Keenan, had played for years at Burnley, whilst there were several arrivals, like Jack Yates from Accrington.

One of the highlights of the Burnley team in those early League days was the left-wing partnership of Pat Gallocher ('the artful dodger') and Jack Yates. Later in the season, Yates became the first Burnley player ever to figure in an International match, when he played for England against Ireland. England won 6–1, and though Jack Yates scored a hat-trick, strangely enough he was never chosen for England again! Soon after the start of the season, three Burnley players, Bury, Tait and Abrahams, were suspended by the club for taking a holiday and not coming back in time for training!

Victories were few and far between in 1888, and defeats were often and heavy. One player called Jardine scored five for Notts County against Burnley, whilst Blackburn Rovers came to Turf Moor and won 7–1! And then, when they were next to the bottom, having conceded more goals than any other team in the League, Burnley beat the current Cup-holders, West Bromwich Albion 2–0, to register their third victory in the League after ten games. The importance of the League could already be seen on that occasion, because that same day, Burnley had to play Halliwell in the Lancashire Cup, and the club's Reserve side was well beaten, 9–4. Already, the League fixture list was taking priority over other games.

In December, Burnley beat another lowly team, Stoke 2–1, and after 14 games, they were eighth, but still with the worst defensive record. The season's best result came early in the new year, when Burnley drew 2–2 with the League leaders, Preston North End. (It was only the third game all season that Preston had failed to win, and as a reward, the Burnley committee gave ten shillings to each player, and treated them to a free supper at the Bull Hotel in town.) From this fine performance, Burnley's form improved; they beat Notts County, they drew with Accrington, and they recorded a 1–0 win over the bottom club Derby County. Burnley even won a Cup-tie, when they beat the London Amateurs, Old Westminsters, 4–3.

But the club's most famous victory in 1888–89 was when they beat the famous Aston Villa, 4–1, at Turf Moor. (The secret of Burnley's success was that on the way to the game, three Aston Villa players got lost in a Manchester fog whilst changing trains, and the team were only able to field eight men!) In the second round of the F.A. Cup, Burnley were drawn away to Cup holders West Brom. In preparation for this game, C. J. Massey, the Burnley President, paid for the team to go to Ingleton to train. (This was, as far as we know, the first occasion that the club ever went away for special training, but it didn't seem to make much difference because West Brom won the game 5–1.)

During the season, the League fixtures were interspersed with the usual large number of friendly games, and one of these friendlies was played at Easter, when Celtic came down from Scotland and beat the Turf Moor team 3–1.

And so Burnley came to the close of their first League season. They finished in a very modest position—fourth from the bottom out of the twelve clubs. The club's record was:

P 22 W 7 D 3 L 12 goals for 42, against 62, Pts 17

Their last game was against Derby County, the bottom club, who won 1–0. This victory meant that Stoke City finished as the bottom team in the League's first season. Altogether in 1888–89, 'Keenan's men' played in 52 games, winning 25, drawing five and losing 22. The team scored 145 goals and conceded 118.

1889–90

If 1888–89 had an average beginning, 1889–90 almost turned out to be the club's last! Things weren't so bad to begin with, for though Everton beat Burnley 1–0, the club managed to squeeze a point from Aston Villa (2–2) and Accrington (2–2). But at the same time, the club lost a lot of friends in the town, by raising admission charges in 1889 from fourpence to sixpence. These days, that may not appear too much, but in 1889 it was a fair amount, and letters poured in to the local papers objecting to these extravagant and exorbitant charges, 'especially as we are not winning anything!', said one correspondent. More fuel was added to the controversy by the fact that Rovers, Preston and Everton only charged threepence, whilst at Turf Moor to watch the least successful team in Lancashire, it cost twice as much! However the increased prices did not stop 7,000 people coming to Turf Moor to see Aston Villa win 6–2. After six games, only Bolton Wanderers and Burnley still hadn't won a game, and after eight matches, it was only Burnley!

P 8 W 0 D 3 L 5 goals for 11, against 26, Pts 3

Blackburn Rovers came to Burnley and won 7–0, after being six ahead at half-time! Preston beat Burnley 6–0, and West Bromwich Albion beat them 6–1. After ten games, Burnley were still without a win, and still bottom! The team that was struggling through that sad season was: Cox; Bury and Lang; McFetteridge, White and Keenan; Haresnape, Duckworth, Murray, Heys and Crabtree. 'Are Burnley ever going to win a match this season?' asked the *Burnley Gazette* despairingly in December 1889, after Wolverhampton had beaten them 9–1! Fortunately, the previous season's bottom club, Stoke, were also hovering near the bottom keeping the Burnley team company, but in January, even Stoke beat Burnley, 2–1!

Simply because two teams turned out to play a game did not mean that it constituted a League match in those far off days. Many games were unfinished, most clubs objected every Saturday over the result, the referee, the conditions, or really anything at all. At regular intervals, the Football League published lists of games they ordered to be replayed. So even though Bolton beat Burnley 6–3 in January 1890, both clubs appealed against playing owing to the frozen state of the ground. The League upheld the objection, which was to prove a blessing for Burnley.

There was some general improvement in the team's play in the new year of 1890, and this was mainly due to the arrival in town of five Scotsmen—Lambie, Stewart, Hill, McColl and McLardie. Soon after their arrival, Burnley went on a northern tour, and as the local paper said 'surprised themselves, and everyone else' by beating Middlesborough 4–1, Newcastle West End 3–2, and Darlington 2–0. But still that first League victory eluded them, and it was March 1 in 1890, before they won, in their eighteenth game. It was in the replayed Bolton game, which the Wanderers had originally won, that Burnley recorded their first success, winning by seven goals to nothing, (Claude Lambie getting three). And suddenly after months of defeat and anxiety, Burnley hit form. In their three remaining League matches, they beat Derby, Stoke, and Notts County, thus leaving Stoke trailing at the bottom again by three points.

If 1889–90 was a season that the Burnley followers would be happy to forget, then there was another reason why they would always remember that year. For at the same time as they were floundering in the League, the team were flourishing in the Lancashire Cup. In the first round, they beat Rossendale 4–3, and in the second round, they created history by scoring 15 against Haydock (January 20, 1890). In this game, which still remains Burnley's highest score in any really competitive match, Murray scored five, whilst Haresnape, McColl, Campbell, Lang and Heys, all got two each. That enormous score saw them into the semi-final, where they thrashed Higher Walton 7–0. Perhaps Burnley had had a fortunate draw, drawing Rossendale, Haydock, and Higher Walton, but the Final saw Burnley up against the 'old enemy' Blackburn Rovers.

It was typically the Rovers seventh Lancashire Cup-Final, whilst Burnley up to that season had never even won a Lancashire Cup *First Round* tie! Up to that season, they had been beaten in round one four times; once they had scratched without playing; twice they had received a bye, whilst once their opponents had scratched! What a success story! No one expected Burnley to even exist on the same field as the mighty Rovers. Blackburn had finished third in the League that season, whilst humble Burnley were next to the bottom! But that day saw Burnley rise to the occasion with a glorious 2–0 victory in the Final at Accrington.

'FOR 'TWAS A GLORIOUS VICTORY!' sang out the Burnley papers, with such headlines as 'ROUT OF THE ENGLISH CUP HOLDERS' and 'TODAY, BURNLEY FOOTBALL CLUB STANDS ON A HIGHER RUNG THAN IT HAS EVER STOOD BEFORE'. Local supporters worked out that as Blackburn Rovers had won the F.A. Cup, and now Burnley had beaten the Rovers, this meant that Burnley had 'the best team in the Kingdom'.

Over 15,000, a Lancashire Cup record crowd, saw Scotsman Stewart score both goals in the 2–0 victory. Back in Burnley, 'Lang's eleven' received a tremendous reception from the townspeople, with large crowds gathering at the Mitre, down Westgate, and through St James's Street into the town centre, cheering the horse-drawn coach all the way.

Of course, one mustn't expect that Blackburn took the defeat lying down; like anyone else would have done, they protested! But the protest came to nothing, and the *Burnley Gazette* summed up their attitude in the following couched terms: 'The Rovers' captain lodged a protest against the encroachment of the spectators, though how he could possibly expect to succeed with it, it is rather hard to understand. The only encroachment of note occurred 3 or 4 minutes before the finish, and the game was stopped till the crowd were put back. It would be interesting to know how many Blackburn people were amongst this band of encroachers, and whether they received no encouragement from the losing team?'

But let no Burnley supporter smile at the idea of the Rovers lodging a protest. Protests and appeals against the conditions, the referee, the other team, the pitch, the supporters, anyone and anything, were commonplace in those far-off days, and Burnley used to appeal and protest as often and as loudly as anyone!

Only two months prior to the Lancashire Cup Final, Burnley had played the Rovers at Turf Moor. Burnley scored in the very first minute, and soon after Claude Lambie had another disallowed by the referee. Eventually, the Rovers won the game 2–1, thanks mainly, said the *Burnley Gazette*, to the referee, a Mr Richard Horne of Accrington. In the game, the Rovers' goalkeeper was a player called John Horne, and naturally Burnley's suspicions were aroused. It turned out that the referee and Blackburn's goalkeeper were brothers, and so naturally Burnley lodged a protest to the League. But the Rovers had *already* appealed to the League, objecting about the threatening Burnley crowd after the game, saying that the referee had been intimidated. Both appeals were dismissed, but the Burnley club were warned to keep their crowd in better conduct.

And so this topsy-turvy season of 1889–90 came to a close with Burnley, for the second season, having to compete with other teams in the bottom four, and other prospective League teams in the ballot for places in the League the following season. But at the same time as this humiliation, they had reached the heights with the greatest success in their history until then, the winning of the County Cup.

1890–91

The season 1890–91 saw the beginning of a minor revival in the club's playing fortunes. Admittedly, they couldn't have finished much lower other than bottom, but in the League's third season, Burnley improved to eighth, almost breaking even with 21 points from 22 games. They were still playing a great number of friendly games, and these often resulted in high scoring, with the great contrast between League standards and non-league standards. So it was when in 1890, Burnley beat Nelson 9–2 in a Hospital Cup-Tie, and then on Christmas Day 1890, they rattled in 12 against 2 by Wrexham.

Already there were beginning to appear local idols, and two of the early personalities at Turf Moor were Claude Lambie (known in Burnley as 'Lambie the Leap') and Tom Nichol. As an example of their prowess, in 1890 in the match against Bolton Wanderers at Turf Moor, Lambie, later described as the best ever centre-forward', hit the post twice, had two more disallowed, and scored three; whilst Tom Nichol on his first appearance for Burnley at Turf Moor scored four, in Burnley's 6–2 victory over Preston North End. But then after losing two games, there was some dispute between the committee and Lambie, and the player was suspended for a fortnight. Whilst he was off, and with Lang and Hill injured, the old enemy Blackburn came to Turf Moor and won 6–1! Burnley were again disgusted with the referee, a Mr Roberts. (He disallowed two Burnley goals, and then allowed a rather doubtful Rovers goal.) So once more, Burnley protested to the League, but again without success.

Two giant characters, both in physique and personality, made their appearance on the Turf Moor scene in 1890–91—Walter Place ('Big Walter') and Jack Hillman ('the burly one'). Place made his debut at outside-left, but was to figure in most positions in later years, whilst goalkeeper Jack Hillman made his first appearance in a friendly against Linfield Athletic, the Irish champions, at Turf Moor, when Burnley won 6–2.

Mention of goalkeeper Hillman reminds us of alterations in the laws of the game which particularly affected goalkeepers. Players like Jack Hillman must have witnessed many changes over the years. No doubt as a boy he had seen tapes across the posts, whereas by 1890 the cross-bar had almost completely taken over. In 1890 the penalty-kick was introduced, though kickers were allowed to play the ball more than once. If we think it strange that a player could dribble the ball into the goal from a penalty-kick, matters were levelled up by the fact that the goalkeeper could come out to the limits of his goal-area, whilst the kick was being taken. (It was only in 1905 that the goalkeeper was ordered to remain on his line.) By 1892, the rule had been changed so that penalty-kickers must not play the ball twice; and then in 1891, goal-nets were introduced for the first time. Cross-bars, penalty-areas, goal-nets; association football changed in many ways during the last ten years of Queen Victoria's reign. Umpires disappeared in 1891 when they were replaced by linesmen, and then in 1894 the referee was given complete control of the game, (it was no longer necessary for players to appeal to him to make a decision).

1891–95

The season 1891–92 saw Burnley 'break even' for the first time, winning as many games as they lost, and scoring four more goals than they conceded. That season, they created another 'mini-record' for the club, when in one spell of four matches, they scored 29 goals! They beat Sunderland Albion 6–1, Brierfield 6–2, Belfast Distillery 8–3, and Darwen 9–0. Admittedly, the first three games were all friendly matches, but the Darwen result still stands to this day, as Burnley's highest ever League score.

It was not until the meeting at Ewood Park, in the League's fourth season, that Burnley managed to gain a point at the expense of their great rivals Blackburn Rovers. The date was December 12, 1891. That day, Burnley found things going all their own way, and at half-time the score was 3–0 in their favour. But midway through the second half, the Rovers player Lofthouse kicked Stewart, who at once struck back. Both men were immediately sent off by the referee, and shortly afterwards, all the Rovers players, with the exception of Herbie Arthur, their goalkeeper, walked off the field. Down the field stormed Burnley once again and Arthur claimed they were all offside! However, the referee stopped the game and awarded it to Burnley. The Blackburn team insisted after the game that they had left the field, neither because they were losing, nor because Lofthouse had been sent off, but because of the extreme cold. As a result of the ensuing League enquiry, the Rovers had to play a penalty match, with the receipts being divided between the two clubs and the League.

There was trouble at the Rovers–Burnley game the following season too. The date was December 17, 1892, and the game was played at Ewood Park. Burnley's team for the record was: Hillman; Nichol and Lang; King, Matthew and Bowes; Crabtree, Chambers, Lambie, Hill, and Place (Senior). Five minutes from the end, Lang, the Burnley captain, was knocked down and kicked. Getting up, he butted Southworth, the Rovers centre-forward, in the face. Soon they were standing toe to toe, and the referee ordered both of them off the field. As the Burnley players left the field at the end, they were met with a shower of stones and mud, and several players were struck.

That season saw a further improvement as the club climbed to sixth position in the League table, which was even more creditable because there were now sixteen teams in the League, as well as a Second Division of twelve new clubs. The five year spell of progress up the League table reached its climax in 1893–94, when the Burnley team reached fifth position in the League, scoring a new high total for the club of 61 goals (in 30 games that season). At one time, in October 1893, and again in February 1894, Burnley were third in the League.

	Played	*Points*
Aston Villa	25	37
Rovers	23	30
Burnley	23	29

But the Lancashire teams both fell away, and Aston Villa finished easy champions, with Burnley in fifth position.

Burnley still held the reputation of attracting more Scots south of the border, than any other team in the country. In 1891–92, they had 64 Scots on their books, and three seasons later in 1894–95, there were still 57 Scotsmen registered with the East Lancashire club. Of course, not all of them played for the first team, and most of them only got as far as Burnley Swifts, the reserve team which in those days played in the N. E. Lancs League.

It is hard to imagine just what the Turf looked like in those far off days, but we do know that when Burnley played the Rovers in December 1893, 13,000 gathered for the match, with the then record receipts of £339. That money must have been very welcome, because the first 20 years of League competition were financially sticky years for the Turf Moor team. But there was another way of raising money quickly, a means by which Burnley were to become famous in later years, and that was by transferring their players. In 1894, Burnley were beginning to collect a few big names in their ranks, players who were sure to attract the larger and more affluent league clubs, international players like Jack Hillman, James Crabtree, and Tom 'Ching' Morrison.

It was in 1895 that Burnley once again got their names in the history books by being involved in the first transfer fee, when they sold the redoubtable James Crabtree to Aston Villa. Crabtree had originally been a full back, but during his career he performed with prowess in every position from goal to centre-forward. Burnley's reason for transferring Crabtree was their objection to paying him the 'exorbitant terms' which he demanded. We don't know what he asked for, but we do know that after all the bother, he went to Aston Villa for the same terms, but with promises of better things to come.

1895–97

The sale of Crabtree may have solved some financial headaches, but it caused problems in the Burnley team. That year saw the end of Burnley's gradual improvement, for in 1895, they were back in the bottom half, finishing ninth out of 16 teams, and the following season, they were tenth. But worse, and much worse was to come during season 1896–97. That season, Burnley finished bottom of the League for the first and indeed the only time in their history, winning only six out of their 30 games. The team that played out most of that sad season read: Hillman; Reynolds and McLintock; Place (Senior), Longair, Taylor; Beveridge, Black, Toman, Bowes and Place (Junior). It was during that season that another great favourite of the Turf Moor crowd, Jack Hillman, left the club, when he was transferred to Everton.

But with the arrival of a Second Division had come problems. How could teams who finished at the bottom in Division One be penalised, and how were teams who finished at the top of Division Two to be rewarded? One suggestion was a series of Test Matches, and this system was tried over a period of six seasons (1893–98). These games were staged between the bottom teams of Division One and the top teams of Division Two, and so it was that Burnley were involved in this struggle for survival in 1896–97. Sunderland, who had finished four points ahead of Burnley at the bottom were also involved, whilst at the top of Division Two, Notts County had finished three points ahead of Newton Heath (Manchester United). In the first game of the Test Match series, Burnley did very well and beat Newton Heath 2–0, but later they were beaten in the return game by the same score. A draw away to Notts County seemed to assure Burnley of First Division status, but their hopes were dashed when once again they failed at home, being beaten

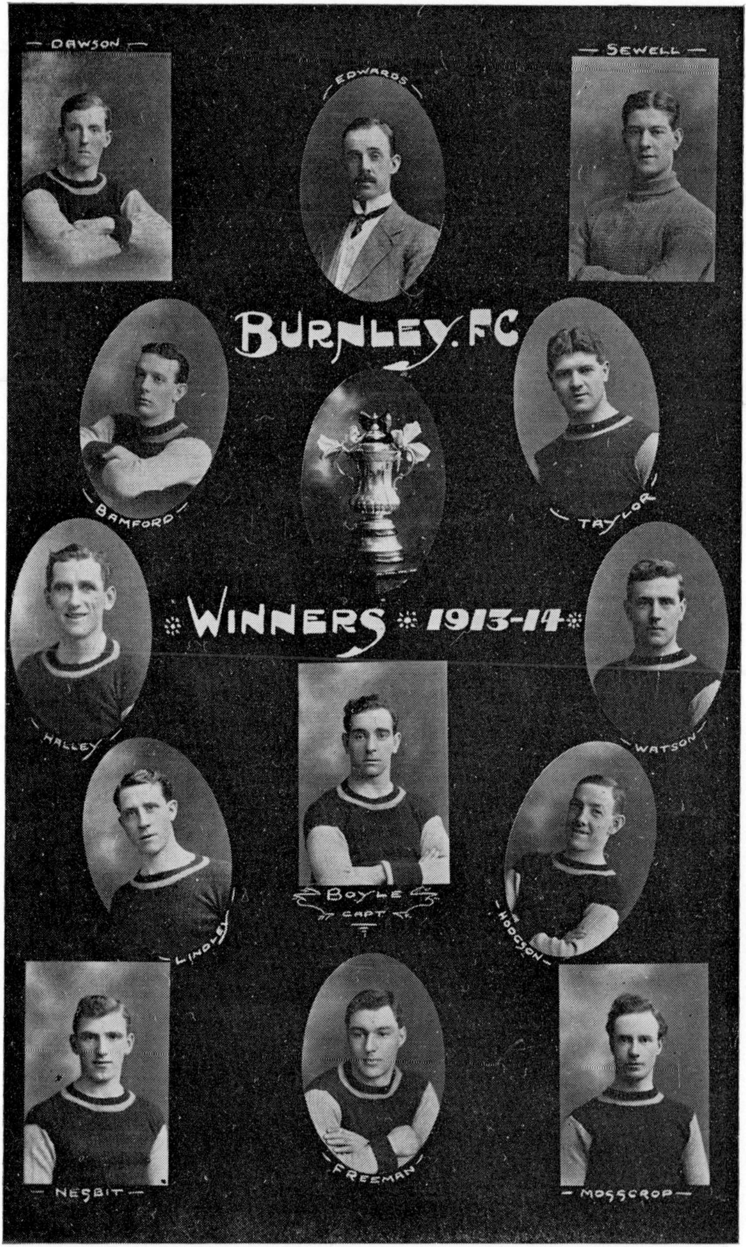

CUP WINNERS, 1914. (left to right, top to bottom) Dawson, Edwards, Sewell; Bamford, Taylor; Halley, Watson; Lindley, Boyle (capt.), Hodgson; Nesbit, Freeman (who scored the only goal), Mosscrop

THE GOAL THAT WON THE CUP IN 1914. Bert Freeman turns away from the goal as Boyle, Watson and Hodgson rush in to congratulate him

A MOMENT OF HISTORY. Tommy Boyle, the Burnley captain is the first player ever to receive the F.A. Cup from the King

1–0 by Notts County at Turf Moor. So along with Newton Heath, Burnley were compelled to compete for the first time in Second Division football in 1897–98.

1897–98

That season proved to be the most successful yet for Burnley, because they finished Champions of Division Two. Under their trainer, an ex-professional runner called Stuttard, the team played their first eight League matches without defeat. By the end of the season, they had won 20 of their 30 games, they had scored 80 goals in the process, and they had only lost twice. That season, Burnley scored goals like nobody's business, and over the year they recorded victories over Blackpool 5–1, Wolves 5–0, Grimsby 6–0, Kilmarnock 6–0, Nelson 7–3, Newton Heath 6–3 and Loughborough 9–3. Of course they weren't all League games, but it must have been great stuff to watch!

But being Division Two champions was only half the story; Burnley then had to compete in the Test Matches. Along with them in the series were Newcastle United (runners-up in Division Two), whilst the bottom clubs in Division One were Stoke and Blackburn Rovers. What an occasion that must have been in East Lancashire, with Rovers and Burnley meeting in do or die fashion to either get up or stay up in Division One. The games proved a great success for Burnley. They won 3–1 at Blackburn, and again 2–0 at Turf Moor in front of a record crowd. But their promotion hopes received a set-back when Stoke came to Burnley and beat the home team 2–0. And so, the position with just one game to play, was:

	Played	*Points*
Stoke	3	4
Burnley	3	4
Newcastle	3	2
Rovers	3	2

Both Stoke and Burnley needed just one point to achieve First Division status the following season, and from all accounts it would seem that both clubs came to a 'gentlemen's agreement' before the game at Stoke. The ground was in a shocking state, and had it not been the last day of the season, so the referee declared, the game would not have been played. All in all, five balls were used, and in an attempt to stop either team from scoring, the spectators kept possession of them whenever they went into the crowd. The proceedings ended on a note of high comedy with the score 0–0, and everyone went home happy. The Football League had learned its lesson, and Test Matches were never tried again; automatic promotion and relegation of the top and bottom teams followed the next season. (In fact, Burnley and Stoke didn't gain anything by fair means or foul, because the League took the opportunity in 1898 to enlarge Division One from 16 to 18 clubs, and the new Division One included all the four teams who had fought out those last historic Test Matches.)

1897–98 seems to have been quite a season, because besides regaining their place in the First Division, Burnley had their first F.A. Cup run of any note. Previously, of the 18 Cup-ties they had played, they had lost 12! However, in 1898, they reached the third round for the first time in their history, and they were drawn at home against Everton. The game was a great attraction in Burnley, and a record attendance, some 20,500 people paid an unprecedented £794 for admission at Turf Moor. Unfortunately the home team lost 3–1, but the game and the gate were recalled for many a year afterward. One man for whom the game was particularly memorable was big Jack Hillman. Hillman, who had gone to Everton from Turf Moor, had later been transferred up to Dundee in Scotland. At the end of the 1897–98 season, he had permission to play for Burnley, who were paying Dundee for his services, and he fitted back into his old team so well that he never returned to Scotland.

1898–1900

The season after their promotion to Division One, saw the best Burnley performance until that time, when the team from Turf Moor finished third behind Aston Villa and Liverpool. At one time in that season, they even reached second place, when on December 10, 1898, after having beaten Preston, the League position read:

	Played	*Points*
Aston Villa	16	25
Burnley	17	23
Everton	18	22

But after Christmas, they faded a little, and the final table was:

	Played	*Points*
Aston Villa	34	45
Liverpool	34	43
Burnley	34	39

Towards the end of the season, captain Jimmy Ross was transferred to Manchester City, whilst centre-forward Wilf Toman went to Everton. Toman was a brilliant player who came from Bishop Auckland. Previous to his time at Burnley, he had played for Aberdeen Strollers and Dundee. The team that finished in third place usually read: Hillman, Reynolds and McLintock; Barron,

Place (Senior), and Livingstone; Morrison, McInnes, Bowes, Place (Junior) and Robertson.

But 1898–99 seems to have been very much a flash in the pan, because the turn of the century saw Burnley struggling yet again. This time they finished next to the bottom team Glossop, and together they were relegated. Those days in the Football League were still a long way off the present days of floodlight soccer, high organisation and world competition. At almost every match, there were reports of goalposts collapsing, games starting late, referees not turning up, and the like. The regular team at the turn of the century at Turf Moor looked like: Hillman, Woolfall and McLintock; Barron, Taylor and Livingstone; Morrison, Bowes, Hartley, Chadwick and Miller. Of that team, Hillman (England) and Morrison (Ireland) were international players, McLintock and Livingstone had been fine servants of the club for over ten seasons, whilst Fred Barron was to stay with Burnley until the era of Halley, Boyle and Watson. Besides being relegated that season, the club had a disappointment in the Lancashire Cup, when they were beaten 1–0 by Preston in the Final. In fact, other than reaching the County Cup Final, it is doubtful if anything successful occurred to Burnley in that last season of the nineteenth century.

The season ended with relegation and scandal. In their last match, they went to Notts Forest, desperately needing a win in order to stay in the First Division. They did not achieve anything like a win, being well beaten by the Forest team, 4–0. The match report of the game said : 'Hillman was not to blame for the score'. Indeed he was not! After the game, Notts Forest officials alleged that Hillman had tried to bribe the Forest players to lose the match, offering the players £2 each, if they allowed Burnley to win. The offer was indignantly declined, but when Forest were winning 2–0 at half-time, Hillman increased the amount to £5 a man! The Forest team still refused the handsome offer, and Burnley lost and were duly relegated! Jack Hillman, who had a great reputation for humour, admitted that he had said the words, but simply in jest! The Forest team were not amused, and at a meeting of the Football League Disciplinary Committee, Burnley's goalkeeper was suspended for the whole of the 1900–01 season.

THREE

GRIM DAYS

1900–02

THE SEASON that Jack Hillman was absent from Turf Moor saw almost a repeat performance of the last occasion that Burnley had been relegated, when they bounced straight back into Division One. However, this time, after a good season, they only managed to finish third behind Grimsby and Small Heath (Birmingham).

Now they were firmly entrenched in Division Two, and the next ten years were critical days at Turf Moor. Division Two and extremely poor gates caused great financial problems, and not for the last time, Burnley were compelled to sell valuable and important players.

For the second successive season, they were beaten in the Lancashire Cup Final, this time by the 'old enemy', Blackburn Rovers, 4–0. In 1901–02, Burnley applied to have Jack Hillman reinstated as a player, and the team that usually played was: Hillman; Ross and Lockhart; Barron, Bannister and Taylor; Morrison, Watkins, Brunton, Davidson and McLintock. That season, winger Billy Bannister was chosen for the England team to play Wales, and at the time he was getting paid 27s 6d a week by Burnley! (Jack Hillman was the best paid man on the books, and he only took home a fiver, the maximum wage at the time). And once again, for the third season running, Burnley were beaten in the Lancashire Cup Final, once again by Blackburn Rovers, 1–0.

What big names Burnley had, they sold in 1902. English international and captain of the Burnley team, Jack Hillman, went to Manchester City for £350; English international Billy Bannister went to Bolton Wanderers for £375, and Irish international 'Ching' Morrison, who had come to Burnley via Glentoran and Glasgow Celtic, went from Turf Moor to Manchester United.

1902–08

The season after these stalwarts of the Burnley side had left Turf Moor, Burnley, for the first and only time in their history, finished bottom of the Second Division. In doing so, they conceded what was till then a record for the club of 77 goals in a season, and they only managed to win six of their 34 games. Fortunately, there was no Division Three in those days, or else Burnley might well have gone the way of Accrington Stanley, many years before their demise. There was the risk, however, of their being voted out of the League, and in 1902–03, there were eight applicants and three vacancies at the bottom of Division Two. Just how close Burnley came to losing their position can be seen by the result of the ballot: Bradford 30 votes, Stockport 20, Burnley 19, Doncaster 14.

Newspaper headlines of the day sum up the sad state of the club's affairs . . . 'Turfites towelled at Toffeeopolis', 'Turfites topple over at Teeside', and 'Bolton batter baffled Burnley'. Between December 7, 1901, and October 24, 1903, Burnley played 33 consecutive League matches away from home without winning. Gates of 300 and 400 people were the order of the day in 1903, and on one occasion, the local paper said there was 'a mere handful'. Appeals were made in the local press, public meetings were called in the town, raffles were held, and bazaars were organised, in order to raise money to keep the club afloat. One player who did not cost the club a penny was the amateur international Arthur Bell, who came from the neighbouring Burnley Belvedere club. Bell, who joined Burnley in 1902–03 came as an inside-left, but later played on the left wing. He was also an outstanding cricketer with the Turf Moor club. In 1904–05, another much changed Burnley team usually turned out looking like: Green; Henderson and Moffatt; Barron, D. Walders and Taylor; J. Walders, Hogan, Smith, McFarlane and Ross.

To emphasise just how difficult it was to raise money in 1904, the entrance fee for the pre-season practice matches was a penny per person! The first ten years of the twentieth century were very average years in Division Two for Burnley performances, and very precarious concerning finances. It might be said that things began to brighten gradually in 1907. That year, on February 2, a young local unknown, employed as a blacksmith's striker at nearby Cliviger, signed on for Burnley. His name was Jeremiah Dawson, and his first wages for Burnley were 7s 6d.

Dick Lindley signed on in 1908, and believe it or not, after winning Cup-winners medals and Second Division Championship medals with Manchester City, 'the burly one', old Jack Hillman returned to Turf Moor in 1908. But the most sensational buy that year took place in December, when the English international half-back, Alex Leake, who had made his name with Aston Villa, winning a Cup medal in 1905, signed on for Burnley. That signing was the turning point. Years later in 1921, people looked back and said that it was the signing of Alex Leake that put Burnley on their feet again.

With the arrival of Leake, attendances increased, and in 1908, even the Reserve team were attracting gates averaging 5,000. Season tickets that season were priced as follows: Brunshaw Road stand 21s, Star Stand & Enclosure 12s 6d, whilst a ground ticket cost just 9s for the season! On January 11, 1908, Burnley were drawn against Southampton in Round One of the F.A. Cup, and prices for that game were: Higher Ground 1s, Lower Ground 6d, Star Stand 2s and Old stand 3s 6d. Southampton won the game 2–1, but 15,702 people paid £603 to see the game. It was the largest gate for nearly ten years, since the Everton cup-tie of 1899, and the future was beginning to look brighter for Burnley soccer. The team that day read: Dawson; Barron and Moffatt; Cretney, Leake and Wolstenholme; McFarlane, Whittaker, Smith (R), Mayson and Smith (A).

But playing conditions were still very different from the present day, and some other standards were a little different too; witness the following extract from a Burnley paper in 1908. 'Last Saturday, the referee had to stop the Reserve match at Turf Moor, in order to speak to one of the spectators for having used bad language to one of the players. It is generally these dirty-mouthed members who are the severest critics, men who never did a day's training in their lives, and who could not run a hundred yards if they wanted. Obscene barracking of this kind, which is becoming common, must be stopped at all costs'.

1908–09

The season 1908–09 was to be one of the club's most historic seasons ever, and people in Burnley still talk about it. Not so much because of their League record (Burnley finished a very modest fourteenth in Division Two), but because of their record in the F.A. Cup.

The first round saw Burnley drawn away to Bristol Rovers, and the Lancashire team won fairly convincingly, 4–1. Excitement was very high, as it was the first time for five seasons that Burnley had won a cup-tie, and Burnley found themselves drawn away again in round two, this time at Crystal Palace.

The *Burnley Gazette* for February 10, 1909, reports about the team: 'They entrained on Friday afternoon at 12.30, a horse shoe being thrown into the railway carriage as they started, but fortunately it did not strike anyone'. Eighteen thousand, including over 1,000 people from Burnley, saw the teams play out a 0–0 draw, and Burnley earn a replay. The following week, 14,000 people rolled up at Turf Moor to see Burnley strike form for the first time for seasons. Dick Smith played the game of his life at centre-forward and scored a hat-trick. The other scorers were Abbott (2), Cretney (2), Smethams, and an own goal. The team was superbly generalled by Alex Leake who commanded the whole of the middle of the field, whilst the entire half-back line of Cretney, Leake and Moffatt were in superb form that day. The final result was 9–0 for Burnley, and the club were a step nearer to their first ever Cup-Final at Crystal Palace.

Unfortunately, the third round draw found Burnley away from home once again, this time at Tottenham. Over 21,000 people were at the Spurs v Burnley game, and again Burnley earned a replay with a 0–0 draw. Never had anticipation been so high as that day in February 1909, when Burnley and Tottenham took the field at Turf Moor. An attendance of 25,000 people created a new ground record, thus beating the 20,500 of eleven years earlier at the Everton Cup-Tie.

Once again, their Cup opponents were no match for the Turfites, as they were called in those days, and Burnley ran out convincing 3–1 winners. For the first time in their history, Burnley were in the Fourth Round (which in 1909 was the Quarter-Final stage). The fourth round draw saw them at home for the first time that season . . . against Manchester United, the current League champions.

What a draw! The whole town was gripped with 'cup-fever', football writers summed up each team's chances over the preceding weeks, supporters wrote to the local press, expressing their faith, hope, and love of their favourites. Strong-armed weavers and tough little lads were even moved to poetry to express their feelings.

'The Palace' and the 'Spurs'
Were laid beneath the earth,
With nine to nought, and three to one
Were mangled on the Turf.

If United come on Saturday
And suffer same as Spurs.
There will be great rejoicing,
For the Cup will sure be ours.

We then will trim our badges
And paint all green and white,
And Burnley'll roll their sleeves up,
And for the Cup will fight.

It may not be nine-nothing,
Or even three to one,
But let us hope it's something,
If only one to none.

Let's hope we get to London
And in the Final play;
Here's luck to good old Burnley,
We every team will slay.

Edgar Hewitt (aged 12) of Trafalgar Street, Burnley.

A total of £600 was spent by the club in providing extra banking and barricading at the ground. Much of the money went towards moving the Star Stand several yards backwards to create an enclosure in front. (Whoever these days would dream of moving a stand?) Work went on until late in the night, until the official capacity was said to be 32,000, an undreamed of figure in Burnley's history.

On the day of the great match, an item in the correspondence column of the local paper read simply: 'Sir, Burnley expects every man this day will do his duty. Yours, Burnley'.

The Burnley team that memorable day of March 6, 1909, read: Dawson; Barron and McLean; Cretney, Leake and Moffatt; Morley, Ogden, Smith, Abbott and Smethams. Jerry Dawson was already well established in the Burnley team, whilst Fred Barron had now made almost 400 appearances in a Burnley jersey (green in those days), and Moffatt had played for over five seasons in the Burnley team. He had captained the side before Alex Leake arrived, and he was to resume the captaincy once again when Leake retired.

Dick Smith was the local goal-scoring idol of the times, whilst Walter Abbott, a veteran international, had appeared in two Cup Finals with Everton before coming to Burnley in 1908. United's captain was international Charlie Roberts, in the middle of the famous Duckworth, Roberts, Bell, half-back line, whilst the legendary Billy Meredith was on the right wing (one of the long awaited clashes was that between Meredith and Burnley left-back Jimmy McLean, who always played Meredith well).

The night before the game, it began to snow. All that night and throughout the day of the big match, how it snowed! Several inches fell during the morning alone, whilst 22 men worked full-time trying to clear the town centre. Altogether, it was estimated that over 800 cartloads of snow were removed from the Burnley town-centre alone!

There was some doubt as to whether the game would start at all, but referee Bamlett decided to make the effort. Burnley played with the gale behind them in the first half, and the wind was so strong that once a Jerry Dawson goal-kick went straight off the other end for a goal-kick to United. Late in the first half, an Ogden header from Charlie Smetham's centre gave Burnley the lead. In the second half, with the storm on their backs, United threw everything they had at the Burnley defence. Full back Fred Barron was injured, but still it seemed as if the local team were going to hold the League Champions. But then, with the snow driving harder than ever into the faces of the Burnley team, and with little over a quarter of an hour to go, the referee called the players off the field and abandoned the game! After the match, naturally opinions were divided. Alex Leake said that seeing they had persevered with the conditions so long, the game should have been completed, and anyhow, Burnley had more than held everything that United had to offer. United's captain Charlie Roberts, said that the game should never have been started anyway!

Fred Barron missed the replay through his injury, and though Dick Smith was taken ill just before the game, he insisted on playing. Once again, Arthur Ogden put Burnley ahead, but United replied with two goals just before half-time. They added a third in the second half, and just before full-time, Ogden made it 3–2.

Manchester United had won, and they went on to win the F.A. Cup for the first time in their history, but the abandoned cup-tie was to remain in the memory of Burnley's supporters for long over sixty years. To this day, whenever United play at Turf Moor, some of the older generation raise the cry, 'Stop the game, it's snowing!'

The fine cup run was over, but besides raising the hopes of Burnley followers for the future, it had also more than helped to raise the bank balance of the club. Over £6,000 had been realised at the Cup-ties, and Burnley received their fair share of the takings. For the first time for many years, Burnley were out of debt, and they were able to say to their creditors, 'Here's your money . . . come and get it!' This flush of wealth helped to lay the foundations of Burnley's prosperity in the years that followed. And Burnley gained revenge over Manchester United the following season, when they knocked them out in the first round, only to be beaten in the second round by Swindon Town.

1909–11

The team in 1909–10 usually read something like: Dawson; Barron and McClean; Cretney, Leake and Watson; Clarke, Lomas, Green, Abbott and Smethams. Of those names, just Dawson and half-back Billy Watson, were to see the years of Burnley's greatest triumphs, whilst others like Dick Lindley, and Tom Bamford (who had come from Darwen) were in the Reserves at the time, about to be promoted. Sadly, Burnley's great leader, Alex Leake, had to retire from football in October 1910, after being involved in an accident on a London bus.

The club showed a definite improvement in Division Two in

1910–11, but it was only a preview of the following season. If 1908–09 had been a historic season for Cup performances, then most certainly, 1911–12 was in every way as memorable, first of all for the players who joined the club, and then in their performances in the League. First of all, in April 1911, there was Bert Freeman's arrival. The headlines in the local press ran: SENSATIONAL CAPTURE—FREEMAN SECURED FROM EVERTON! Centre-forward Bert Freeman, an English international, was already a goal-scoring legend when he came to Turf Moor, having scored more than a century of goals in his previous six seasons with Arsenal and Everton. He also held the League goal-scoring record with 38 goals in one season for Everton. The great Bert Freeman made the first of his many appearances with Burnley on April 15, 1911, in the game against Wolves.

One story that has often been told since those days concerns Burnley's colours. At the time, they played in green jerseys, but after a fairly bad run in the first ten seasons of the twentieth century, a suggestion was made that their green colours were unlucky. It was proposed that if they adopted the colours of a First Division Club who were doing well, their fortunes might improve. This they did, and they chose the colours of the current League Champions in 1909–10, Aston Villa, who wore claret and blue. What truth there is in this story we cannot tell, but certainly their fortunes began to change from 1911.

1911–12

Another fine player, inside-forward Teddy Hodgson signed for Burnley in September, 1911, and the same month, winger Billy Nesbitt came to the club from nearby Hebden Bridge. Then in October, there arrived at Turf Moor, one of the most legendary figures ever to play for Burnley . . . Tommy Boyle. Tommy Boyle was captain of the Barnsley team, and part of the Glendinning, Boyle, Utley half-back line that had faced Newcastle United in the 1910 Cup-Final. It may have been on February 4, 1911, that Boyle first came to the notice of the Burnley directors, when Burnley went to Barnsley for an F.A. Cup-Tie. (Burnley won the game 2–0, and a curiosity piece is that Jerry Dawson took a penalty kick for Burnley, and missed!) Anyway, Boyle signed for Burnley on October 1, 1911, for the highest price that the club had ever paid for a player (£1,150), and by coincidence, his first game for his new club was against Barnsley on October 4, 1911. And just before Christmas, 1911, full back Dave Taylor appeared on the Turf Moor scene, being transferred from Bradford City, with whom he had won a Cup-winner's medal the previous season.

Now, with players like Dawson, Taylor, Boyle, Watson, Nesbitt,

Lindley, Freeman and Hodgson in their ranks, Burnley's performances improved by leaps and bounds, and with their successes, the crowds rolled up in even greater numbers. Three times in the 1911–12 season, the gate receipts record was shattered by hundreds of pounds. (The Blackpool game in 1910 had set the record at £388.) When the Wolves came in 1911, the receipts were £464; then in 1912, Blackpool came to Turf Moor again, and a crowd of 27,000 paid over £719 to see the match. Then on March 16, 1912, came a high-water mark for the Turf Moor ground, the first gate over 30,000, when Derby County came to play at Burnley. At the time, Derby complete with Steve Bloomer, were lying third in Division Two, whilst Burnley were on top of the Division. The attendance was 31,000 ('among whom were an unprecedented number of ladies') and the receipts were again a Turf Moor League record of £831. The result was 0–0.

That was in March, and by April 6, Burnley had increased the League lead they had held since Christmas to a full six points.

	Played	*Points*
Burnley	34	50
Chelsea	32	44
Derby Co.	31	42

Bert Freeman was once again the country's leading goal-scorer, and Burnley had been undefeated at home all season. Hopes of promotion were high in the town. But then Burnley, with just four games to go began to lose their grip on the title. First of all, they went to Birmingham and lost 4–0. And then to Leicester, where Leicester Fosse won 3–2. Whilst Burnley dropped these four points, Derby had gained eight points out of a possible ten, and so with only two games to play, the table read :

	Played	*Points*
Derby Co.	36	50
Burnley	36	50
Chelsea	35	48

In their last game at Turf Moor, Burnley rediscovered their promotion form, and beat Huddersfield Town, 3–0. But by this time, Derby had won their last two games, and so ensured promotion. In the last week of the 1911–12 season, the Division Two table read :

	Played	*Points*
Derby Co.	38	54
Burnley	37	52
Chelsea	36	50

Everything depended upon Burnley's last game; with a superior goal-average to Chelsea, a win would make promotion a certainty.

But the headlines in the *Burnley Gazette* the following week tell the story:

LAST HURDLE FALL.
BURNLEY'S FATAL ERROR.
CHARMED CIRCLE AS FAR OFF AS EVER.

Burnley had been beaten 2–0 at Wolverhampton, whilst Chelsea had won their last two games.

	Played	*Points*
Derby Co.	38	54
Chelsea	38	54
Burnley	38	52

Burnley were still in the Second Division, but only for one more season. And what a season that was going to be!

FOUR

HALLEY, BOYLE'N WATSON

1912–13

Interest was very high at the start of the 1912–13 season, and 8,000 paid twopence each to see the public practice match. The Burnley team that kicked off their thirteenth consecutive season in Division Two was: Dawson; Reid and Taylor; Swift, Boyle and Watson; Mosscrop, Lindley, Freeman, Hodgson and Husband. The season began in a very average fashion, with Burnley only gaining eight points from their first nine games, and October found them in the bottom half of Division Two.

Then the team suddenly struck form again, and in five games, Burnley scored 21 goals against 3. In one game against Leicester Fosse, Bert Freeman scored four out of five, and by Christmas, the team from the banks of the Brun were points clear at the top of Division Two. To reinforce their already redoubtable attack, Burnley entered the transfer market once again, and this time they bought Jim Bellamy, 'the crack inside-right of Motherwell' for £1,000. Earlier in the season, they had signed Will Husband from St Mirren, whilst a local schoolteacher called Mosscrop played his first game for Burnley against Glossop at the start of the 1912–13 season. Eddie Mosscrop, a very skilful winger was unable to play in midweek games, or in games involving long weekend journeys, owing to his teaching commitments.

Burnley's successful run continued until January 25, 1913. On that day, *the* surprise result in the country was: Burnley 3 Notts Forest 5. Previous to this shock home defeat, Burnley had won eleven consecutive matches (ten League and a Cup-tie). It was their first home defeat since March 20, 1911, 22 months earlier, when Bolton Wanderers had beaten them 3–1 in a League game.

Meanwhile, besides Burnley's great promotion run, the team was quietly progressing in the F.A. Cup. In round one, Burnley were drawn away to Leeds City, but unfortunately there was a repetition of the Manchester United 'stop the game, it's snowing' fiasco, when the game was abandoned late in the second half with

Burnley leading 4–2. How the minds of the Burnley supporters must have gone back to that week in 1909, when Burnley had lost the replay. However, all turned out right this time, for Burnley won the return game the following week, 3–2.

The second round saw them drawn at home against the Midland League club, Gainsborough Trinity. It is to be remembered that at that time, there was no Third Division, but Leagues like the Southern League and the Midland League had a very high reputation, and many League clubs developed from their ranks. Gainsborough were one of the leading Midland League clubs, but Burnley didn't have too much difficulty in beating them 3–1.

More sensational than the match itself was the sequel, when Burnley caused a stir throughout the whole football world by signing the entire Gainsborough defence, goalkeeper Sewell, and full backs, Gunton and Jones. The three that Burnley signed, that February day in 1913, were generally described at the time as the best defence in the Midland League. Perhaps as big a sensation at Turf Moor itself, was the fact that the following Saturday, the regular Burnley defence of Dawson, Bamford and Taylor, were all 'rested', and the three new signings made their debut against Bristol City.

The third round created a great amount of interest, when Burnley were drawn at home again, this time to Middlesbrough. The club raised the ground charges to 1s for the big occasion, but this did not deter 27,824 people turning up (paying £1,679) to see Burnley win once more, this time 3–1. For the third time in five seasons, 1909, 1911 and 1913, Burnley had reached the Quarter-Finals (round four), and for the first time in their history, they were drawn in the F.A. Cup against their oldest and greatest rivals, Blackburn Rovers, who at that time were a leading team in Division One.

Seventeen thousand people went from Burnley to Ewood Park for the Cup-Tie, and in a classic game, Burnley beat the Rovers 'on their own midden', 1–0. Captain Tommy Boyle scored the winner by heading home a corner kick, and for the first time Burnley had won their way through to the Semi-Finals of the competition.

Burnley continued to try and improve the strength of their team, and in March, 1913, they made what had to be one of their most significant signings of all time, when they signed George Halley, a right-half, for 'a large sum of money' from Bradford Park Avenue. What was significant about this move was that it brought together for the first time George Halley, Tommy Boyle, and Billy Watson, who have gone down in history as the legendary 'Halley, Boyle'n Watson'. For the time being, suffice it to say that Halley, Boyle'n

Watson made their first appearance together in March, 1913, when Burnley beat Bury 2–1 at Turf Moor. How many people who saw that game, realised that they were in at the beginning of a new era in the history of Burnley Football Club?

Tommy Boyle made his International debut for England v Ireland, the same month as George Halley arrived at Turf Moor, whilst Billy Watson also made his International debut that season, when he played for England against Scotland. Previous to the International, he had played in over a hundred consecutive games for Burnley, but unfortunately he was injured in the International match, and missed most of the remaining games for his club that season.

Meanwhile, Burnley were in the Semi-Final of the F.A. Cup, as well as being at the top of Division Two. In the Semi-Final, Burnley were drawn to play Sunderland, a tower of strength in the soccer world in those days, with international players like Cuggy, Ness and Buchan scattered among their ranks. They were a team of near giants in stature, with only two men under 5ft 9ins, and the average weight of their players well over 12 stone. In contrast, Burnley were a team of midgets, with only two men, Dawson and Taylor standing over 5ft 9in, and only three men, Bamford, Taylor and Freeman weighing over 12 stone.

The first game at Bramhall Lane ended in a goal-less draw, but in the replay at St. Andrew's, Burnley's Cup hopes came to an unlucky end, the Second Division team going down 3–2 to the team who only failed to achieve the double in 1913 by narrowly losing in the F.A. Cup Final. After the Semi-Final defeat, the season came to a slightly disappointing conclusion, when Burnley were pipped for the Second Division title by Preston North End, who had been relegated the season before.

But, the great feat of promotion had been achieved. Burnley were back in Division One, once again. In winning promotion, they had scored a record 88 goals of which Bert Freeman had scored 31 (in the 37 games he had played). Add to that, the seven he had chalked up in the seven cup-ties, and altogether 'Gentleman' Bert had scored 77 goals in 83 matches over the two seasons 1911–12 and 1912–13. For the second season running, he was the top scorer in Division Two, and he was the only player in the country to have scored over 30 goals in two consecutive seasons. It is perhaps facts like those which make people dwell upon 'the good old days!'

To celebrate the great event of promotion, Mr Philip Morrell, the M.P. for Burnley, gave a dinner at the Mechanics Hall in Burnley. During the speeches, C. E. Sutcliffe recalled his old rugby days when he played on Calder Vale, when if they wanted a bath after the match, they had to go in the river! He also recalled the 'dark days' of the club when one game had resulted in a £15 gate, whilst there was a £2,000 overdraft at the bank! Later in the evening, there was a presentation to Billy Watson on the occasion of his playing 100 consecutive League games for the club. He was presented with a gold watch and chain, and a specially inscribed medal. For their successes in 1912–13, the Burnley players shared between them £220 for being runners-up in Division Two, and £165 for reaching the Semi-Final.

1913–14

In September, 1913, after a very modest start on their return to Division One, Burnley had a £940 home gate against the Rovers, a new record for Turf Moor. Yet another big signing occurred in 1913, for after Freeman, Boyle, Halley and company, Burnley signed on perhaps the biggest name in their entire history . . . Bob Kelly. In November 1913, Robert Kelly was signed from St Helen's Town, for what was said to be the highest fee ever paid for a Lancashire Combination player. 'The most talked of player in Lancashire junior football circles—a second Buchan', was the way in which one newspaper described the 19-year-old Kelly.

Inside a week, Bob Kelly was playing his first game for the first team, when Teddy Hodgson was injured, and he scored in the 4–0 trouncing of the Cup-holders, Aston Villa. In November 1913, the Burnley papers spoke of 'this young man's sensational debut . . . a born footballer'.

Meanwhile, round one of the F.A. Cup had seen Burnley drawn at home against South Shields: 'practically a walk-over', said the confident *Burnley Gazette*. Fifteen thousand people turned up to see the 'walk-over' on January 10, and Burnley lined up: Dawson; Bamford and Taylor; Halley, Boyle and Watson; Nesbitt, Lindley, Freeman, Hodgson and Mosscrop. In the first five minutes, Burnley should have gone into the lead, but Tommy Boyle hit the post with a penalty kick. After that Jerry Dawson had to show some brilliant form to keep the keen South Shields forwards out, but then Dick Lindley scored two just before half-time. Bert Freeman added a third and the South Shields team scored a consolation goal near the end.

Burnley were back on the road to Crystal Palace, and round two saw them at home again, this time against Derby County. Burnley fielded the same team against Derby as had won in the previous round, whilst Derby were playing the great Steve Bloomer, for probably his last appearance at Turf Moor. He turned out at centre-forward, now 40 years old, and in his 22nd year with Derby. A total of 30,000 people paid £1,025 to see the match; and in what turned out to be the roughest game seen at Turf Moor for many years, Teddy Hodgson scored all three in the 3–2 win that took Burnley into the third round. The winner came only six minutes from the end.

Now Burnley were in the last sixteen, and they found themselves drawn at home yet again, this time against their neighbours, Bolton Wanderers. Prices were slightly raised for the game. Ground 1s, Enclosure 2s, Stand 3s and 4s. Meanwhile, during their Cup run, Burnley had been gradually climbing the League table. During January and February, they went eleven games without defeat, and February saw them lying fourth in the First Division, behind Blackburn, Sunderland and Manchester United. In preparation for the Bolton game, the Burnley team went to Lytham, taking many long walks and brine baths. The day before the game, the players returned to Burnley. The same team played for the third Cup-tie running and 32, 734 paid £2,153 at Turf Moor on a fine February afternoon to see the local 'derby'. Many walked from Bolton, arriving long before ten in the morning, whilst nine excursion trains made the trip from Bolton to Burnley.

The game proved a great triumph for the home team, with Bert Freeman scoring after half-an-hour and Hodgson and Halley making it 3–0 in the second half. MAGNIFICENT VICTORY, ran the newspaper headlines, as Burnley beat the team who were third in Division One at the time, and who included such stars as Vizard and Smith. The *Burnley Gazette* reported 'Dawson did his job to perfection; Bamford and Taylor were towers of strength; the half-backs were superb; Nesbitt had his best game of the season—all three goals coming from his wing. Exit Bolton!'

The draw for round four was:

Sunderland v Burnley
Manchester City v Sheffield United
Liverpool v QPR
Sheffield Wednesday v Aston Villa

The Sunderland game was going to be the biggest hurdle of the season. Brilliant though their victory over Bolton had been, Sunderland were the League Champions; they were second in Division One at the time, and they had beaten Burnley in the semi-final the previous season. Back to Lytham Burnley went in preparation for the visit to Roker Park. It was about that time that several of the Burnley team were chosen for representative honours. Taylor and Halley for the Anglo Scots; Watson, Freeman and Mosscrop for the English League, whilst both Watson and Mosscrop were English internationals that season.

A record crowd for Sunderland of 34,581 paid £2,196 at Roker that day in March, 1914, with over 4,000 making the long journey from Burnley. Once again, Burnley lined up with the same team, whilst Sunderland had their usual galaxy of stars, Ness, Cuggy, Mordue, Buchan & Co. In a closely fought game, Burnley came away with a 0–0 draw, and earned a replay the following Wednesday.

History was made again at Turf Moor the following week, when a crowd over 10,000 greater than any previous attendance, jammed into the ground to see the replayed Cup-tie. Altogether 49,734 people filled Turf Moor, and they paid a record £2,838. 'In the history of Burnley Football Club, it will be recorded that one of the most brilliant achievements was the victory over Sunderland, which paved the way to the semi-final for the second season in succession'. So wrote one local paper in retrospect. The Wearsiders were routed; Hodgson scored within four minutes, and then Lindley got a second. Conner scored a late goal for Sunderland, but the result was never in doubt. The *Daily News* said: 'It was a great triumph for Burnley—one of the best in the club's history, looked at from whatever point of view one likes. They were a great side, fore and aft. Admirably captained by that great centre-half back, Tommy Boyle, they had not a weak spot. There was nothing better in the match than the wing play of new international Mosscrop—easily the best forward on view'. Soon afterwards, Boyle, Hodgson and Mosscrop were chosen to play for the English League against the Scottish League, which was played on Turf Moor, March 21, 1914.

The semi-final draw saw Burnley, who were eighth, paired with Sheffield United, who were fighting against relegation; whilst Aston Villa, second in the League table, were drawn against Liverpool, who were also in the relegation struggle. After another spell at Lytham, Burnley met Sheffield United at Old Trafford, but the game resulted in a very boring 0–0 draw; 55,812 paid £3,777. Commented one paper: 'It is hard to imagine a duller game—without a goal and without a feature'. One feature, however, was that Jerry Dawson badly wrenched a thigh muscle, and for the first time in the Cup games that season, Burnley were compelled to make a change, Ronnie Sewell coming in as goalkeeper.

Meanwhile, Liverpool had beaten Aston Villa, 2–0, to enter their first ever Cup Final.

The Burnley–Sheffield United replay at Everton on April 1, 1914, was a much brighter occasion than the first encounter. The score was 0–0, when with 17 minutes to go, 'Nesbitt, who had scarcely played up to his true form, centred brilliantly, right to the feet of Mosscrop. Mosscrop trapped the ball and touched it back to Boyle, who espying an opening amid the players, shot the ball into the net with terrific force'. It was the winning goal, and Burnley, like

Liverpool, were through to their first ever F.A. Cup Final at Crystal Palace. Said the Burnley press: 'Individually, Boyle was a wonder, whilst Sewell played the game of his life'.

Jerry Dawson came back a month later after his thigh injury, to play in the first team at Manchester, just a week before the Final. But soon in the game, he collided with a Manchester City forward, and was forced to retire with severe rib injuries. (Dave Taylor went into goal for the rest of the game, but Burnley went down 4–1.)

Straight after the City game, Burnley set off for their training headquarters at Lytham again, where they had stayed before every Cup-tie. They returned to Burnley on the day before the Final, and then embarked on the train at Bank Top station. They were given a great send-off by hundreds of local people. The team was followed later in the day by 14 excursion trains which travelled down to London after work on Friday evening. Around 15,000 people (including my grandfather!) were on those trains (return fare 12s!), and because so many of the town's working population were away, most mills closed down for the weekend. There was especial local excitement because King George V would be at the match, the first time a reigning monarch had ever attended such an event. 'The King will arrive by motor-car at 3.20 (ten minutes before the kick-off), and it is still hoped that he may be persuaded to present the Cup to the winners'.

From early on the Saturday morning thousands of Burnley and Liverpool fans were all over London, especially around the Houses of Parliament, where Burnley's M.P., Philip Morrell, was showing large parties of people around. Three regimental bands provided music from one oclock at the Crystal Palace ground. And then, just an hour before the kick-off, Burnley hearts sank, when it was announced that Ronnie Sewell, who had only played seven League games for Burnley, would be taking the place of stalwart Jerry Dawson in the Burnley goal. Dawson had met the directors, and voluntarily stood down from the team, as he felt that his injury had not sufficiently recovered for the big test. The King arrived five minutes before the kick-off, at 3.25, and the huge crowd greeted his arrival with great cheers which completely drowned the playing of the national anthem.

Played upon a very hard, dry ground, the 1914 Cup Final was not a great game by any standards, but it was a very sporting game. The score was still 0–0 at half-time, and Bert Freeman's goal came 13 minutes after the interval.

'From a throw-in on the right, Nesbitt banged the ball across to Hodgson, who had to compete with Longworth. It was a great leap that Hodgson made before he reached the ball above the head of Longworth, but he managed to get his head to the ball, and directed it across to Freeman. Like a flash, the Burnley centre was on the ball, and he snapped up the opportunity without hesitation. Campbell in the Liverpool goal had no chance of saving, and Freeman was almost overwhelmed by the exuberance of the Burnley team who swarmed around him'—*Burnley Gazette*.

Tommy Boyle's voice could be heard all over the ground as he urged his team on in the second half in their supreme effort to capture the Cup. Teddy Hodgson later struck the cross-bar, and 12 minutes from the end, Boyle collapsed with a chest injury, but after treatment, he was able to continue. And so it was that Sewell; Bamford, Taylor; Halley, Boyle and Watson; Nesbitt, Lindley, Freeman, Hodgson and Mosscrop, won the F.A. Cup for the first, and as yet, the only time in Burnley's history.

Meanwhile, there had been a Reserve game at Turf Moor, where a board had been carried around at intervals giving the Crystal Palace news, 'NO SCORE'. We can only imagine the great roar that spread around the ground as news of Bert Freeman's goal came through. The progress of the game was also relayed to the offices of the *Lancashire Daily Post* in St James' Street, and throughout the afternoon, the town centre was so packed with people that the traffic had to be diverted. Thousands stayed out in the streets all that night celebrating the victory. Local papers told of 'gentleman' Jerry Dawson's brave decision not to play, Bert Freeman's opportunist goal, Tommy Boyle's leadership, and how greatly the King had enjoyed the occasion. The *Burnley Express's* headline ran . . . BURNLEY'S CROWNING TRIUMPH.

Local schools and mills closed for the day on Monday. The train carrying the team arrived at Rosegrove station, where the players boarded a wagonette. From the station, the triumphant procession made its way into Burnley, down Accrington Road, and on Trafalgar. When they turned the corner of Trafalgar into Manchester Road, a great crowd of well over 50,000 people greeted them with a loud roar. And so, Tommy Boyle, sitting in his shirt-sleeves at the front of the wagonette, next to Dave Taylor, brought the F.A. Cup back to Burnley. At the Town Hall, cheer after cheer rose from the gathered crowd, bands played and hats were thrown into the air. The crowd was so large that the players weren't able to leave their coach, so they stopped whilst the Mayor of Burnley, James Sellers Kay, called for three hearty cheers for the victorious team. Then they proceeded to Turf Moor, where they were due to play Bradford City in their last League game, kick-off 6.15 p.m. The proceedings were somewhat light-hearted after all the weeks of tension and preparation for the Cup Final, and no one was over-worried at the result, a 2–2 draw. During the course of the following week, the team made daily tours around the district, as far afield as their training headquarters at Lytham, and on the Wednesday, even to Liverpool, their Cup-Final opponents, where the clubs met again in a charity match, which Liverpool won 1–0.

Earlier in the season, Burnley F.C. received the following letter from the Deutscher Fussball Club in Prag: 'We ask courteous if you were not willing to come on the continent for 14 days (in the time from middle May to June 1) and 6 plays in this time in diverse towns, and what you wish for travel compensations. We are praying you send us answer by return of post and sign with exquisite respect. D.F.C. Prag'.

Very few teams could have resisted such an offer (if they understood it!) and so in the close-season of 1914, Burnley made their first overseas tour, an 18-day visit to Austria, Hungary, and Germany. During their six games, Burnley beat Berlin 2–1, and Rapid Vienna 2–1, but lost in Hungary to Glasgow Celtic, in a match for the 'Buda Pesth' Cup. Burnley were the last team to visit Germany before the World War hostilities commenced, and indeed they only returned to England, less than a month before the outbreak. From all reports, it would appear that hostilities began during the tour, because the club returned with 13 of the players on the injured list. Only goalkeepers Sewell and Dawson returned unscathed from the conflict!

1914–15

The 1914–15 season began after war had commenced. There was a sense of anti-climax in the Burnley camp after their Cup triumph, and because of weakened teams due to war-time service, form fluctuated. The week after Burnley had beaten Bolton Wanderers 5–0, Blackburn put six past the Clarets without reply. Already by late 1914, the Halley, Boyle and Watson formation had broken up, when George Halley was one of the first to volunteer for the forces. Burnley were fortunate in having such an able deputy for Halley, as Levy Thorpe, and early in 1915, he was chosen for the English League against the Scottish League. Billy Watson also came in for honours, when he played for the English League against the Irish League, whilst Bert Freeman scored his hundredth goal in little over three seasons at Turf Moor.

A new face, Joe Lindsay, came from the Irish club Glentoran, and Tommy Boyle had a spate of penalty misses . . . in the match report against Bolton Wanderers, the local paper reported, 'for a change, Tommy Boyle was successful from the penalty spot!' The player who was capturing all the attention in 1915 was Bob Kelly, by now established in the first team, and the local papers were regularly printing sensational reports of this 21-year-old. The year after the Crystal Palace victory, 42,938 saw Bolton Wanderers gain revenge for the previous season when they beat Burnley 2–1 in the third round of the Cup.

Fourteen points won out of the final 16 lifted Burnley into fourth position behind Everton, Oldham Athletic and Blackburn. The 1914–15 season was certainly a great one for the Lancashire teams. Mention of Lancashire, reminds us that Burnley won the Lancashire Cup for the second time in their history, when they beat Rochdale 4–1 in the Final at Hyde Road, Manchester, after they had beaten Manchester United, Liverpool and Rovers on the way to the Final.

1915–19

Every attempt was made to keep footballers at home during the early days of the war, and this policy sparked off no small controversy, locally and nationally, because already the war had been costly in lives for the ordinary families. However, for the entertainment of the wounded, and to keep morale as high as possible, it was decided to continue with organised football, though on a more local level, thus cutting costs.

The game had continued to develop over the years, and two changes in the rules that came about during the years of 1912–13 greatly affected defensive play. In 1912, the Laws were changed so that the goalkeeper was not permitted to handle the ball outside his own penalty area, whilst in 1913 the distance from the ball at which opponents must stand at free kicks was altered from six to ten yards. No doubt in their day, these changes brought about various experiments, and Burnley's defence developed an interesting and adventurous system when facing up to free-kicks. When the opposing team were taking a free kick anywhere near the Burnley penalty area, Jerry Dawson would come out and stand as near to the ball as possible (ten yards), in order to narrow the angle, whilst Tommy Boyle and Dave Taylor would stand on the goal-line to cover him. Amazingly, the idea usually worked.

Bob Kelly continued to capture local and national headlines in 1915–16 . . . 'Lindley and Kelly were a magnificent wing' . . . 'No one was better on the field than Kelly' . . . 'Kelly improves every game he plays'. In those days, it was quite usual for forwards to change positions regularly; Bob Kelly had quite a spell at outside-right, whilst Billy Nesbitt proved a sensation for a season at centre-forward. In 1916 the Football Club helped the war effort by sending out footballs and jerseys to the men fighting in France. But by this time, the war was becoming even more costly, and it seemed imperative that even footballers should be ready to offer themselves for their country. Because of this, regulars like Kelly, Boyle and Dawson began to appear less frequently. It was one of the most remarkable features of 1916 that when Jerry Dawson had to leave the team, who should fill his place in goal, but 'the burly one' himself, old Jack Hillman, who had first appeared on Turf Moor over 25 years previously.

Because of war-time conditions, it was impossible to keep a settled team; 19 players played in the first four games of 1916–17. Because of where they were stationed, many Burnley players were playing for other teams, Eddie Mosscrop for Reading, Dave Taylor for Chelsea, and Billy Watson for Southport. One player, Hastie, played centre-forward, inside-right, outside-left, right and left-half, right and left-back . . . seven different positions in 19 matches that season! Gates fell disastrously, and without their regular players, Burnley had no success. At the end of the 1916–17 season, there was great doubt as to whether it was worth playing another season under war-time conditions. Anyway after all the deliberations, football nationally and Burnley F.C. locally, soldiered on with the added burden of an increase in admission fees to eightpence. A. Lorrimer and W. Pickering, both ex-Burnley players had been killed in action; Tommy Boyle had been hit with a shell in France and was now in hospital; ex-player, Jimmy Hogan had been imprisoned in Austria; Levy Thorpe returned home badly wounded in the knee, whilst Charlie Bates, ex-player and first team trainer, had been a prisoner in Germany for nearly four years.

One statistic stands out in 1917–18; the fact that 76 players played for the first team that season, and 37 of them appeared for just a single game!

But with the end of the war in 1918, the team's performances began to improve with the return of men like Bob Kelly and Teddy Hodgson. February, 1919, saw 10,000 people at Turf Moor, the largest crowd at Burnley for four years, and to celebrate the occasion, Burnley beat Manchester United 4–2, after being two goals down at one time. The team that day read: Dawson; Splitt and Newton; Yates, Taylor and Watson; Kelly, Lindley, Freeman, Hodgson and Mosscrop, and for the first time that day, Billy Watson and Eddie Mosscrop were making their return to the side. Tommy Boyle returned to the game in March, 1919, and that same week, full-back Len Smelt, who had turned out several times for the Clarets during the war, signed on for them from his native Rotherham.

1919–20

Despite Burnley's miserable war-time record, optimism was high at Turf Moor at the beginning of the 1919–20 season. A practice match was held, and left-winger Walt Weaver and defender Alf Basnett were described as 'promising juniors'.

Eyebrows and voices were raised in protest when admission prices were increased again in 1919. The admission to Stand A went up from 1s 3d to 2s; the Enclosure increased from 8d to 1s, whilst the Ground was 9d. One sad point at the start of the 1919–20 season, was that neither Dave Taylor nor Teddy Hodgson were available, as both were quite seriously ill; also George Halley, who had been one of the first to volunteer in 1914, was still away. But worse was to come, for in August, Teddy Hodgson died, aged 33, because of kidney trouble which had been brought on by the war. A great local favourite, he was greatly mourned in the town, and many hundreds of people turned out in the town for his funeral.

Gates were higher than at any time since the war began, and 15,000 on an average came to the 1919 games. Burnley began well, and after six games, they were third in the First Division, behind Middlesbrough and West Brom. 'Boyle is playing better than ever' the paper reported. A testimonial match was arranged for the family of Teddy Hodgson, in which a League XI played a Burnley team strengthened with guest players. The League XI won 5–1, but the match was long remembered by the locals because of the Burnley right-wing pair . . . Bob Kelly and Billy Meredith (the legendary Manchester United player, who had taken part in the 'Stop the game, it's snowing' epic). Said the *Burnley News*, 'The pair appeared to have a thorough understanding of each other, and they manoeuvred with a braininess and artistry, such as has not been seen at Burnley for a long time'.

Billy Watson was chosen at the time for the England team to play Wales, whilst Levy Thorpe, who had now recovered from his war injuries, was selected as a reserve for the international. A national paper reported that 'Watson was the pick of the English half-backs', and immediately after the game, he was chosen again to play against Ireland. Whilst Billy Watson was away on international duty, George Halley returned to Burnley after two and a half years away in India and Mesopotamia, and he played his first game at left-half in place of Watson.

By November, Burnley were second in the table:

	Played	*Points*
Newcastle	14	21
Burnley	14	19
West Brom	13	18

Billy Watson was certainly capturing the headlines in 1919, because after his international appearance, he was chosen again, this time for the English League to play the Irish League. And then in November, he scored a spectacular goal in the game against Manchester United.

Eddie Mosscrop put the ball into the penalty area, and it was headed out; then came Watson's 20-yard shot from outside the penalty area. 'Who can recall Watson's goal, without at the same time remembering Watson's action as he thundered down the field with big hefty strides, uttering at the same time, his long drawn out cry of 'Hey-up!' It was an action which in a manner, hypnotised the whole of the players, and they practically stood still waiting for him to shoot. Nearly all the players stood transfixed watching the ball go in the net, having moved their heads more as an act of curiosity to see what the ball would do, more than anything else'. (*Burnley News*, November 15, 1919.)

Despite Burnley's run of success, they had achieved it very much without the talents of Tommy Boyle, who was out of the team injured for many weeks. But then, with Burnley challenging for the First Division leadership, there came the bottom of the table team, Bradford, to Turf Moor, and they beat Burnley 6–2! 'It is a somewhat peculiar feature that if Jerry Dawson happens to make a bloomer, the rest of the Burnley team go flop, their hearts sink in their shoes, and everything goes wrong. It was so on Saturday, when Dawson allowed a corner kick to slip through his hands'.

But the following week, Tommy Boyle returned, and the 'old firm' of Halley, Boyle'n Watson played together again for the first time for five years. The result was that Burnley beat Bradford 1–0 at Bradford, and for the first time in the whole of their history, they were on top of Division One!

	Played	*Points*
Burnley	17	23
West Brom	16	22
Newcastle	16	21

Now, they were being regularly referred to as 'The Clarets' in place of their older nickname 'The Turfites'. Another interesting incident that happened prior to the Bradford game, was that Tommy Boyle received a letter offering the team £1,000 if they lost. Fortunately, to dispel any rumours, it was a game which they went out and won, but the sender of the letter was never traced.

In December, 1919, Cliff Jones, the full-back, was sent off for kicking an opponent in the game against Oldham. Burnley lost the game 1–0, and also lost the lead in Division One. It was the third time in the last ten years that a Burnley player had been given marching orders. In January, 1911, Bob Reid was sent off for fouling Anthony in the first replay against Rovers in the Lancashire Cup Final, whilst in November, 1918, Dick Lindley was ordered off the field, for kicking the ball away from the penalty spot in the match against Manchester City.

After the Jones incident at Oldham, the Oldham team came to Burnley to play the return game the following Saturday, as was the custom in those days. A DISGRACEFUL GAME ran the headlines in the local paper the following Wednesday. 'Tommy Boyle fell on top of Dolphin, who had been involved with Jones the previous week, and broke bones in Dolphin's shoulder. Watson caught Bradbury on the instep, and he had to go off too. Oldham now had nine men . . . now ball or man was their motto, and they usually chose the man. Nesbitt received several bad kicks, and once Lindley luckily escaped being kicked on the head with a back-heeler, as he bent down to pick up the ball for a throw-in'. They bred them tough in those days! Burnley went on to win the Oldham game 2–1, despite the fact that George Halley missed two penalties. However, Tommy Boyle made no mistake with the third one!

In January, 1920, the League positions read:

	Played	*Points*
West Brom	22	32
Burnley	24	31
Newcastle	23	29

The F.A. Cup was back in business after a break of four seasons, and Burnley had an unusual draw away against Thorneycrofts (Woolston), a team who played in the South-Eastern League. Because the pitch of this torpedo works team was too small, the game was transferred to the Portsmouth ground, and in a hard game, the little works team forced a 0–0 draw with the First Division challengers. However, Burnley won the replay, 5–0, and went on to be drawn against Sunderland.

Meanwhile in February, Burnley's title hopes disappeared when they were beaten 3–1 by Sheffield Wednesday, who were then at the bottom. Sunderland came to Turf Moor for the Cup-tie, and though Travers gave them the lead, Bob Kelly equalised soon afterwards. Eddie Mosscrop had a goal disallowed, whilst Tommy Boyle had to miss the game through illness. It was perhaps typical of the strain of playing in those days, and of the efforts of Bob Kelly that he had to take to his bed after the match, and was there for several days.

That same day, a fascinating thing happened in the Reserve team. Sewell was chosen, but objected to playing for the Reserves, so who should turn out for Burnley Reserves, but old Jack Hillman! Another headline that day, was that the old favourite of the Burnley crowd, Dave Taylor, returned to Burnley, and started training again. He had been seriously ill for many months at his home in Scotland.

Burnley were going through a bad spell in early 1920, for they lost the Cup replay at Sunderland 2–0. Not for the first time, it was Charlie Buchan who was the master-mind of the Sunderland team that day. Then on the day that Burnley were beaten at Hyde Road (as usual!) by Manchester City, reserve goalkeeper Sewell, who had played in the Cup winning team, requested a transfer as he didn't want to become a permanent reserve to Jerry Dawson. No fewer than 42 goalkeepers had come and gone in the Reserves during Dawson's 13 years as Burnley's regular first-team choice, and I don't suppose that Ronnie Sewell wanted to become just another of the also-rans. The League position in February read:

	Played	*Points*
West Brom	28	40
Burnley	31	39
Sunderland	28	34

Another instance of violence on the pitch can be seen from the *Burnley News* in March 1920 . . . 'Personally, I do not think Boyle looks quite fit, but for all that I regretted the action he took with regard to Peart on one occasion. One Burnley player has just finished two months' suspension for retaliation, and the fact that Boyle had been kicked did not justify him seizing Peart by the throat!'

The deciding week for the League Championship came in March when Burnley met West Brom. The game at Turf Moor resulted in a 2–2 draw, but just as memorable were the gate receipts of £1,962, a Turf Moor League record. In the return game, West Brom won easily, 4–1, and so clinched the title. The League position now read:

	Played	*Points*
West Brom	32	46
Burnley	34	42
Sunderland	32	37

Two individuals caught the headlines at Burnley in March, 1920. First of all, a new centre-forward, Joe Anderson, was bought from Clydesbank for £2,000. Joe 'Andy', who was to become a real Turf Moor personality, made his first appearance on March 20, 1920, against Sunderland at Turf Moor. The team that day read: Dawson; Smelt and Halley; Basnett, Boyle and Watson; Nesbitt, Freeman, Anderson, Lindsay and Mosscrop. One personality was missing from the team that day . . . Bob Kelly. Kelly was playing for the English League against the Scottish League, his first major honour since coming to Burnley. One report read 'Bob Kelly played a brilliant game and appears to have taken over the inside forward position from Buchan'. Kelly scored in the English League's 4–1 win.

As a result of his spectacular debut, he was chosen for England, and played his first international against Scotland at Sheffield in

April, 1920. England won 5–4, and Bob Kelly scored two of his country's goals. 'THE GREATNESS OF KELLY' was the headline in the *Athletic News:* 'The best forward on the field' was the way the *Sunday Chronicle* described him, whilst the *Daily News* reported the following: 'England's strength was in attack, all five players were first class, with Kelly touching greatness. The Burnley man has a turn of speed, an elusive swerve, and perfect ball-control, and England has not had a better inside-forward since Bloomer at his best'.

Meanwhile, as the League programme drew to a close, Burnley beat Everton 5–0; Joe Anderson scored his first hat-trick for the club, and Bert Freeman turned in a superb performance at outside-right. The forward line that day read: Freeman, Kelly, Anderson, Lindsay and Weaver (who was introduced at the end of the season when Eddie Mosscrop was injured).

The final League table read:

	P	W	D	L	f	a	Pts
West Brom.	42	28	4	10	104	47	60
Burnley	42	21	9	12	65	59	51
Chelsea	42	22	5	15	56	51	49

Burnley had finished runners-up in Division One for the first time in their history. Three more of the Cup-winning team bid farewell to Turf Moor . . . goalkeeper Ronnie Sewell went to Blackburn Rovers for £1,600; inside-forward Dick Lindley went to Bradford City; whilst full-back Tom Bamford went out of football. Levy Thorpe also went to Blackburn, for a fee of £2,000, whilst at the same time, a young promising forward called Benjamin Cross came to Turf Moor.

1920–21

The new season started off in a very spectacular, if somewhat disappointing fashion for Burnley. They entertained Bradford City, who included the old Burnley stalwart, Dick Lindley, and despite a late Joe 'Andy' goal, Burnley went down 4–1 at home. Two days later, Burnley went to Huddersfield and were beaten 1–0. After this game, Jerry Dawson was dropped and reserve 'keeper Birchenough came in. Tommy Boyle was injured in the Bradford game, and he missed the next two matches. Burnley fans were staggered after their performance of the previous season. It was their worst start to a season since 1893. But then, Burnley went to Bradford and were beaten again by the City team, 2–0. After three games, Burnley were bottom of Division One!

And then came the turning point on September 6, 1920 . . . Burnley 3 Huddersfield 0. 'BOYLE'S GREATNESS, A BIG

FACTOR IN VICTORY' ran the headlines, and the team that played in that first winning side was, Dawson; Smelt and Taylor; Halley, Boyle and Watson; Nesbitt, Kelly, Anderson, Cross and Weaver. Kelly, Boyle and Nesbitt scored the all important goals.

'Will Burnley maintain their newly found form?' asked the *Burnley News*. Little did anyone at the time realise how long they *were* going to maintain that form!

Middlesbrough came to Burnley, and at half-time were one up. But then Benny Cross headed the equaliser, and Joe 'Andy' hit the winner. A 0–0 draw in the return game at Middlesbrough put Burnley five points behind the leaders Huddersfield. And then Chelsea were beaten 4–0 at Turf Moor. Benny Cross had an outstanding game, and he and Walt Weaver were beginning to form a real partnership. Tommy Boyle scored from a penalty, Cross, Kelly scored others, and Billy Nesbitt made it four, just three minutes from the end.

On October 2, 1920, Burnley Football Club fielded three teams for the first time on the same day . . . the First team were away to Chelsea, the Reserves away to Stockport, whilst the Third team were at home to Northern Nomads. The seniors were almost beaten at Chelsea, and were 0–1 down, until Joe 'Andy' equalised with twelve minutes to go. A big feature in Burnley's play at this period, was that big Dave Taylor was really back to his best form at full-back.

And then to Park Avenue, where Bradford scored first, but Bob Kelly scored a hat-trick to make it 3–1. In that game full-back Bob McGrory came in for Len Smelt who was ill. Now Burnley were in the top half, though still five points behind the League leaders, Aston Villa. In October, Bob Kelly was chosen to play for England v Ireland at Sunderland. The next Saturday, Burnley completed the double over Bradford with a Joe 'Andy' goal.

Because of the international, Burnley went to Tottenham without Kelly, Joe Lindsay the Irishman taking his place. Spurs numbered in their team such stars as Dimmock, Clay and Walden, and though they scored first, two more Anderson specials were enough to gain the points for Burnley. Now Burnley were sixth, just three points behind Villa. Meanwhile at Sunderland, Bob Kelly continued on his historic way by scoring one of the two goals that beat Ireland.

The next week, Tottenham came to Burnley and lost 2–0 through goals by Kelly and Cross. One newspaper reported that Jerry Dawson was at his best, 'diving low, quick to run out, tipping over the bar'. The Clarets had now risen to fourth place, two points behind the joint leaders, Newcastle, Liverpool and Aston Villa, and the next game was away at St James' Park, Newcastle!

Over 50,000 people came that day in November to see Burnley win 2–1, through goals by Boyle (penalty) and of course, Kelly. 'The finest team in England' was the verdict on Burnley by many of the Geordie fans that night.

The return match between these two League leaders was greatly anticipated, and the number of seats was increased in the stand. A total of 38,860 people were present, a new League record for Turf Moor, beating the Rovers gate of 38,000 in 1913. 'AND THAT WAS THE MUCH VAUNTED NEWCASTLE TEAM!' ran the headlines after the match. Again, Burnley were triumphant, for though Jerry Dawson allowed an easy one early on, goals by Kelly, Cross, and another penalty by Boyle made Burnley joint League leaders with Liverpool, just a point ahead of Villa.

This was now easily the best unbeaten run in Division One for any Burnley team, and the *Burnley News* commented: 'This team looks like beating a lot of records'. How true!

And then there came a surprise for Burnley. They went to Oldham, and when Joe 'Andy' and Walt Weaver put them two up, they appeared to be on the usual victorious road. But Oldham came back and equalised, and almost scored a late winner. However, the point that Burnley gained at Oldham was enough to put them at the top of Division One.

'THE WIZARDRY OF BURNLEY' ran the headlines after Burnley had beaten Oldham 7–1 at Turf Moor. Listen to this! . . . 'Not many times in the life of a football spectator is it permitted to watch football such as that of Saturday, which gained Burnley the biggest bag of goals which has fallen to their lot in 19 years. Saturday's display will live in history—not merely for the glut of goals, but for all the glorious football that the team showed. "I have been following football for 38 years," said a well-known Burnley man at the close, "I have seen it in all parts of England and Scotland, but I never saw such wonderful football in the whole course of my life, as I saw in the first 15 minutes of the game today". The play of the Burnley side was too staggering for words. Kelly was surely an inspiration to see, swaying like a reed in the wind, deceiving, feinting, then slipping through the defence on his own, or co-operating with Nesbitt in a manner which brought the pair cheer after cheer. Theirs was surely the acme of scientific skill . . .' (*Burnley News*). To sum up, Bob Kelly scored four, Benny Cross got a couple, and Tommy Boyle added the seventh, and Burnley had now played 13 games without defeat.

The attack had starred; in the next game, a goalless draw at Liverpool, it was the turn of the defence. It is interesting to note, that all this time, there were men of the calibre of Alf Basnett, Eddie Mosscrop and Bert Freeman, playing in the Reserves!

A rising shot from Walt Weaver was sufficient to give Burnley the points in the return match against Liverpool. The position at the top of Division One now read :

	P	W	D	L	f	a	Pts
Burnley	18	11	4	3	34	16	26
Newcastle	18	11	3	4	35	17	25
Bolton W.	19	9	6	4	36	21	24

And then Burnley increased their lead to three points, when they beat Preston North End 2–0 at Turf Moor. Joe 'Andy' scored two in a minute, both coming from Weaver centres. This was the first season where the bonus system for players had operated, whereby players received £2 for a win, and £1 for a draw. And because of Burnley's successes, there was great interest in the town, as to which of the Burnley players was earning the most!

Burnley celebrated Christmas 1920, by beating Sheffield United 6–0, (Anderson 4, Kelly and Cross). Sixty thousand saw the return game at Bramhall Lane, a 1–1 draw. Sheffield gained for themselves the miniature honour of being the first team to score against Burnley in a month, but Bob Kelly got the equaliser. Now Burnley were beginning to tighten their hold on the championship . . . four points ahead of Newcastle, with a game in hand! When the New Year was heralded in, Kelly and Anderson both had 13 goals to their credit—more than any Burnley player had scored in all the previous season.

They made it 14–14, when the team went to Preston, and won 3–0. Benny Cross scored the third, and this was a particularly satisfying victory, as it gave Burnley the first 'double' over their old rivals at North End since 1893–94.

The town even began to talk of winning the 'Double' of Cup and League, when Burnley went to Leicester, and won 7–3 in the First Round of the Cup. (For the second time in a fortnight, Joe 'Andy' scored 4, whilst Kelly, Cross, and an own goal made up the number.)

After Preston, came the Rovers! And the Clarets took their East Lancashire rivals in their stride, winning 4–1. Burnley had previously played 13 games without a team change, but the 13th proved unlucky for Walt Weaver who was injured. Eddie Mosscrop came back into the side, and there was a newcomer in the Burnley side. Joe 'Andy' was given a monkey wearing the Burnley colours as a mascot, and for several games, it would make its appearance before the game, and climb upon the crossbar.

In the Blackburn game, Tommy Boyle shot from over 30 yards out, but the ex-Burnley player, Sewell, misjudged the ball, and Burnley were ahead! The other scorers that day were Cross (2) and Kelly. Then, just as they had done the double over Tottenham,

Newcastle and Preston, Burnley accomplished the feat against the Rovers, when they beat Blackburn at Ewood through goals by Kelly, Anderson and Mosscrop.

February saw them back in the battle for the Cup. Burnley were drawn at home against Queens Park Rangers. 'THE MASTERY OF MOSSCROP' ran the headlines, as Burnley advanced into the third round by means of a 4–2 win; 41,007 people, paying £2,582, saw the goals shared by Anderson and Kelly.

Benny Cross and Walt Weaver were both injured, so Joe Lindsay and Eddie Mosscrop came in for the game against Aston Villa. This again was a memorable match, as Burnley raced to a 7–1 win, and thus equalled Preston's 32-year-old record of having gone 22 games without defeat. Billy Watson was captain for the day in place of the injured Tommy Boyle, and he celebrated by scoring from the penalty spot. Joe Lindsay also got one, but the day belonged to Joe 'Andy' with five goals to his name! Even against the famed Sam Hardy, Anderson was unstoppable. The *Burnley News* recorded that as the referee prepared to blow his whistle for full-time, 'Hardy, with a look of disgust and weariness, came out of his goal—never bothered to stop Anderson getting his fifth, and walked straight off the pitch, leaving the ball in the net!' 'One of these days, we shall lose Andy in the netting!', ran a Burnley cartoon the following week. Now the club were seven points ahead of Newcastle with two games in hand!

Burnley Football Club were *the* topic of conversation in the barber's shop, in the Church vestry, in the smoking room, and on the trams. 'THE NEW INVINCIBLES' ran the headline of February 12. Of course there was always the occasional lucky break, such as when Derby missed a penalty at Turf Moor. Burnley went on to win 2–1, with goals by Anderson and Lindsay, but if Derby had scored the penalty, it could have been a different story. George Halley was more unlucky, for although he was chosen to play for Scotland against Ireland, he had to step down because of a bout of pneumonia, which also kept him out of the Burnley team for several weeks.

A week after the 'New Invincibles' headline, the press had to take back their words, when they were compelled to print 'THEIR WATERLOO AT LONG LAST'. It was the third round of the Cup at Hull, a ground on which Burnley had never won, and against a team who were struggling at the bottom of Division Two. Burnley went into the game without Anderson who had a badly damaged cheek bone after being carried off in the Derby game, and without George Halley, still down with pneumonia. Bert Freeman came back to fill his old centre-forward spot.

'Hull went into it hammer and tongs; they kicked the ball any-

CUP IN HAND. Tommy Boyle arrives back in Burnley with the F.A. Cup

" HAIL THE CONQUERING HEROES." (*above*) 1914: Burnley fans welcome home Tommy Boyle and his team with the F.A. Cup. (*below*) 1960: the town turns out to cheer the 1959–60 League Champions, led by Jimmy Adamson

where, raced about for it, and whenever it came their way, it had to be either man or ball, or both. The Turf Moor side were not simply thrown off their game; they were knocked off it with bounce, bustle and speed'. The result, a 3–0 victory for Hull, is remembered to this day, as one of the greatest giant-killing acts of the century, ranking alongside all the tales of Colchester, Yeovil, and Walsall.

Perhaps knocked a little off their perch, Burnley were glad to take a point in a 0–0 draw at Derby, and then the following Saturday, when Bolton were the visitors at Turf Moor, the Wanderers were ahead at half-time. But goals by Cross, Kelly and Nesbitt put the result beyond doubt . . . Burnley were back on Championship course!

For the away game at Bolton 3s 9d rail returns were run for the first time since the war. Both the excursion trains and Burnden Park ground were packed like herrings, as 54,809 squeezed into the Bolton ground, beating the previous record of 52,000. That day was an outstanding one for Burnley's defence, against a team which included David Jack, Joe Smith and Ted Vizard. With Dawson and Smelt particularly outstanding, Joe 'Andy' scored, and Joe Smith equalised in a 1–1 draw. Now after 30 games, Burnley were still six points ahead of Newcastle, and after the Bolton game, Joe 'Andy' was chosen for the Anglo-Scots team to play Scotland.

A penalty goal by Billy Watson was enough to beat the Arsenal at Turf Moor, and by this time, Burnley had won their last 15 home games. There were problems in the playing staff . . . 'Watson is sorely in need of a rest, Anderson dare not head a ball, and George Halley is still down with pneumonia'. (Alf Basnett had taken over the right-half position with great success.)

In the return game at Highbury, a Joe 'Andy' goal gave Burnley a point, whilst on Good Friday 1921, a Benny Cross goal was enough to secure both points at home against Manchester United. Now the Turf Moor side were eight points ahead of Liverpool in second place.

And then came Easter Saturday (March 26) 1921, and Burnley were to be seen that afternoon at Hyde Road, Manchester. The gates were closed long before the kick-off, house tops around the ground were crowded with people, great numbers of people climbed upon the stand roofs, and the crowd poured over the barriers until there was scarcely a yard of space around the touch line. Everything went wrong that day for the Clarets . . . Bob Kelly was completely subdued by Hamill, Alf Basnett was knocked out twice in the second half, Tommy Boyle missed a penalty. City ran out 3–0 winners, and all there agreed that on the day, Burnley were well beaten by the City team who were fourth in the League at the time.

But came Easter Monday, and it was 'business as usual' for the Burnley team. They were still in Manchester, but this time at Old Trafford—an Old Trafford ankle deep in mud, to play the United team. 'THE REAL BURNLEY AGAIN—THE MAGIC OF KELLY' roared the local papers. Tommy Boyle, Bob Kelly, and Joe Anderson were the scorers to give Burnley two more valuable points, but it would be almost sinful to omit the following account which appeared the week after in the *Burnley News*.

'THE MAGIC OF KELLY'

'. . . And so Kelly took matters into his own hands, and thrilled the crowd by his stupendous individualism. Swerving, writhing, wriggling through obstacles, jumping over extended feet, and carrying the ball with him all the time, he electrified the crowd by some of the most magnificent runs it has ever been their lot to see. Not once or twice, but a host of times, he broke away like a fox with the hounds streaming in full cry behind him, and the crowd hugged themselves in ecstasy, and the cry of 'He's off again' could be clearly heard. Wildly fascinated, the crowd waited for these exciting runs. They commenced towards the close of the first half. Just one minute was wanted till half-time, and then Kelly set off again. He worked right away from his own position to the left, dodging and dribbling cleverly, and avoiding the defence till he was well within the penalty area, and an almost certain scorer. And then Silcock kicked his legs from under him. Referee! Spot! BOYLE! Goal!!!'

Let the last word about the 30 games without defeat come from a man of the times, 'Kestrel', who wrote all the Burnley F.C. articles in the *Burnley News*. 'So an end has been put to Burnley's record-breaking run. But do we mind? Not a bit of it! We have been partners with the greatest team that ever was. We know full well that never in our time will such a thing be accomplished again, and we like to think that we live in an age that will be remembered when we personally are forgotten'. How true you were, Kestrel old friend!

The successful run was ended, but the season was now reaching its climax. Manchester City came to Turf Moor, and Burnley recorded their 17th successive win at Turf Moor. City scored first, and for a time it appeared that they might be going to do the 'double' over Burnley, but goals by Nesbitt and Anderson saw Burnley through again. Now with only six games to play, Burnley were nine points ahead of Liverpool, and seemed assured of the title.

But with Kelly away, playing for England, Burnley went down 2–0 at West Brom, and only just saved a point with a last minute Bob Kelly goal in the return match at Turf Moor. Then on April 23, 1921, came the crowning point of a record-making season, when a Benny Cross goal gave Burnley a point against Everton at Goodison, and Burnley were CHAMPIONS for the first time in their 40 years' history.

It was just as Burnley clinched the title that the local press carried a news item that must have caused a tinge of regret for all true Burnley fans. 'EXIT BERT FREEMAN', the headline read. 'Gentleman Bert', as he was known throughout the game, had announced his retirement from the game. 'The name of Bert Freeman, a real sporting type, will live in football as long as the game continues', said the report.

The Burnley–Everton 1–1 result was repeated at Turf Moor with another goal by Benny Cross, but then Sunderland put paid to Burnley's hopes of establishing a new record of points, when they won 1–0 with a Charlie Buchan goal.

The final match of this memorable season was at home against Sunderland. Strangely, just as Jerry Dawson had missed the final honour in the 1914 Cup Final so, once again, he was missing the day that Burnley received the League Championship trophy. He missed the match because of a pulled thigh muscle, and Moorwood deputised. Nesbitt and Kelly levelled the scores for Burnley after Sunderland had gone two ahead. 'Rarely have Kelly and Nesbitt operated better than on Saturday. Nesbitt had the Sunderland defence in a hopeless tangle, and seemed able to do just as he liked, whilst Kelly let himself go thoroughly, and played what is known in football parlance as a "blinder". He dragged the Sunderland defence over half the field with him on many occasions'.

And so Burnley, the League Champions, came to the end of probably their most glorious season. Besides the regular eleven of Dawson; Smelt and Jones; Halley, Boyle and Watson; Nesbitt, Kelly, Anderson, Cross and Weaver; Eddie Mosscrop (who played in 14 games), Dave Taylor (who played in 11 games), and Alf Basnett (who played in 15 games) were also presented with Championship medals. Billy Watson was the only player to have played in all their 62 games, League, Cup and Lancashire Cup.

The average gate at Burnley's games in 1920–21 was 32,850 and because the gates had been so great, the club made a profit of £13,040.

The last word of a remarkable season comes from the report on the F.A. Charity Shield game played that May between Tottenham, the Cup Winners, and Burnley, the League Champions. Spurs won by two goals to one, but the match report includes a paragraph with the familiar heading 'KELLY THE WIZARD'. 'Kelly, of course! There was not another like him. He was a gay spark, full of humour, and often his way of running around the ball, side-stepping, and dodging, aroused great peals of laughter and cheers'.

And to celebrate the Championship coming to Burnley for the first time, the club treated all its players and officials to a picnic. Two charabancs went off to Morecambe for the day!

1921–22

The price of a season ticket in Stand A at Burnley in 1921–22 was 50s, and many who bought season tickets that season saw Burnley set off to a great start again . . . much better indeed than the Championship year when they had lost the first three games. First, a 3–2 win at Birmingham, and though this was followed by a 3–2 defeat at Sunderland, the club rattled off three fine victories at Turf Moor, against Sunderland, Birmingham and Newcastle. After playing five games, Burnley were back on top of the League table.

But Newcastle knocked Burnley off the top with a 2–1 beating, and only Jerry Dawson saved them from a bigger beating. Twice in October, 1921, Burnley met Glasgow Celtic. They beat them 2–1 in Glasgow, and 3–0 on the Turf, recalling memories of the Buda Pesth Cup they had competed for in Hungary in 1914.

At the start of the new season, there was great local controversy as to who was the club's best left-winger, Eddie Mosscrop or Walt Weaver . . . but for the time being it was Weaver who held the position.

The Clarets went back to the top when they beat Bradford City 4–0 twice in a week, first at Turf Moor, and then at Bradford. Jerry Dawson and Billy Watson were chosen to play for the English League against the Irish League, and then at last, after 15 seasons with Burnley, Jerry Dawson was chosen to keep goal in the England v Ireland match. For this game, Bob Kelly was dropped by the English selectors, much to the disgust of his many admirers.

And then with a 1–0 win over Sheffield United at Bramhall Lane, Burnley were now two points ahead of Liverpool after the first ten games. Everything seemed to be going well for the champions, when they put five past Chelsea, but perhaps the turning point in Burnley's history came with a 4–1 defeat at Stamford Bridge. In that game, both Boyle and Watson were injured, and with captain Boyle absent from the side, a weakened Burnley let in nine goals in the next three games. Burnley only gained four points from their next six games, and after 17 games, Burnley, Huddersfield, and Liverpool were all level with 22 points.

Jerry Dawson and Bob Kelly were both chosen for the international trial, England v The North, and afterwards, they played again in the England v The South trial. But at Turf Moor, Burnley were falling behind Liverpool in the title race. They lost at Ewood, when the Rovers won 3–2, and this put them six points behind Liverpool.

And then on February 11, 1922, Burnley's great home record was broken by, of all teams, Rovers, when the Clarets went down 2–1. It was the first ' double ' achieved over Burnley, since Bradford City had done the trick in the first few days of September, 1920. The team that day, read as usual: Dawson; Smelt and Taylor, Halley, Boyle and Watson; Nesbitt, Kelly, Anderson, Cross and Weaver, whilst ex-Claret Ronnie Sewell was in the Rovers' goals.

' DECLINE OF BURNLEY ' and ' AN INFUSION OF YOUNG BLOOD IS THE PRIME NEED ' ran the local headlines. There *were* changes made for the next games, but it would seem only because of injuries . . . Astin came in for Dave Taylor, Billy Morgan for Billy Watson, and Douglas for Billy Nesbitt. Bob Kelly continued his international career when he was chosen for the England v Wales game in 1922, and a further honour came to Turf Moor as a ground, when it was chosen as the venue for the F.A. Cup semi-final on 25 March between Huddersfield Town and Notts County. Huddersfield won the game 3–1, and went on to the Final where they met Preston, who had beaten the Spurs, 2–1. At Turf Moor 46,323 saw the game and the receipts came to £3,266.

Burnley dipped into the transfer market in March, when they signed an outside-right, John Fisher from Chesterfield, and an Irish international full-back, William Emerson from Glentoran. There was a slight hangover from the Emerson transfer, when Burnley were fined £50 for playing him before his registration had gone through the proper channels! He played for Ireland, within a fortnight of his signing for Burnley. April was a memorable month for veteran goalkeeper Jerry Dawson, now in his 15th season at Turf Moor. First of all along with Bob Kelly, he was chosen for the England team to play Scotland at Villa Park, and then he was presented with a gold watch by the club on the completion of 500 appearances with the Burnley first team.

Injuries cost Burnley dearly in their bid to keep the title, and the season came to a disappointing close, as they finished third.

	Played	*Points*
Liverpool	42	57
Spurs	42	51
Burnley	42	49

Billy Nesbitt was out of the team from February until the season's end; Billy Watson had been out for over a month, and their great captain, Tommy Boyle, had spent the rest of the season on the injured list. It was to be the last that the Burnley crowd would see of Tommy Boyle, for in May, 1922, the *Burnley News* reported: 'Boyle has signed on as coach, but it is very unlikely that the condition of his leg will permit him to play again'.

It was the end of a glorious decade, summed up by the local paper. 'The greatest regret of the season was the break-up of the grand old line of half-backs—Halley, Boyle and Watson'. Their last game together had been the home defeat against Blackburn Rovers on February 11th, 1922. Despite their lasting fame in East Lancashire soccer circles, it is a fact (though the old-timers will probably shake their heads and say 'Never!') that they only played 115 games together as a half-back line; less than three complete seasons. Their longest run of consecutive appearances was 23 during the great 30 game sequence in 1920–21 before George Halley went down with pneumonia.

FIVE

DECLINE AND FALL OF THE BURNLEY EMPIRE

1922–23

The team that began the 1922–23 season looked like: Dawson; Smelt and Taylor; Emerson, Sims and Watson; Fisher, Kelly, Anderson, Cross and Mosscrop.

But it was a different Burnley these days, from the 'old guard'. Tommy Boyle had retired, though he still expressed hopes of making a come-back; Bill Nesbitt had broken down again in training, whilst George Halley and Cliff Jones were involved in a dispute with the club over wages.

Meanwhile after their modest start, Burnley found their old form again, and an 8–2 victory over Notts Forest (Cross 3, Kelly 2, Watson 2, Weaver) in November, put them two points behind Champions and League leaders, Liverpool. That same week, George Halley, who had failed to come to terms with the club, was transferred to Southend. The old firm of Halley, Boyle and Watson, now looked like Emerson, Basnett and Watson.

But something was lacking from the club's play, and several dropped points at home meant that when Christmas, 1922, came around, Burnley were sixth, eight points behind Liverpool, who were galloping to their second successive League title.

The new year saw the return of the F.A. Cup, and as had been their custom since before they won the trophy in 1914, Burnley were at Lytham for special training. But before the Cup-tie at Sunderland, there was the League. Home and away defeats by Sheffield United put Burnley in the bottom half of the table for the first time since February, 1915, and the Sunderland Cup-tie began to take on vital proportions. 'SERIOUS ISSUES AT STAKE FOR TURF MOOR CLUB', screamed the local press.

There was no instant recovery in the Cup either, for Burnley went down fighting at Roker Park, beaten 3–1. It was the usual story for the two clubs who were meeting in the Cup for the fourth time in seven seasons . . . Buchan v Kelly! For many seasons they were compared and contrasted as they competed for the inside-forward berth in the England team. In the Sunderland Cup-tie, one paper recorded: 'Despite Kelly being one of the greatest men on the field, and giving Joe Anderson his goal, it was Charles Buchan who once again proved to be the master-mind whom Burnley could not hold'.

Things continued to get worse for Burnley, and local interest declined until gates had dwindled in March, 1923, to 14,000. There was even talk of relegation, (a strange word for Burnley over the last ten years) and a demand for new blood. Even Jerry Dawson was dropped after a bad spell, and Moorwood came in for eleven games. Seven games produced a single point during February and March, 1923, and in an attempt to bring success, the club plunged into the transfer again. Winger Jack Fisher went back to Chesterfield in exchange for their top scorer George Beel. But it was to no avail . . . Burnley, who at one time had challenged the leaders Liverpool, finished 22 points behind them, and only eight points off relegation.

Kelly and Emerson continued on their international careers, playing against Scotland and Wales for their respective countries. But it proved to be the last season at Burnley for two more Turf Moor stalwarts . . . Billy Nesbitt (who had only managed eight games in the season) and Eddie Mosscrop (16 games). After 174 games for Burnley, Mosscrop's retirement was a particularly tragic one, as he was taken ill in November, 1922, with sciatica. More new faces arrived at Turf Moor in preparation for the 1923–24 season. Burnley paid a four figure fee to Albion Rovers for outside-right Peter Bennie (only 5ft 2½ins), but they really shook the football world when they signed one of their tallest ever players and biggest ever names, the 6ft 3½ins tall centre-half from Plymouth Argyle, Jack Hill. The fee was the highest that Burnley had ever paid, and a League record at the time, around £5,000.

1923–24

Both Bennie and Hill proved to be great favourites with the Burnley crowd. Though Burnley went down 2–1 at Notts County, the press headlines ran, 'HILL MAKES SATISFACTORY DEBUT', and then in his second game against Everton, he scored with a header. The team at the start of the new season read: Dawson; Smelt and Taylor; Watson, Hill and Emerson; Bennie, Kelly, Beel, Cross and Weaver.

But popularity didn't bring success, for after six games, only Burnley and Preston hadn't registered a victory in Division One. Then at last, two Joe Anderson goals did the trick against Liverpool, and soon afterwards, Joe 'Andy' left Turf Moor to return to his native Clydebank. The Liverpool game proved to be very much a flash in the Turf Moor pan. After nine games, Burnley still only had seven points, and then defeats by Sheffield United and Aston Villa brought the headlines, 'BURNLEY HEADING FOR SECOND DIVISION'. One win in eleven games had resulted in the position:

	Played	*Points*
Middlesbrough	11	7
Burnley	11	7
Preston N. E.	11	4

Again, in desperation this time, Burnley spent money on a player, and this time, what a bargain! £450 was forked out on George Waterfield, a 22-year-old outside-left from Mexborough in the Midland League. Waterfield came to Burnley in October, 1923, and Burnley celebrated his debut with a win over Sheffield United at Turf Moor.

Stalwart full-back, Len Smelt, made his 100th consecutive appearance for the first team against West Ham, but in contrast to Billy Watson who had accomplished the feat in 1913, the club was refused permission by the League to present Smelt with a suitable memento. George Beel scored his first hat-trick in that game against West Ham, which Burnley won 5–1. But even Len Smelt was made to look a raw newcomer the following game, also against West Ham, when Jerry Dawson chalked up his six hundredth appearance.

Now Burnley were fielding four teams every week, the First and the Reserves, the 'A' team and a midweek team. The club didn't have a very happy Christmas in 1923, gaining only one point from the three holiday games, and even bottom team Preston beat them 5–0!

The shaky League position was reflected in the Cup, when Burnley narrowly beat non-league team South Shields, 3–2, with goals by Kelly (2) and Cross. Burnley had never managed to win at Hyde Road, and when Manchester City moved to their new ground at Maine Road, Burnley were still unsuccessful with a 2–2 draw. After a goal-less draw in the second round of the Cup against Fulham at Turf Moor, Burnley won through to round three by the single goal in the replay.

Probably the high-light of the entire 1923–24 season was in February, 1924, when Huddersfield Town came to Turf Moor for the third round Cup-tie. Stand seats were increased to 5s for the game, but despite this, a crowd of 54,775 came to Turf Moor for the game. Never before, and never since has such a crowd invaded the ground on Brunshaw Road, and they saw one of the most thrilling Cup-ties witnessed at Burnley. Burnley (who were in the bottom six) beat Huddersfield (who were in the top six) 1–0.

Jack Hill dominated the game; Walt Weaver was the best winger on view, and George Beel led the Burnley attack with great spirit. One spectator, James Dodd, aged 69, was killed in the great crush of the crowd.

Len Smelt was injured in the Burnley v Huddersfield Cup-tie, and his absence the following week brought to an end his run of 117 consecutive appearances for the first team. Meanwhile, both Kelly and Hill were included in the English League team to play the Scottish League.

Burnley continued shakily towards the new towers of Wembley, when they forced a draw at Swindon, through a Walt Weaver goal. In the replay, two goals from George Beel and another by Weaver saw them through to the semi-final for the first time since they had won the Cup ten years previously.

Still hovering dangerously near the foot of the table, Burnley entered the transfer market again, buying George Parkin, Ernest Dixon, and Ben Wheelhouse from Halifax Town, and Evans, a Welsh international full-back from Cardiff. Billy Morgan, the club's left-half, broke his leg, whilst playing in the 0–3 home defeat by Sunderland, but the following week, lowly Burnley caused the surprise of the season when they visited League leaders Sunderland, without the injured Smelt, captain Hill, Morgan, Weaver and Cross, and yet came away with the points thanks to a George Beel goal.

The two questions in the minds of Burnley fans in March, 1924, were 'Will the club be relegated?' and 'Will the team win the Cup?'

The second question was the first to be answered, when Aston Villa were easy 3–0 winners over Burnley in the Cup semi-final at Sheffield. But the relegation struggle continued and when 36 games had been played, Burnley were sixth from the bottom, with Arsenal, Forest, Preston, Chelsea and Middlesbrough below them.

Looking back, it would seem that just one thing saved them in those closing games, the discovery of a new right-wing partnership of Benny Cross and Bob Kelly. With these two fine players just clicking at the right time, Burnley drew at Tottenham and Huddersfield, and won at home against Arsenal. In the end they just escaped relegation by four points.

Towards the end of the season, gates hit rock-bottom at Turf Moor. Only 5,058 saw the Bolton game, whilst a mere 3,685, paying £126, turned up for the Arsenal game. Because of the greatly decreased gates and the cost of transfers, Burnley made another loss of over £6,000, following on the £6,500 they had been in debt the previous season.

Again, the end of the season brought another nostalgic farewell to Turf Moor, and this time it was the veteran left-half Billy Watson who was retiring after 468 appearances in the first team. Watson, one of the most popular and talented men ever to play at Turf Moor, made his final appearance for the team in the F.A. Cup semi-final against Aston Villa. Another old favourite who had played in that game and who had graced the Turf Moor scene for many seasons, Dave Taylor, also left at the close of the season to return to Scotland to manage the St Johnstone team.

1924–25

The new season began with many of the locals prophesying relegation after the previous disappointing season. The Clarets began with a 0–0 draw against Cardiff, and the team was: Dawson; Smelt and Evans; Basnett, Hill and Parkin; Kelly, Cross, Beel, Drummond and Weaver. 'There are few changes in the Burnley team' read a local cartoon—'Kelly still wears the longest trousers —and Hill the longest legs!' One important change in the football code that season was that goals could be scored direct from corner kicks for the first time, but the law didn't affect Burnley too much as they didn't score many goals to begin with, one way or the other. Another goal-less draw was made against Everton, and then an away win at Preston, 2–0, gave them 'a good defensive start', according to the press at the time.

But then came a 'SHOCK FOR BURNLEY'. Against their oldest rivals, Blackburn Rovers, Burnley were three up after only fifteen minutes, and seemingly on the way to a famous victory. But the Rovers pulled one back by half-time, and in the second half, went on to score another four, and win 5–3 in the end. 'We would rather have lost to anybody in this manner, but to Blackburn', said the local reporter.

A home point against Liverpool, saw Burnley seventh from the bottom after six games. In an attempt to stem the flow, the Turf Moor club made an important signing in October, 1924; Tom Roberts, a centre-forward, was signed for over £4,000 from bottom team Preston; Roberts was already an English international, and was one of the League's leading scorers. James Tonner was also signed that week. Tonner, a speedy outside-right, came from Bo'ness, the Scottish Second Division club.

With their two new signings, and without Bob Kelly, away playing for the Football League, Burnley gained a very welcome away point at Tottenham, with Roberts scoring the all important goal. Later Bob Kelly was chosen for his ninth cap against Ireland. 'There is no doubt that Kelly is one of the greatest artists in the game. In fact one is sometimes inclined to think that he is too great an artist for his colleagues, and that his super-brilliance does not tend towards a harmonious working of the side'. So said the *Burnley News* in 1924.

Another goal-less home draw against Bolton Wanderers meant that after ten games, only Everton, Sheffield United, and Preston were now beneath them. Of course the Championship side of 1921 had undergone many changes in three years, and only Dawson and Kelly were still in the first team, whilst Smelt, Watson, Basnett and Weaver were regulars in the second team; Benny Cross was on the injured list.

Burnley went to Upton Park and lost 2–0 to West Ham, and then a foolish mistake cost them a point at Turf Moor. Alf Basnett, thinking an opponent was offside, stopped the ball with his hand, and from the resulting penalty (!), Sheffield United took away a valuable point. Several team changes didn't stop them losing 3–0 to Newcastle, and now Burnley were next to the bottom.

But then came a welcome change in the club's fortunes; in their ninth home game of the season, Burnley won for the first time. Their run of eight consecutive home games without a win equalled the record they set up in 1889 when they had gone until March without winning. And Tom Roberts helped to pay back some of his transfer fee, when he scored his first hat-trick in the 4–0 win over Bury.

Sadly, Burnley's mini-revival came to a halt when Everton knocked them out of the Cup in round one, and now the fight for Division One survival was on!

	Played	*Points*
Everton	25	20
Burnley	23	18
Notts. For.	24	16
Preston N. E.	24	14

Two more goals by Roberts gave Burnley a 2–0 revenge win over Blackburn, and again local hopes began to soar. Jack Hill was tried at right-half, and George Waterfield was moved to left-back, and both were great successes in their new roles. Their best performance of the season came when they went to West Brom, the League leaders, and won 4–1. So successful was Jack Hill at right-half that he was chosen for England in that position, along with Bob Kelly in front of him. But again bad luck struck at Burnley, when newcomer Roberts who had fitted into the team so well, was seriously injured in the game against Spurs. The Tottenham goalkeeper went up for a ball with the Burnley striker, and Roberts hit the ground and broke his hip-bone, which put him out for the rest of the season. In 23 games, he had scored 16 goals, and had become a real favourite of the Turf Moor crowd. Burnley's policy of buying continued, when they bought Jack Bruton, an outside-right, from Horwich in March 1925.

The season limped along to its close, with Burnley picking up an occasional point, and a draw in the last match, saw the final position for 1924–25:

	Played	*Points*
Burnley	42	34
Arsenal	42	33
Preston N. E.	42	26
Notts. For.	42	24

It was Burnley's worst season in Division One since their return in 1913, and on top of their miserable first team record, the Reserves finished bottom in the Central League. No doubt, Roberts' injury played an important part in their struggle, and so to strengthen their forward line, Burnley made another memorable signing in the close season, when they signed 25-year-old Louis Page, the Northampton Town left-winger. Within a week, Burnley tightened their defence, when Irish international full-back, Andy McCluggage, was signed as a 25-year-old from Bradford. Like Bruton, both these players were to become household names in Burnley.

Once again, Burnley made a big financial loss on the season. Average gates had dropped to 15,000 and over £16,000 had been lost over the past three seasons. The writing was beginning to appear in bold capitals on the wall!

1925–26

The big talking point at the start of the 1925–26 season was the change in the offside rule. Burnley tried it out in a public practice game, and Bob Kelly opened up the opposing defence so much that local opinion turned against the new rule. 'Who wants to see one team win 20–0?' asked 'Kestrel' of the *Burnley News*. Well, in the opening game of the new season, the crowd at Villa Park nearly did see such a score. Burnley were the visitors, and Capewell scored for the Villa in the first half minute. He went on to get a hat-trick by half-time, and with Jack Hill off the field injured for the best part of the game, Aston Villa went on to win 10–0. 'It could have been twenty!' said one Aston Villa player after the match. The Burnley team in that historic game was: Dawson; McCluggage and Waterfield; Basnett, Hill and Parkin; Kelly, Freeman, Roberts, Beel and Page. The following week, Burnley bounced back to beat Leicester City 4–0, and Tom Roberts scored his second hat-trick for the club. But it was a flash in the pan, for in the next game, Manchester United beat the Turf Moor team 6–1. This early season flood of goals was merely a foretaste of things to come.

Strangely, despite the defensive lapses, Andy McCluggage was an instant success in the team, and it was a pity that Burnley had to refuse to release him to play for Ireland against England, because of a crucial league game on the same day.

Goals continued to pour into the Burnley net, and when Manchester City beat them 8–3, (Tom Browell getting five), they sank into the bottom three.

	Played	*Points*
Burnley	13	9
Bury	10	8
Cardiff	13	7

Ignominy was piled upon ignominy, for Burnley's 'pet antagonists', the Rovers came to Turf Moor and won 3–1. And Burnley hit the bottom of the ladder.

	Played	*Points*
Man. City	13	10
Cardiff	14	9
Burnley	14	9

'WILL THE CLUB ESCAPE THE SECOND DIVISION?' asked the local press. And then, almost predictably they went and drew with the League leaders Sunderland, 2–2, at Roker. Something had to be done to stem the flow of goals, and despite their serious financial position, Burnley bought John Steel, a right-half from Hamilton Academicals for around £3,000. This purchase naturally plunged the club into deeper financial waters, and rumours began to circulate about the possibility of players like Roberts, and even Bob Kelly himself being sold.

After only 17 games, Burnley had conceded 50 goals, and were now at the bottom of the table.

	Played	*Points*
Bury	16	12
Cardiff	17	12
Man. City	17	11
Burnley	17	11

But then on top of everything, after a few bad games, Jerry Dawson was dropped. But worse was to come. A brief stop press paragraph on the back page of the *Burnley News* of December 2, 1925, created the biggest news of the season, and people still talk of it in the town.

BOB KELLY TRANSFERRED TO SUNDERLAND

During the following week, the reports of his departure read like an obituary; 'DEPARTURE OF KELLY' . . . 'BLOW TO BURNLEY FOOTBALL PUBLIC' . . . 'Never has a greater blow been administered to the Burnley public than the transfer of Bob Kelly' . . . 'He was the first player ever to be brought through the Burnley teams, and sold for any amount' . . . 'No man has ever been so greatly honoured whilst playing with Burnley' . . . 'To those who saw him, the memory of his brilliant play will remain for life, the sinuous moves, his deceptive body swerve, his speed off the mark, the spectacular shot, his ball jugglery, all in all—a football wizard'. Whilst 'Kestrel' of the *Burnley News* summed up Bob Kelly's transfer in his usual prophetic way . . . 'We part with him with regret, fearing that we may never see his like again'. Very few players have done anything to make 'Kestrel' eat his sad words, since that day in December, 1926. Once again, the transfer fee was a record one at the time, amounting to £6,550.

But life went on at Turf Moor. The idol of the crowd had gone, and the club were still at the bottom of the First Division, with the worst defensive record in the whole Football League. So once again, Burnley entered the transfer market . . . Roberts, Tonner, Tresadern, Bruton, Page, McCluggage, Steel had all arrived at Turf Moor inside 12 months, and now they signed a goalkeeper, 27-year-old Tommy Hampson from West Ham United.

The new arrival had a very unhappy debut, for the Clarets went down 8–1 against Bury in a Division One game. Hampson was injured early on, so Jack Hill took over until half-time, when left-half Leonard Hughes replaced him, thus giving Burnley the unusual record of having three goalkeepers in one game. Jack Hill even saved a penalty during his time between the posts, but very little went right for the Turf Moor team that day. Soon after Hampson left the field, Roberts was injured, and Burnley were reduced to nine men for the second half. Late in the game, Andy McCluggage missed a penalty, just to add to Burnley's cup of woe.

However, Christmas, 1925, proved to be a happier time for the East Lancashire team, for they managed to take three points from fellow strugglers, Leeds United, and so lift themselves off the foot of the table.

	Played	*Points*
Burnley	23	18
Man. City	23	16
Leeds Utd.	22	16

Louis Page was the man who did most of the damage to Leeds that Christmas, and he was beginning to score goals regularly from the outside-left position. Life was getting tougher than ever at the bottom, for after 29 games, only two points separated the bottom eight clubs, whilst Notts County at the bottom were only ten points off Arsenal at the top!

	Played	Points
Leeds Utd.	29	24
Cardiff	29	24
Man. City	30	23
Burnley	30	23
Notts. Co.	28	22

The position looked very grim now, and so, desperately, Burnley spent some more of the Bob Kelly transfer fee. 'MIDNIGHT TRANSFER' ran the headlines in the *Burnley News* and the arrival at Turf Moor the following day was Billy Dougall, a versatile forward from Falkirk. The date was February 27, 1926, and it was the beginning of one of the longest player-club relationships in the club's history. Big Jack Hill was chosen for the English League to play the Scottish League, and because of this, the Burnley captain missed the important game against Blackburn. Rovers were one up at half-time, and two up after the hour, and then seven goals came in the last eighteen minutes, with Blackburn emerging 6–3 winners. Local headlines ran 'HOPES OF ESCAPING RELEGATION RUNNING THIN', for the bottom of the League table now appeared:

	Played	Points
Man. City	32	26
Notts. Co.	32	25
Burnley	33	25

The immortal Kelly returned to Turf Moor with Sunderland, and although he scored, Burnley surprised everyone by running out 5–2 winners. It seemed that the club were just going to stave off the drop into the Second Division, but there were shocks in store over the Easter weekend in 1926. West Brom visited Turf Moor, and despite two successful McCluggage penalties, the Midlanders took home two points with a 4–3 win. And then fellow strugglers, Manchester City, came to Burnley, and they too won, 2–1. Prospects were now bleak. The team was bottom, and there didn't seem much hope of any improvement in form. The last game that Easter was away to Birmingham, and Burnley announced six team changes in the side to play at St Andrew's. Dawson was dropped and back came Tommy Hampson; Fred Blinkhorn was brought in at left-back for George Waterfield; Bruton came in on the right in place of Tonner, who was moved onto the left wing. Beel and Roberts were dropped, and Benny Cross and Louis Page took their positions in the middle.

Louis Page, very much at home on the left-wing, didn't want the centre-forward position, but he was persuaded to play, very much against his will. He remarked casually before the game, 'I'll get six goals and stop at that!' 'PAGE THE PROPHET!' ran the headlines after the game, for he created football history that afternoon by scoring three in each half. Briggs, the Birmingham centre-forward, was injured for the best part of the game, and this disorganised the home team completely. Benny Cross was the complete schemer, and he reduced the Birmingham defence to shreds. Besides scoring a hat-trick before half-time, Louis Page also hit the bar twice, and after Jackie Bruton had made it 4–0, Page scored three goals in little over three minutes! Page's six goals remains the club's individual scoring record to this day.

The converted centre-forward scored another important goal the following Saturday, when he hit the equaliser in a 2–2 draw against Bury at Turf Moor. And again he scored in the next match against Sheffield United, but the Blades hammered six in reply, which only underlined Burnley's grave plight with two games to go.

	Played	*Points*
Leeds Utd.	40	34
Man. City	40	33
Burnley	40	32
Notts. Co.	40	31

Burnley simply had to win their last two games, and the first was away to Tottenham, who were riding high in the League table. In an amazing performance, Burnley came away from White Hart Lane winners by two goals to none, Andy McCluggage (penalty) and George Beel being the scorers. With just one game to play, one thing was certain: Notts County were relegated. But who went with them?

	Played	*Points*
Man. City	41	35
Leeds Utd.	41	34
Burnley	41	34
Notts. Co.	41	31

And of the three, Burnley had by far the worst goal average. On the last day of the season, these were the vital fixtures:

Burnley v Cardiff City
Leeds Utd. v Spurs
Newcastle v Manchester City

It was a game that Burnley simply had to win, and they did. Goals by Beel (2), Bruton and Page (his 26th of the season) gave them a 4–1 win, much to the relief of one of the biggest crowds of the season. The fate of the club now hung in the balance as they waited to hear how Leeds and Manchester City had fared. The news came through that Leeds had also won 4–1, and then a swelling cheer from a corner of the ground told the Burnley team gathered in the dressing-room what they wanted to hear. Manchester

City had lost, and were relegated. Newcastle had beaten them 3–2, but just before the end, Austin had missed a penalty for Manchester. If he had scored, and City had gained the point, Burnley would have gone down on goal average. The final table in 1925–26 showed:

	Played	*Points*
Leeds Utd.	42	36
Burnley	42	36
Man. City	42	35
Notts. Co.	42	32

And shortly afterwards, came the General Strike.

1926–27

But life went on at Turf Moor. Preparations were made for the new season, and season tickets were on sale, £3 3s for Stand A and £1 for the Ground. There were the usual close season comings and goings, and the two main names who left Turf Moor that summer were the old stalwarts, Len Smelt, who was transferred to Barrow, and the goalscorer Tom Roberts, who returned to his previous club, Preston North End. The only signing of any significance was George Sommerville, a goalkeeper, who came from Hamilton Academicals, and altogether 30 professionals were on Burnley's books at the start of 1926–27.

The team started off, where they finished the previous season, playing Cardiff. A goal four minutes from the end by Hargreaves made the score 4–3 in Burnley's favour, and set them off on the right footing. The team read: Sommerville; McCluggage and Blinkhorn; Steel, Hill and Dougall; Bruton, Cross, Beel, Hargreaves and Page.

The club had started well, but the best was yet to come! Away to Newcastle at St James' Park, Burnley won 5–1. George Beel scored a hat-trick, and never before had Burnley won their first two games in a Division One season. After almost being relegated in April, here they were in September, riding high at the top of Division One. And Beel scored another hat-trick when the Clarets beat Bolton Wanderers 4–3. George Beel now headed the League's goalscorers with nine goals in five games.

But after such a fine start, Burnley were kicked off the top by a 2–1 defeat at Old Trafford. Benny Cross, (who had been ill the previous season), was now playing at inside-right and performing brilliantly. Jim Tonner was transferred to Hamilton Academicals, and in the meantime, Burnley picked up three more points from Derby and Sheffield United. But when Burnley met their old colleague Bob Kelly again at Roker Park, he bewildered Waterfield and Dougall so much that Sunderland ran out 7–1 victors.

Still, Burnley kept up with the leaders with a 2–0 win over the Arsenal, who included Joe Hulme and Charles Buchan.

For the third time, Jack Hill was chosen for England, but to the consternation of the Burnley fans, Benny Cross, now playing better than ever before, was passed over yet again.

League leaders Sunderland were beaten 4–2 at Turf Moor, and Burnley took over from the Wearsiders at the top. Steel, Hill and Dougall were proving the most regular half-back line since the glory days of Halley, Boyle and Watson. In the Rovers–Burnley game played at Ewood that October, with nine minutes to go, the score was 1–1. But then Andy McCluggage obliged with his usual penalty, and Paddy Freeman and Louis Page (2) went on to make it 5–1 in the end. The Clarets were still at the top, and gates were averaging about 22,000. The mood was a much brighter one than the previous season, which had been one long struggle for success and money.

November proved a crucial month for the club's Championship hopes, for on November 13, Burnley lost the leadership when they went down by the odd goal at Birmingham. But more important than two lost points was the loss of players. Beel and Devine were both badly injured, whilst Benny Cross was so seriously hurt that he would be off for at least a month. And on top of these injuries, Andy McCluggage was sent off for hacking at an opponent. There were many injuries for those playing football in the 1920's, and as an example, Spurs came to Burnley the week after and finished the game with only eight men on the field. Burnley emerged 5–0 winners, but the talking point in the town centre that week was the form of the new boy, Joe Devine, who had come from the Scottish Second Division club Bathgate. Meanwhile, Andy McCluggage was suspended by the League for a month.

Three points from Liverpool over Christmas, 1926, saw Burnley back at the top as they entered the New Year.

	Played	*Points*
Burnley	23	30
Newcastle	22	29
Sunderland	24	29
Huddersfield	22	27

The big name in Burnley that first week in January, 1927, was Dixie Dean, and his two goals helped the bottom team Everton to beat the League leaders, Burnley, 3–2.

Louis Page and George Waterfield were both chosen for the English international trial match, and the next week, Burnley easily beat Grimsby Town, 3–1, in the third round of the F.A. Cup, after Grimsby had scored in the first minute. January 15, 1927, was a historic day in the story of Burnley Football Club, for the club fielded four teams on the same day for the first time, the First team, the Reserves, the 'A' team, and a team of amateurs and juniors were invited to play nearby Portsmouth Rovers in a friendly.

There was great anticipation amongst the supporters for the Cup-tie at Fulham in the fourth round. A local cartoon showed Jack Hill sitting down to a meal, 'Now I've eaten the fish course (Grimsby), I think I could polish off the (Ful)ham!' And they did, 4–0. The fifth round saw the Clarets drawn away in London again, this time to Second Division Chelsea. Waterfield, Page, and Cross were all chosen for the next international Trial, after which Waterfield and Page were selected for the England team to meet Wales, and just as predictably, Benny Cross was passed over again.

Many hundreds of visitors made the trip from Burnley to London, for the meeting between Chelsea and Burnley in the F.A. Cup. One of them, Henry Waters of Ivy Street, Burnley, set off nearly a fortnight previously, and walked to London for the game. A photograph appeared in the local paper showing Henry walking down the street complete with flat cap, rosette, and his coat over his arm, as if out for a Sunday afternoon stroll in the park! He got there alright, and was among the 63,300 people who saw Chelsea win 2–1.

Andy McCluggage was chosen to play for Ireland against the Scots. But after the Cup defeat, Burnley were beginning to lose touch with the leaders. Arsenal beat them 6–2, and now the Turf Moor team were four points behind Newcastle. The club gained some new heart from the 3–1 win which gave them the 'double' over the Rovers, and a glance at the scorers each week seems to suggest that Louis Page and George Beel were the scorers in practically every other game.

Benny Cross led the attack with great flair in the game against Bury. Three down at one time, Burnley recovered to snatch a 3–3 draw. Jack Hill (captain) and Louis Page were chosen for the England team to play Scotland, and during the last week of March, 1927, the club signed both full-backs, Andrew Reid and Alex Forrest from Bo'ness, the Second Division leaders in Scotland.

And then whilst Hill and Page were away on international duty, Burnley lost to Birmingham, and the club dropped to fifth in the League table. After a run of bad results which had cost them any chance of honours, the season came to a quietly disappointing end, with Burnley occupying fifth position.

1927–28

Two more Scottish players arrived at Turf Moor, Andrew Haddow, a centre-forward from Greenock, and Jim Brown, a centre-half from East Fife. Newcomer Haddow created quite an impression in the practice matches, and he was included in the opening match of the new season. Unfortunately, both Steel and McCluggage missed the start owing to illness. In 1926, Burnley had won their first two games for the first time ever in Division One. In 1927 there was another first . . . they lost their first *five* games! Injuries played a big part in the disastrous beginning, for besides Steel and McCluggage both being off, Cross and Page were both badly injured in the opening games, Haddow broke his collar bone, whilst even Jerry Dawson broke his arm playing for the Reserves.

But the Clarets turned the corner, and three consecutive victories did wonders for the team; 4–2 against Villa, 3–2 at Sunderland, and a George Beel hat-trick in the 4–2 rout of Derby gave the Burnley supporters every reason to smile again.

On top of all their injuries, the first team goalkeeper, George Sommerville broke his collar bone as Bolton went on to crush the Clarets 7–1 (Blackmore 4 and David Jack 3). Once again, as on previous occasions, big Jack Hill went in goal, but not even the captain of England could stem the flow of goals that day! How fortunate for Burnley that the day before Sommerville was injured, Billy Down, who had previously played with Doncaster Rovers, was signed on by the directors as a replacement keeper. Down made his debut for Burnley the following week against Birmingham City.

Turf Moor had another debut of its own in November 1927, an international debut, when England played Wales at Burnley's ground (November 28, 1927). Wales won the game 2–1 and 32,089 people paid £2,039 to see the game. There was very much of a Burnley flavour about the occasion for C. E. Sutcliffe was in charge of the England team, Charlie Bates was the England trainer, and Jack Hill was the England captain (who also chose this auspicious occasion to put through his own goal!).

In December, Billy Dougall came back into the team at inside-left, to play against Leicester City who won 5–0. The following day, things were turned around as Billy's brother, Peter Dougall, took over the inside-left berth, and scored in Burnley's 5–1 victory over Leicester at Turf Moor!

Billy Down was proving a great success in goal, but he wasn't good enough to save Burnley going down 2–0 to Aston Villa in the F.A. Cup third round. Jackie Bruton became the fourth Burnley player to take part in an international Trial and Burnley came back to form to beat Sheffield United 5–3. George Beel (3) and Jackie Bruton (2) scored the ones that mattered, whilst Andy McCluggage uncharacteristically, missed a penalty. George Beel had now scored 23 goals in 25 games. Now amazingly, Burnley had risen to sixth position, only five points behind the leaders, Everton.

But any chance of finishing amongst the leaders disappeared when the bottom club, Sheffield Wednesday, beat them 5–0. Altogether, Burnley went through a spell of six games, and only gained three points. And so after another 4–0 beating by Birmingham, the team went for a fortnight's special training to Cleveleys. The Burnley team that were finding life in Division One so difficult in 1928 usually looked like: Down; McCluggage and Waterfield; Steel, Hill and Parkin; Bruton, Pollard, Beel, Dougall and Page. Everton came to Turf Moor, and thanks mainly to Dixie Dean, who scored four, Everton returned to the Mersey 5–3 winners. As usual, Burnley faced Cardiff City in the last game, but this time they weren't as fortunate as the previous occasion, for Cardiff won 3–2. This last defeat almost meant relegation for Burnley, for it cost them ten places in the First Division table, and they finished up only one point off relegation.

	Played	*Points*
Sheff. Wed.	42	39
Sunderland	42	39
Liverpool	42	39
West Ham	42	39
Man. United	42	39
Burnley	42	39
Portsmouth	42	38
Spurs	42	38
Middlesbrough	42	37

Burnley's 98 goals against was the worst defensive record in the First Division. They had never had a settled team because of injuries. Even at the close, Sommerville, Cross, and Dougall were still injured, and Benny Cross had not played since the first game of the season.

1928–29

Four players were signed during the 1928 close season, Stage from Bury, Willighan and Conway from Ireland, and Scott from Grange Rovers in Scotland. Burnley's team which faced Sunderland in the first game of the 1928–29 season was: Down; McCluggage and Waterfield; Steel, Hill and Parkin; Bruton, Steel, Beel, Devine and Page. Benny Cross was still injured and unable to play. Burnley won the game 3–1, and then journeyed up to the North-east to meet Newcastle. In those days, the duels between Hughie Gallacher and Jack Hill were always looked forward to by the crowds, but in September, 1928, it was Hill's day, for Burnley ran riot and were 6–2 ahead by half-time! With Bruton and Page sweeping down both wings and swinging across highly dangerous centres, the game ended 7–2 in Burnley's favour. (Beel 3, Page 2, and Bruton 2 did the damage for Burnley).

But the following Saturday, Burnley were on the receiving end as they were hammered 7–0 by Cardiff, Ferguson scoring five. On October 3, a rumour spreading around town and further afield that Jack Hill was to leave Burnley was fiercely denied. Certainly Hill's form didn't seem quite as consistent as it had been . . . perhaps it was because key players like Sommerville, Dougall, and Cross were still off, and the Burnley captain was over-burdened with responsibility. The rumours continued to grow about big Jack Hill after Burnley lost top place, when they were beaten 4–3 at Turf Moor by the old enemy, Manchester United. In a remarkable game, three penalties were awarded, two being scored by Andy McCluggage, and one by United. And then, three weeks after the first rumour had been denied, another of the greatest personalities ever to grace Turf Moor, left Burnley for the North-east, once again for a record transfer fee. In 1925, it was Bob Kelly who went to Sunderland for £6,550. In 1928, it was Jack Hill who went to Newcastle United for £8,000. It was to be a long time before Burnley saw their like again.

To replace Jack Hill, Parkin was moved to the centre-half position, whilst Alex Forrest came in at left-half. The changes seemed to be successful when Everton came to Turf Moor, and Parkin subdued Dixie Dean as the Clarets won 2–0. But Burnley's troubles reappeared when Huddersfield Town, with players like Bob Kelly and Sam Wadsworth, beat Burnley 7–1. Again Burnley went down, this time to Manchester City, but again the Clarets bounced back with a 6–3 victory at Birmingham. Beel (3), Page (2) and Devine were Burnley's scorers, as the goals continued to mount in the 'for' and 'against' columns of the League table. Another hat-trick came from Beel, as Burnley beat Portsmouth 4–1, and now the team were seventh in the League, just four points behind the leaders, Sheffield Wednesday.

The year didn't provide a very happy Christmas for Burnley; on Boxing Day Liverpool beat them 8–0. As a result of this miserable result, George Sommerville came back into the first team, and gave a brilliant display in the team's narrow win over Sheffield United in the F.A. Cup. But the week after, they slumped to their Christmas form again, when the team they had beaten in the Cup, Sheffield United, gained more than ample revenge, when they thrashed the rapidly failing Burnley side, 10–0! Incidentally, the referee that day was one S. F. Rous—now Sir Stanley Rous, President of F.I.F.A. By now, Burnley had their usually atrocious defensive record, the worst in Division One. In fact, they had conceded 25 more goals than any other team in the Division.

As the club sank gradually down the First Division table, they plunged into the transfer market again. In January, 1929,

Wallace, an inside-forward from Clyde, and Stanley Bowsher, a centre-forward from Newport County, appeared on the Turf Moor scene. Bowsher played for Wales the following week against Ireland, for whom Andy McCluggage scored the equalising goal, naturally from the penalty spot.

But the decline continued. Aston Villa beat Burnley 4–2 at Villa Park, and now the Clarets were in the bottom half, only five points clear of the bottom pair, Portsmouth and Manchester United. Defeat at the hands of Leicester City put Burnley in the bottom six, and then even the bottom club, Manchester United, beat them 1–0.

Andy McCluggage was chosen for his ninth cap, whilst after one game with the Burnley first team, Hugh Flack was selected to partner McCluggage at left-back in the Irish team against Scotland. Now, after the departure of Hill, and Burnley's utter lack of success, Turf Moor gates were falling fast. The 5,936 who turned up for the Burnley v Bury game in February, 1929, was the worst gate at Turf Moor for four years. The financial problems besetting the club gave rise to more rumours concerning a Burnley player, and this time the tales were that Andy McCluggage was seeking a move.

But Burnley didn't sell; instead, they bought! And this time it was Harry Storer who came to Burnley from Derby County. Storer, a left-half and already an English international, proved a good buy, for the team showed an immediate improvement as they beat Leeds United 5–0 with goals from Beel (3) and Page (2). Soon after this game, both Harry Storer and Louis Page were chosen for the English international trial. But Burnley were now in serious financial trouble, and with the overdraft at the bank nearing its limit, the directors, at their meeting in March, 1929, caused a stir throughout the football world, when they announced that all six full-backs on their books, McCluggage, Waterfield, Flack, Knox, Willighan and Heap were on the open to transfer list. Of these, the first three named were all international players.

The League position was as serious as the financial situation, for the team that had topped the table in October, were third from the bottom in April.

	Played	*Points*
Burnley	38	33
Bury	38	30
Cardiff	40	27

'Will Burnley escape?' was the topic about town, but fortunately, a late recovery ensured their presence in Division One, for another season at least.

	Played	*Points*
Burnley	42	38
Portsmouth	42	36
Bury	42	31
Cardiff	42	29

It had been another disappointing season, with the team finishing in the bottom four for the fourth time in five seasons. A fact which emphasised how unsettled the team had been in 1928–29 was that Burnley had eight captains during the season—Hill, McCluggage, Steel, Parkin, Beel, Storer, Stage and Waterfield.

1929–30

In his twenty-third year at Turf Moor, Jerry Dawson announced his retirement from the game. From 1907 to 1929, Jerry had been one of the best-known and most popular players at the club, and he left a legend behind him. His last appearance on Turf Moor was October, 1929, when he appeared in the special benefit match which the club arranged for him.

After a point had been won at Maine Road, and another point at home against Everton, the *Burnley News* headlines read 'A PROMISING START—NO CAUSE FOR PESSIMISM'. But it was early days yet! Hopes soared for the future after two victories over Sunderland and Portsmouth. And so it was that Messrs Down; McCluggage and Waterfield; Brown, Bowsher and Forrest; Bruton, Wallace, Mantle, Devine and Page, found themselves next to Derby County at the top of Division One.

But the rot set in in the fifth game, when Arsenal beat Burnley 6–1, with the help of a superb goal by Alex James. With this defeat, Burnley dropped to sixth position, and then Aston Villa came to Turf Moor and won 4–1! Back into the bottom half Burnley went once again. And then Leeds United beat the Clarets 3–0! Down and down they went.

In an attempt to stop the rot and bring some order into the defence, Burnley bought the English international full-back, Sam Wadsworth, from Huddersfield. Wadsworth had a great reputation for ball control, rarely, if ever, kicked the ball out of play, and had earned a Cup-winners medal, and three consecutive League Championship medals with Huddersfield. It seemed strange for Burnley to buy another full-back, especially after they had announced that all their six existing full-backs were open to transfer. Only one, Hugh Flack, had left the club, but it was hoped that Wadsworth would bring his renowned influence to the team. At £2,000, it seemed that Burnley had made an astute bargain in an effort to steady their creaking defence, which was consistently the worst in Division One. Eight games had now been played, with a net result of eight points, when Sheffield Wednesday came to Turf Moor and won 4–2. Trainer Charlie Bates had a busy time that afternoon, for after Down and Forrest had had attention, Page, Beel, and Bruton were all off the field at the same time. And to crown all their misfortunes, new signing Sam Wadsworth was carried off on a stretcher. With the season almost a quarter over, Burnley were 'back in the old routine', fighting it out in the bottom five clubs.

Louis Page was chosen to play for the English League against the Irish League, whilst Andy McCluggage was capped for the tenth time for Ireland, but Burnley refused to release him for the game. A bolt from the blue came when Burnley had a 5–0 win over Sheffield United. 'THE BRILLIANCE OF BRUTON' ran the headlines, with Beel (2), Devine (2), and Bruton scoring the goals that mattered. Bob Kelly scored for Huddersfield in the 3–0 win which helped to keep Burnley near the foot of the table.

	Played	*Points*
Burnley	12	10
Man. United	12	8
Portsmouth	12	8
Sunderland	11	7

Birmingham's Barkas was sent off the Turf Moor pitch for a foul on Louis Page, as Burnley gained two invaluable points in a 3–1 win. But try as they could, Burnley could not fight clear of the relegation zone, and November 13, 1929, saw them plunged into even deeper despair when they came up against the old enemy Blackburn Rovers. Goalkeeper Billy Down was injured early on, and had to leave the field. In hospital, it was discovered that he had sustained severe internal injuries, and in fact he never played again for the club. Seizing their opportunity, Rovers went to town with a sensational 8–3 victory. Groves (3), Roscamp (3), and McClean (2) were the scorers for Blackburn, whilst McCluggage put home a couple of his specials from the penalty spot, and Louis Page made the score a bit more respectable with a late goal.

The fight at the foot of the table was getting tighter with six teams now involved in the struggle for First Division survival.

	Played	*Points*
Burnley	16	14
Sunderland	15	13
Portsmouth	16	13
Grimsby	16	12
Newcastle	16	12
Man. Utd.	16	12

As usual, along with the team's poor form, the club's finances were suffering badly. The gate of 6,670 at Turf Moor for the West Ham game, realising £314, was the lowest at a Saturday match for six years. Club Secretary, Mr A. Pickles, put the situation fair and square to the public of Burnley, when he said that 'unless gates improve, the Club will be forced to sell players like Page, Devine, and Bruton'. His words were soon followed by action, when international Jackie Bruton was transferred to Blackburn Rovers on December 5, for about £6,000.

Then came a surprise revival in the team's playing fortunes. They won at Anfield with 'a great goalkeeping display by Sommerville'; they had a 4–1 win over Middlesbrough at Turf Moor; a 4–2 home victory over Manchester City, and two Christmas draws against Bolton Wanderers. These eight points from five games saw Burnley enter 1930 halfway up the table, with 23 points from 23 games. 'NEW YEAR HOPES—GROWING CONFIDENCE IN THE CLUB', commented the local football reporter.

A controversial decision in the game at Leicester captured the headlines the following week. Burnley lost the game 4–3, but a 'goal' scored by Hutchinson for Burnley was disallowed by the referee, Mr Mee of Mansfield, because he believed the ball had not crossed the line. But a photograph taken of the incident by the *Leicester Mail*, and reprinted in the Burnley press, showed the ball clearly over the goal-line. The loss of this important point disappointed Burnley very much, and in the next game, after another disputed goal early on by Portsmouth, Burnley cracked up and lost 7–1.

Things began to look black on the Burnley horizon when League leaders Sheffield Wednesday put Burnley out of the Cup. Then despite the absence of Alex James, a David Jack goal gave Arsenal the points, and the next week, Burnley lost 3–0 at home to Leeds.

On the day of the Arsenal defeat, another Burnley favourite, Joe Devine, went to Newcastle United, struggling at the bottom, for a fee of £5,000, whilst on the day of the Leeds defeat, Andy McCluggage was away on international duty for Ireland. For the first time, he captained his national side, and scored with a 30 yard free kick.

When Burnley won at Villa Park for the first time for 33 years (2–1 after being one down), they seemed to be safe. Seven points from the foot of the table, with only 14 games to play. But once again they flattered to deceive, because League leaders Sheffield Wednesday beat Burnley for the third time that season, this time, 4–1. Louis Page's usual goal gained the club a home point against Leicester, and the local press, always keen to offer the slightest encouragement, led with the headlines, 'BURNLEY'S RECORD GIVES LITTLE CAUSE FOR PESSIMISM'. The following week it was a different tale. 'SECOND DIVISION DANGERS' said the *Burnley News* after Burnley had gone down again, this time 3–1 at Bramhall Lane. Local boy, Tom Prest was given his chance at inside-right in the game against Birmingham, but again the Burnley team lost 2–0.

On March 10, Peter O'Dowd arrived at Turf Moor from Blackburn Rovers, and he played at half-back in the Burnley–Rovers clash in 1930. After Page and McCluggage (penalty) had kept Burnley in the game, the ex-Rover scored the winner for his new team. Tales were rife in East Lancashire about the 'old pals act', which inferred that Blackburn had deliberately given Burnley two invaluable points. The victory certainly helped Burnley's cause, but when the bottom club Grimsby Town, beat Burnley 4–0, they not only lifted themselves off the foot of the table, but re-opened the doors of the Second Division to Burnley.

	Played	*Points*
Arsenal	32	30
Burnley	35	30
Newcastle	32	27
Grimsby Town	33	26
Everton	34	26

Seven points from their last twelve games had put Burnley into this plight. When a victory came, it was usually surrounded by half a dozen defeats, such as when Burnley beat Manchester United 4–0 towards the end of the season. It seems that they had all the luck in the world, but they still deserved their priceless victory. But it was the same old story the following week, when only George Sommerville saved Burnley from a heavy defeat against West Ham. As it was, Burnley went down by the solitary goal.

	Played	*Points*
Burnley	38	32
Newcastle	35	29
Grimsby T.	36	27
Everton	36	26

Billy Down was given a transfer, whilst ex-international defenders, Harry Storer and Sam Wadsworth, were both on the injured list. And so to Easter 1930. Louis Page scored a hat-trick in a great 4–1 win over Liverpool at Turf Moor, and Burnley seemed to be safe at last. But the other teams with games in hand were picking up valuable points, and when Burnley lost at Middlesbrough despite another great display by Sommerville, the Lancashire club suddenly found themselves in dire straits; especially when the bottom club Everton beat them 4–0. Easter 1930 proved to be very cold weatherwise, but the local headlines, 'EASTER SHIVERS', could have been applied to the Football Club, looking at the League table with only one game to play.

	Played	*Points*
Middlesbrough	40	35
Grimsby Town	40	35
Newcastle United	40	35
Sheffield United	40	34
Burnley	41	34
Everton	39	29

'Our hopes of escaping are now almost gone' wrote the usually faithful and optimistic 'Kestrel'.

Meanwhile, Sheffield United had lost to Everton, and Newcastle and Grimsby had also lost, and these results made the position at the bottom even tighter. The last day's fixtures in the 1929–30 season were:

Burnley v Derby County
Everton v Sunderland
Huddersfield v Grimsby T.
Manchester Utd. v Sheffield Utd.
Newcastle Utd. v West Ham Utd.

Burnley had perhaps the hardest task of all the struggling clubs, against Derby who were next to the top. But on that last crucial day, Burnley were superb, running out 6–2 victors, with Joe Mantle getting his hat-trick. But alas, in one great desperate effort, *all* of the bottom five teams won in fine style that day.

Burnley 6 Derby County 2
Everton 4 Sunderland 1
Huddersfield 0 Grimsby 1
Man. Utd. 1 Sheffield Utd. 5
Newcastle Utd. 1 West Ham Utd. 0

'BURNLEY IN SECOND DIVISION' shouted the newspaper placards in the town centre, for in one of the closest finishes for years, Burnley went down on goal average.

	Played	*Points*		
Manchester U.	42	38		
Newcastle U.	42	37		
Grimsby T.	42	37		
Sheffield U.	42	36	(for 91	against 96)
Burnley	42	36	(for 79	against 97)
Everton	42	35		

And at the close of that sad season, Burnley fans were left to contemplate two goals, one that counted, and one that didn't. The locals recalled how referee Mee had failed to see the Leicester goal-keeper McClaren pull the ball back from behind his own goal-line. Photographs to be seen in the local library to this day, prove the ball to have been well over the goal-line. A point gained against Leicester would have saved the Clarets. But just as bitter a pill to swallow was the fact that ex-Claret Joe Devine scored the vital winning goal for Newcastle United in their last game.

But after all the arguing and the inquests had died down, the fact was that Burnley were back in Division Two, after a spell of seventeen years at the top. It was to be another seventeen years before they were to emerge into the soccer sunlight again.

SIX

IN THE DOLDRUMS

1930–31

Thirty years to the day, after Burnley had begun their Second Division struggle for the second time in 1900, they kicked off at home against fellow Lancastrians from Bury. Sommerville; McCluggage and Waterfield; Steel, O'Dowd and Forrest; Jenkins, Mays, Mantle, Storer and Page, began the campaign in a rather inauspicious manner by losing at Turf Moor, 2–0. But that was a moral victory compared to the midweek match played at White Hart Lane the following week, when the Clarets went down, 8–1! The clouds were beginning to gather on the Burnley horizons, and the locals began to realise that the relegation of the team the previous April had been justified.

But an O'Dowd goal gave them a point at Southampton, before the team met Notts Forest at Turf Moor. All the Burnley forwards scored, as the team raised their supporter's hopes by winning 5–2. That game was the beginning of a heartening little run for the Clarets. Bottom of the table Reading came north, and were trounced 8–1 (Burnley's best win since they had beaten Notts Forest 8–2 in 1922). But typical of the team's lack of drawing power was the fact that only 9,889 saw the game. After a 3–3 draw at Molineux, Herman Conway made his debut in goal for the return game against Wolves which Burnley won 4–2. Another personality with due cause to recall that game was Louis Page, who scored his hundredth League goal for the Burnley club in that game. The Lancashire team had now scored 20 goals in their last four games, which was a club record. After a 3–2 victory over Bradford, there began to be talk of promotion—but such a possibility was a long time off yet. After scoring two goals, Louis Page was badly injured in a real hacking match at home against Swansea Town, in which Burnley managed to hang on and draw 2–2.

The fine unbeaten run came to an end on the occasion of the fatal thirteenth, when Port Vale won 2–1 at Turf Moor. But the following week, a fine 3–2 win at Bradford City took Burnley up into second place.

	Played	Points
Everton	16	27
Burnley	16	22
West Brom.	16	21
Preston N. E.	16	21

But goals, or the lack of them, were proving the great problem at Turf Moor. Mantle, Mays, Drinnan, Henderson, and even centre-half Bowsher, were all tried in quick succession in the centre-forward berth, but with little success.

Perhaps Burnley's best performance of that first season in Division Two, came when they beat the team who had gone down with them the previous season, and who were destined to bounce straight back into Division One at the first attempt, Everton. The Mersey-siders came to Turf Moor, and after Dixie Dean had scored with a superb 25-yarder that hardly rose from the ground as it shot past Conway, and Stein had added a second, Burnley came back with a vengeance to win 5–2. But despite such results, Burnley were now losing touch with the leading clubs.

Away from the League, Burnley romped into the fourth round of the F.A. Cup with a fine 3–0 win over First Division, Manchester City. Although City included their famed half-backs, Busby, Cowan and Bray, and forwards of the quality of Tilson, Toseland and Brooks, goals by Prest, Jenkins, and a penalty from Andy Mc-Cluggage gave Burnley the victory, and the task of meeting Bradford in round four.

The week after the splendid cup win, Burnley crashed 3–1 to the bottom team, Reading. And then, after several defeats had sent them sliding down the League table, on February 14, Burnley announced that they were prepared to consider offers for *any* of their players, owing to their financial position.

Eight changes didn't help Burnley at Millwall, where Sommer-ville; Wood and Storer; Brown, O'Dowd and Forrest; Jenkins, Kelly, Beel, Drinnan and Jones went down 2–1. And if Burnley were running short of players, they were certainly finding sup-porters in short supply too. Only 4,942 attended the 1–1 draw at Turf Moor between Burnley and Plymouth. It was the lowest attendance for a Saturday game at Turf Moor since the Stockport County game in 1913.

The only other event worth recording in a very disappointing 1930–31 season was the fact that Burnley played six successive draws! Club captain Harry Storer decided to retire from the game in order to concentrate on his county cricket career with Derby-shire. In the end, he became manager of Coventry City, which added to Burnley's disappointment in losing their captain as a player, for they were unable to receive any transfer fee for him, a

CHANGE OF STYLE. Sixty years difference in travelling to football matches. (*above*) A group of Burnley fans on their way to a Cup Tie in 1912, and (*below*) Chairman Bob Lord boarding the League Liner which Burnley supporters used for the Q.P.R. game in 1972

BURNLEY'S CHAMPIONSHIP WINNING TEAM, 1921. A. Basnett, L. Smelt, D. Taylor, C. Bates (trainer), J. Dawson, C. Jones, W. Weaver; W. Nesbit, R. Kelly, J. Anderson, B. Cross, E. Mosscrop, G. Halley, T. Boyle, W. Watson

BURNLEY ENTHUSIASM. Fans awaiting the news of the Swindon v Burnley Cup Tie replay, outside the offices of the *Burnley Express,* January 1929

player who had cost the club over £2,000 not too long before.

The loss of this transfer fee was particularly worrying to the club who were getting into deep waters financially; 4,108 people turned up for the last home game against Cardiff City, and the club announced that they would have to reduce all their players' wages the following season. This caused rumours to circulate about the future of some of the leading players, and both McCluggage and Waterfield threatened to leave the club.

1931–32

Burnley lost their first game of the 1931–32 season, 3–0 away to Southampton. The Clarets' team that day read: Conway; Wood, and Waterfield; Brown, O'Dowd and Forrest; Jenkins, Prest, Beel, Jones and Page. In a very average start to the season, after six games Burnley were just three points off the bottom of Division Two.

About this time, it was announced that the club were losing over £100 a week. So it was that the 23-year-old centre-half, Peter O'Dowd, who had come from Blackburn the year before, and made such an impression with the Burnley crowd, was transferred to Chelsea in October 1931 for a fee of around £5,000. He had a memorable debut for his new team, against Everton, facing the legendary Dixie Dean. Everton ran riot and centre-forward Dean scored five! Nevertheless, Peter O'Dowd went on to play for England later that season.

With Second Division football, the gates gradually declined, and more than once, there were less than 5,000 people on the ground. Somerville conceded 18 goals in four games, and he was dropped in favour of a young goalkeeper called Richard Twist. Meanwhile Andy McCluggage, who had refused Burnley's reduced terms at the end of the previous season, and who had been playing with the Irish club Dundalk, signed for Preston in December, 1931.

There were the usual local hopes of a good Cup run, but in January, 1932, at Turf Moor Burnley were beaten 4–0 by First Division Derby County. Burnley were now in the bottom half-dozen —only Barnsley, Preston, Manchester United, Charlton and Bristol City were below them. At the same time, the Reserve team were next to the bottom in the Central League. The newly formed Supporters Club met the Board to talk about players who might come to Burnley. Several players were suggested, but the club went ahead and signed Sam Jennings, a centre-forward from Stockport County. The Supporters Club promised to pay Jenning's fee within the month; indeed there was no other source of money in those bleak days, as the directors were now paying the players out of their own pockets.

In February, Burnley's leading scorer of all time, 32-year-old George Beel, was transferred to Lincoln. A 5–1 defeat by Manchester United at Old Trafford, saw the position at the foot of Division Two:

	Played	Points
Burnley	28	22
Barnsley	27	22
Charlton	27	21
Bristol City	28	13

Herman Conway came back into the side, but to no avail. Nine men made their first team debut in little over a month, and after a 4–0 beating at Plymouth, the position now was:

	Played	Points
Charlton	33	28
Port Vale	33	27
Barnsley	33	26
Burnley	33	25
Bristol City	33	17

'THIRD DIVISION FOOTBALL IS NOT SO FAR OFF' said 'Sportsman' in the *Burnley Express.* And not only were the club next to the bottom of Division Two, but the Reserves were still next to the foot of the Central League, with little likelihood of improving their position. Then, after George Beel's departure, another Turf Moor favourite, Louis Page, was transferred to Manchester United for over £1,000.

And then the Division's bottom team, Bristol City, came to Turf Moor, and won 2–1! The position was desperate now, but perhaps the most amazing result of the season came the following week, when the Clarets went to Bristol City and won 6–1, with John Kelly scoring three! Talking of Kelly, it was strongly rumoured that Burnley were trying to buy Bob Kelly back, but whether there was any truth in it or not, Kelly stayed at Preston.

With just five games to go, the position according to 'Sportsman' was now hopeless. But two victories near the end of the season helped to improve Burnley's chances. First, they beat Swansea 4–1, but then, even more important, they went to Barnsley and won 1–0. And then in the penultimate game, Burnley seized another point at home in a 1–1 draw against Notts County.

So the 1931–32 season came to a dramatic finale. If Burnley lost their last match 2–0 (at home to Notts Forest), and Port Vale won their last match 2–0, the two teams would finish exactly level on points and goal average, just above the already relegated Bristol City. Port Vale did their part, winning 2–0 at Leeds (who had achieved promotion), but Burnley beat Notts Forest 1–0 at Turf Moor. The final table meant that Barnsley were relegated.

	Played	*Points*
Burnley	42	35
Port Vale	42	33
Barnsley	42	33
Bristol City	42	23

And so came to an end the worst season in Burnley's 50-year history. On top of the nearly disastrous campaign in Division Two, the Reserve team finished next to the bottom in the Central League, conceding 140 goals in 42 games. (Manchester City Reserves beat them 9–0, four times they conceded eight, and another four times, they let in six!)

During the summer of 1932, rumours swept the town that the Football Club would not carry on in 1932–33. However, the fears were dispelled by the Board of Directors at a special Jubilee Meeting held at the Mechanics Institute in July. Leonard Metcalfe, R. B. Chase, and H. Culpan, who had all played in the early Calder Vale days, were still members of the club, and they were present at that meeting.

1932–33

The new season saw a few changes in the staff. Sommerville was put on the transfer list, whilst among several new signings, Cecil Smith (centre-forward) came from Stalybridge Celtic, Wilf Crompton (outside-right, and the great Bob Crompton's son) came from Blackburn Rovers, C. Hillam (goalkeeper) and G. Richmond (full-back) came from Nelson. Len Smelt was appointed assistant trainer to Charlie Bates, whilst Jerry Dawson was retained as coach.

After scoring five goals in the public practice match, 13-stone Cecil Smith was chosen for the first team, which turned out: Conway; Willighan and Waterfield; Brown, Fairhurst and Forest; Crompton, Prest, Smith, Jones and Hall. In that first game against Chesterfield, Jack Hall broke his shin, and in his place George Mee was signed from Derby County. Albert Pickles resigned as Manager/Secretary, and out of 70 applicants, Tom Bromilow, the ex-Liverpool and England left-half, was appointed the new Manager, whilst Alf Boland was appointed Club Secretary, at 21 the youngest official in the Football League.

Early on in the new season, Burnley were beaten 6–1 at Preston, and it was during that match that they became the first team in the country to have had 1,000 goals scored against them since the war. That day, Harper scored four for Preston, but, ironically, the man who scored the one thousandth goal was none other than Bob Kelly himself. 'Bob Kelly is still as great a master as ever' commented the *Burnley Express.* Then to make amends came two 4–0 victories against Bradford and Preston, and after seven games, Burnley had gained seven points. But three successive defeats followed, which made the position at the foot of the League table:

	Played	Points
Burnley	10	7
Charlton	10	6
Chesterfield	9	5
West Ham	10	5

Burnley were back in the doldrums. George Mee was made captain, and in a fine performance, the team pulled back three goals in the last 15 minutes to draw at Fulham. Unfortunately in that game, goalkeeper Conway was once again in the wars, breaking a bone, and new man Hillam took his place. Then came a 4–4 draw at Turf Moor with the bottom club, West Ham United.

Still the club continued to sign players, and a significant signing in the history of the Burnley Football Club took place, in November, 1932, when veteran Welsh international Ray Bennion came from Manchester United. The following week Burnley 'celebrated' two months since their last victory by getting beaten again. At the same time, the club strongly denied that both Arsenal and West Ham were after the signature of George Waterfield. Not only was the team still conceding goals heavily, but they were also finding great difficulty in scoring any themselves. The centre-forward position was still proving a particular thorn in the flesh to the Burnley management, and over a period of less than three seasons, ten different centre-forwards had been tried—Mays, Mantle, Beel, Bowsher, Drinnan, Kelly, Jennings, Page, Edwards, and now Cecil Smith.

After 16 games, the League position was as critical as ever:

	Played	Points
Chesterfield	15	11
Burnley	16	11
West Ham	16	11
Charlton	16	10

A personal honour came the way of full back Tommy Willighan, when he was capped for Ireland in November, and the same week centre-half George Bellis was signed from Wolves. The following week, on December 3, 1932, Burnley won for the first time in three months when they beat Southampton 2–0. One of the deciding factors that day was the experience of the half-back line, Bennion, Bellis and Forrest, and, in his second game, George Bellis was appointed team captain.

During the Christmas period, the club performed the double over Grimsby, and so managed to keep off the bottom. But then the bottom team, Chesterfield, thrashed Burnley to the tune of six goals to none, to remind the Lancashire team of their problems. In the

F.A. Cup, Burnley went to Swindon, and won 2–1, with Cecil Smith scoring the winning goal despite his being lame for two-thirds of the game. In the next round, they beat Sheffield United 3–1 at Turf Moor (George Mee (2) and Cecil Smith being the scorers). Yet another new face appeared in the Burnley team, when inside-right Teddy Hancock was signed from Liverpool, but as he came, so an old familiar face on the Turf Moor scene disappeared, when Len Smelt, who had been performing as assistant trainer, died aged 49. A benefit match was held for his family, for which Bob Kelly, Jackie Bruton, Louis Page, and Paddy Freeman all returned, and in which an International XI beat the Burnley team 8–2. Said the local press after the game, 'Kelly and Bruton showed themselves on the right wing to be still two very great players.' No doubt the club hankered after the days when such personalities graced the team, but the present team were doing their level best to raise Burnley supporters' hopes, despite the League position.

	Played	*Points*
Chesterfield	28	22
Burnley	28	21
Grimsby	28	21
Oldham	28	20
Charlton	27	18

Burnley were drawn at home again in the Cup, this time against fellow-strugglers, Chesterfield. A crowd of 31,699 came to Turf Moor for the game, (the previous best had been in 1928–29, when 35,905 saw the Blackburn Rovers match), and Burnley went through into the last eight with a Teddy Hancock goal. Once again Bennion, Bellis and Forrest proved to be a strong half-back line, but new man Hancock was also creating quite a stir locally.

The draw for the quarter-finals of the F.A. Cup saw Burnley at home once again, this time against the famed Manchester City. Such was the demand for tickets that over £600 had to be returned by post to unlucky applicants. Within nine hours of the draw, every seat in the stand had been sold. The directors increased the size of the ground, so that at least 70,000 people could be accommodated. But then, just like another similar occasion against a Manchester team, the big game was threatened when it began to snow. A couple of days before the Cup-tie, Burnley had the worst snow storm since the United Cup-tie of 1909, and parts of the town were several feet deep in drifts. Thirty men worked overtime to keep Turf Moor clear. However, despite the conditions, the game went on. But against men of the calibre of Busby, Cowan and Bray, Burnley lost the game 1–0, with Tilson scoring the winner after 13 minutes. A crowd of 48,719 people paid £3,275 to see the game, and the *Burnley Express* adjudged Matt Busby and Teddy Hancock as the men of the match. (City went on to lose to Everton in the Final).

But away from the glamour of the F.A. Cup, Burnley now had their annual battle to wage against relegation. Cecil Smith got a hat-trick in a 4–0 win over West Ham, which did nothing except keep Burnley off the bottom.

	Played	*Points*
West Ham	31	24
Grimsby	32	24
Burnley	31	23
Charlton	30	22

And then Charlton Athletic won their game in hand, to put Burnley soundly at the foot of Division Two!

Still the directors continued to sign players at a steady rate . . . J. Mustard, an outside-right, came from Preston, W. Wood, a left-winger, came from Blackburn, Miller, a fast winger, came from Newcastle, Harry O'Grady, an inside-forward, arrived from Leeds, and then a 19-year-old goalkeeper, Alex Scott, was signed from Liverpool. To make way for all these new signings, (and these were only a few of a great many more), Burnley transferred Stan Bowsher to join George Beel, who was now with struggling Rochdale in Division Three North, whilst Alec Forrest, who had been at Turf Moor since 1927, was transferred to Chesterfield.

In place of Len Smelt, Billy Dougall returned to the club as assistant trainer to Charlie Bates. Burnley moved off the foot of the table with a 4–1 win at Lincoln, and then they had a fine run, gaining a point at home against Bradford City, a point at Port Vale, a home win against Millwall, a point from Spurs, and a home win against Bury. Altogether, they lost only two of their last 12 games, and yet despite this fine run of success, they escaped relegation once again by two points only. The club had survived in Division Two for another season, but for how much longer, no one knew!

1933–34

Burnley continued to sign players by the score. Half-back Chedgzoy came from Everton, *another* centre-forward, Meecham arrived, big 6ft 3in Tommy Wallace, a centre-half, came from Sunderland, and inside-forward Douglas, all made their appearance on the Turf Moor scene, but created little impression. The Clarets lost the first game at Grimsby 1–0, and the second one at Preston 3–2, and after eight games, they were once against next to Bury at the bottom of Division Two!

And then came Burnley's most important purchase for a long time, when left-half Alick Robinson came from Bury for nearly

£5,000. He scored on his debut, but the Clarets still lost 5–2 at Brentford. Now Burnley's team usually read like: Conway; Richmond and Waterfield; Brown, Bellis and Robinson; Sellars, Hancock, Smith, Douglas and Crompton. And still Burnley continued to buy players. Alf Charles, a West-Indian left-back, came in November, 1933, and, at the same time, inside-right Arthur Warburton was bought from Manchester United; Wilf Smith, a left-back, came from Liverpool, whilst a left-winger, Thomas Weale, came from Crewe. Alick Robinson followed George Bellis as team captain, but by Christmas, 1933, Burnley were still in deep waters.

	Played	*Points*
Millwall	22	18
Burnley	22	18
Swansea	22	17
Lincoln	22	15

The year 1934 began with a good 2–0 win at Turf Moor against League leaders, Grimsby Town, and then two goals in two minutes from O'Grady gave Burnley the points against Notts Forest. In the Cup, Burnley were drawn against Alick Robinson's old club, Bury. Hillman, Barron, Taylor, Place, and Bowes, who had all played in the Burnley team beaten by Bury in the F.A. Cup of 1900, were all guests of the club at the game on January 13, 1934, which resulted in a 0–0 draw. That day 37,379 people paid £2,094 at Turf Moor, but Bury went on to win the replay 3–2 with a goal scored three minutes from time.

Manchester United, who were now at the bottom of the Second Division, came to Turf Moor and won 4–1, and then Burnley went down 4–1 again, against Bolton at Burnden Park. But despite these failures, the club made a gradual recovery to halfway up the League table. And a spell of eight matches without defeat saw Burnley out of the relegation zone for the first time for three years.

At the end of April, 1934, the club announced that they were £9,000 in debt. Only 3,248 people were at the last match of the season, against Bury, and the axe had to fall. Conway, Smith, Sellars, Prest, Chedgzoy, O'Grady, Crompton, Charles and many others were put on the transfer list at the end of the season, and even Charlie Bates, who had been first team trainer for 24 years, had his contract terminated. In the end, only 16 players were retained for the next season.

1934–35

The new season saw many alterations in the Turf Moor scene. Players came in their usual incredible numbers, a full-back called Readett, Syne and Comrie who both came from Manchester City,

Downes from Stockport, Alderman from Derby, Hornby an inside-left arrived from Stalybridge Celtic, and Bob Johnson, a tall local centre-half was also signed. It was at that time that the Billy Dougall–Ray Bennion partnership really began, Dougall taking over the trainer's bench from Charlie Bates, and Ray Bennion becoming player-coach. Frank Hudspeth, the ex-Newcastle and England full-back, became assistant trainer at Turf Moor. Apart from players and staff, the pitch was altered, four yards being added to the length and the width of Turf Moor, so that the full measurements were now 115 yards by 75 yards. And even the club colours were changed! For some reason, the team turned out in the 1934–35 season wearing blue jerseys with claret sleeves, instead of their usual claret jerseys with blue sleeves. The side in 1934 was: Scott; Richmond and Bellis; Brown, Wallace and Robinson; Hancock, Comrie, Syne, Douglas and Downes.

Wins against Southampton, West Ham (twice), Bradford City, Barnsley, and a draw at Sheffield United in their first seven games, put Burnley in the strange position of being amongst the Second Division leaders. Perhaps as a result of this successful sequence, Alick Robinson was chosen to play for the English League to meet the Irish League, alongside Cliff Britton (Everton) and Sam Cowan (Manchester City). Still the players arrived at Turf Moor; George Brown, an English international centre-forward came from Aston Villa, whilst others like Swain, Billington and Kiddy, were also signed around that time. But after their very promising start to the season, several injuries resulted in the team going down the League table. But, as usual, Burnley were doing well in the Cup competition. They beat Mansfield 4–2, and then in the next round defeated Luton Town, 3–1. After a 0–0 draw at Nottingham, Burnley beat the Forest 3–0 in the Turf Moor replay, and once again, Burnley found themselves in the sixth round, at home against Birmingham City.

About that time, 15-year-old Fred Taylor scored 11 goals for Briercliffe St James' in a 24–1 victory in the Burnley Sunday School League. He had already scored over 100 goals that season, and Burnley signed him on as an amateur. The signing of such a young player was so unusual in those days that the local papers were full of it. Yet again, departing from their usual custom of signing players who were rejects from other clubs, Burnley signed another schoolboy goal-scoring centre-forward, Tommy Lawton, in February, 1935. (In his first game for the 'A' team on February 23, 1935, Tommy Lawton gave a hint of things to come, and scored twice.) Three other signings that same month were Frank Raynor from Mexborough, and two full-backs from Spennymoor, Hubbick and Bott.

Meanwhile, the club were preparing for a record crowd for the Birmingham Cup-tie. In a memorable game, recalled by many to this day, Burnley came back from being two down, to win 3–2. Though the ground had accommodation for well over 60,000 only 47,670 paid £3,480 to see the game that day. 'WEMBLEY LOOMING ON BURNLEY'S HORIZON' shouted the *Burnley Express*, but it was not to be. In the semi-final, Burnley were drawn against the favourites, Sheffield Wednesday, and went down 3–0 at Villa Park.

A benefit match for George Waterfield, who was completing twelve years at Turf Moor, was poorly attended, but there was very little interest in professional football in Burnley in the mid-thirties. Crowds came for the big Cup occasions, but for the bread and butter of the League, attendances were often appalling. The lowest gate for 24 years was recorded at the Burnley–Norwich game (2,800), though three hours later, 3,333 saw the Hospital Cup semi-final at Turf Moor!

At the end of the season, amongst those who were placed on the transfer list were Waterfield, Bellis and Prest, whilst in July, Mr Tom Bromilow left Turf Moor, to take over the Manager's post at Crystal Palace.

1935–36

Once again, there was a change of colours with the new season. The blue and claret colours gave way to white jerseys and black shorts with white stripes. More signings included Syred from Gillingham, Kilcar from Chester and Storey from Nelson. The Burnley team that kicked off the new season, and which went down 4–0 at Charlton was: Hetherington; Nevin and Richmond; Clacher, Wallace and Robinson; Hancock, Raynor, Brown (G), Hornby and Downes. Jimmy Brown, who had been a fine right-half over many seasons at Burnley, had been transferred to Manchester United for just over £1,000.

On September 7, 1935, Tommy Lawton made his first appearance for Burnley Reserves in the team at Huddersfield, and what probably helped his rise to fame was the fact that recent signing George Brown, who had established himself as a goal-scoring favourite with the crowd, was suddenly transferred to Leeds United for £3,000. Brown was a very popular figure, but it appears that the offer of £3,000 was just too good to be refused by a team in Burnley's financial position. There was very little to shout about in the mid-thirties, and after nine games, the position at the bottom of Division Two read:

	Played	Points
Burnley	9	7
Bradford	9	5
Hull City	9	5
Norwich	9	3

'GIVE THE RESERVES A CHANCE' pleaded the local paper in October, 1935, and two were soon brought into the first team, inside-right Jack Toll, and centre-half Bob Johnson, when Tommy Wallace was injured. Two more purchases, in an attempt to increase the team's goal-scoring, were George Oliver, an outside-left from Spennymoor United, and J. G. Liggins, a 23-year-old centre-forward, who cost Burnley £1,000, from Leicester City. The lack of support was emphasised by the fact that the club regularly collected more from their share of away gates (like the 35,000 at the Spurs v Burnley game) than they did from home matches (such as from the 4,200 who attended the Notts Forest game at Turf Moor).

When 1936 came, the League position was as usual far from healthy:

	Played	Points
Burnley	21	17
Bradford	21	16
Port Vale	21	14
Hull City	21	13

In January, 25,444 people paid £1,347 at Turf Moor for the Burnley v Sheffield United Cup-tie. The result was a 0–0 draw, and Sheffield went on to win the replay 2–1 at Bramhall Lane. The 22-year-old goalkeeper, Alex Scott, was sold to the Wolves for what was stated at that time to be the highest fee ever paid for a goalkeeper. It came to light that Burnley enquired about Peter Doherty in 1936, but the directors confessed that was as far as it went! Instead, Doherty went from Blackpool to Manchester City, whilst Burnley bought Charles Fletcher, an outside-left from Brentford, and Edward Adams, a goalkeeper from Southport.

It was in 1935–36 that the club began to encourage local youngsters to train with the team, and in 1936, a 'B' team was formed of local 14-17-year-old players. Over 200 lads wrote in for trials in the first week, and several teams were formed to take part in local leagues.

But still Burnley continued to buy players who had gained experience with other clubs, and in March their latest acquisition was Bob Brocklebank, an inside-right who came from Aston Villa for a large fee. But the biggest story of the month was headlined, on March 28, in the *Burnley Express*, 'BURNLEY'S BOY LEADER'. Tommy Lawton was chosen to lead the Burnley attack at the ripe 'old' age of 16, an incredible age, in those days, to play in a First or Second Division side. He had been only 15 when he had first appeared in the Reserve team, and during the 1935–36 season, he had already scored 21 goals in the junior sides. The team that played against Doncaster Rovers that day was: Adams; Richmond and Hubbick; Hindmarsh, Johnson and Robinson; Hancock, Brocklebank, Lawton, Hornby and Fletcher. The result was a 1–1 draw, which did little to relieve Burnley's plight.

	Played	*Points*
Burnley	34	29
Port Vale	35	28
Barnsley	35	27
Hull City	35	18

But it may well be that the introduction of Tommy Lawton at that stage in the season made just that bit of difference that mattered. He scored in his second game, a 3–1 away victory at Swansea, and went on to score five in his first five games. In the end, Burnley finished five points clear of relegation, leaving Port Vale and Hull City to take the drop in the Third Division.

Towards the close of the season, Bob Johnson broke his leg in the game against Spurs, whilst at the end of the season, Cecil Smith was transferred to Cardiff, and Percy Downes went to Oldham.

1936–37

Tommy Lawton continued to make local headlines at Turf Moor during the summer, for he proved to be an exceptional batsman with the Burnley Cricket Club. The outstanding player in the pre-season practice match proved to be another new signing, centre-half, Arthur Woodruff, who had come to Turf Moor from Bradford City. The team that began the new season was: Hetherington; Richmond and Hubbick; Hindmarsh, Johnson and Robinson; Carson, Brocklebank, Lawton, Kilcar and Fletcher, and Tommy Lawton scored twice in the 3–0 win over Norwich City.

Mainly due to injuries, the good start was not maintained, and Burnley as usual began to slide down the table. Arthur Woodruff made his debut for the club in 1936 in the game against Plymouth; but again the club dipped into the transfer market. This time they bought Billy Miller (inside-left) and Jimmy Stein (outside-left) from Everton. The fee that Burnley paid for the pair was the highest since Jack Hill had come from Plymouth. The week afterwards, Tommy Lawton was 17, and he signed professional forms for the club. The day after becoming a professional footballer, Lawton celebrated with a glorious hat-trick in the 3–1 beating of Tottenham, (the first coming in only 30 seconds).

The next player in the comings and goings that were constantly happening at Turf Moor in the 1930's was Teddy Hancock, who went to Luton Town. And then came another of those transfers that has kept Burnley in the headlines over the years, when the up-and-coming Tommy Lawton was transferred to Everton in the first week of 1937. Once again, as on so many other occasions, it was a sale that Burnley were compelled to make because of their financial problems. The £7,000 fee that Lawton brought in was a League record at that time for a seventeen-year-old, and the income most certainly helped to keep Burnley afloat in the 1930's. (Strangely, his first game for his new club was for the Everton Reserve team in the Central League game against Burnley Reserves, and of course he scored in the 2–0 win!)

In the F.A. Cup, Burnley beat Aston Villa 3–2, and then Bury, 4–1. The fifth round saw them drawn at home to the Arsenal. Arsenal were very much *the* team in the country at that period, having won the Division One title four times in five seasons; they were also the current Cup holders, so it is easy to imagine the excitement that the draw brought to Burnley. There was talk of the club record attendance of 54,775 being broken, and one reporter described the Burnley–Arsenal Cup-tie as the greatest match ever to take place at Turf Moor. But as on previous occasions, the record attendance was *not* broken; the 54,445 were just 330 short, but the gate receipts of £4,025 were a new record for the club. The teams on that historic day were: Burnley—Adams; Richmond and Hubbick; Rayner, Wood and Robinson (captain); Stein, Toll, Richardson, Brocklebank and Fletcher. Arsenal—Boulton; Hapgood and Male; Crayston, Roberts and Copping; Kirchen, Bowden, Drake, James (captain) and Bastin.

To this day, Burnley fans who saw that game, swear that a 'goal' which Bob Brocklebank 'scored' after ten minutes was a genuine effort. The referee said that the ball did not cross the goal-line, and when the ball was cleared by the Arsenal defence, he waved play on. What might have happened if that goal had been allowed, no one will ever know. What *did* happen is now history, and no one at Turf Moor that day will ever forget it! The Arsenal team turned on one of the finest performances ever seen on the Turf, and wiped the floor with gallant Burnley. Ted Drake scored three minutes after the disallowed Brocklebank effort, and he got a second two minutes later. Within another five minutes, Jack Crayston had made it 3–0, and in the next minute, Ted Drake completed his hat-trick, making the score 4–0 after 21 minutes. Richardson scored a consolation goal, but Arsenal registered three more in the second half to leave Turf Moor, 7–1 victors. Kirchen on the right-wing was described in the *Burnley Express* as 'the fastest thing on two legs that has ever been on Turf Moor', and the newspaper commented that Arsenal just gave up trying when the score reached six!

Certainly the money was beginning to pour back into the Turf Moor coffers, with the Lawton transfer fee and the Arsenal Cup gate. Another £6,000 came Burnley's way, when Bolton signed the Burnley full-back Harry Hubbick. At the same time, Burnley signed on Len Martindale, an ex-school pal of Tommy Lawton at Bolton, Rimmer, an outside-right from Bolton, Tom Chester a right-back from Bury, and young Fred Taylor also signed professional forms with the club.

At this time the Turf Moor club persisted, for a period, in playing an offside trap, which was not particularly successful; it was particularly unsuccessful at Leicester, where Burnley went down 7–3.

An England trial, Possibles v Probables, was held on Turf Moor on March 17, 1937. Only 6,024 people attended the game, which was most notable for the fact that the players wore numbered shirts for the first time in a game at Burnley. We need to remember that it was not until 1939 that the numbering of players became compulsory; even in 1937, it was still a novelty. The 1930's had seen a few more developments in the Laws of the game. It was only in 1929 that the goalkeeper was compelled to stand still on his goal-line whilst a penalty-kick was being taken; in 1931, the goalkeeper was allowed to carry the ball for four steps instead of two; in 1931, instead of a free-kick for foul throw-ins, the throw reverted to the other side. In 1936, defending players were no longer permitted to tap the ball into the goalkeeper's hands when a goalkick was being taken. The ball had to travel outside the penalty area. Whilst in 1937, the same rule was made to apply for free-kicks taken inside the penalty area. The game had come a long way from tapes between the goalposts and handlebar moustaches. But the Laws of the game were rewritten in 1938.

The old Burnley first team trainer, and ex-player, Charlie Bates, died in 1937, aged 52. Arthur Cunliffe, ex-English international outside-left was signed from Middlesbrough, whilst at the end of the season, the club captain, Alick Robinson, was not retained. Later the club changed their mind and kept this fine player on their books. Burnley managed in the end to finish in thirteenth League position, and because of the Lawton and Hubbick transfers and the receipts of the Arsenal Cup-tie, the Club was far better off financially than at any other time since 1930.

1937–38

Season tickets for the new season were priced as usual, Stand 'A' £3 3s; Enclosure £1 10s, and Ground £1, with the demand the best since 1928. There were rumours that Burnley were about to sign Dixie Dean. But they didn't! The first team that kicked off the new season read: Adams; Robinson and Richmond; Rayner, Woodruff and Smith; Cunliffe, Toll, Brocklebank, Miller, and Fletcher.

The club made their usual very mediocre start to the season, and two youngsters made their League debut. Len Martindale played for the first time against Swansea Town, and the following week Fred Taylor came into the team against Norwich. 'I wouldn't have missed this game for a gold clock', said 'Sportsman' of the *Burnley Express* afterwards, for Burnley won 3–0, and Taylor scored two goals on his debut. More and more young players were being brought up through the junior teams now. An 18-year-old, George Bray, brother of the famous Jack Bray of Manchester City, signed on as a professional, as did 17-year-old Harry Potts from Hetton-le-Hole that November. When Sunderland tried to buy Fred Taylor, an offer of £10,000 was mentioned in the press, but now Burnley were in a much better financial position, and they were able to hold onto their players.

Burnley visited Sheffield Wednesday in the third round of the Cup; a 0–0 draw at Hillsborough was followed by a 3–1 victory in the replay, when Brocklebank (2) and Hornby were the scorers. But the Turf Moor team lost 3–2 at Chesterfield in round four against a team which included the old Burnley favourite, Joe Devine.

There was a spate of players asking for transfers in the early part of 1938; Gastall, Richardson, Cunliffe, Toll, and even Arthur Woodruff had their names put on the transfer list. April seemed to connect Burnley with Aston Villa on several occasions. First of all, 66-year-old Alex Leake, the ex-Villa and Burnley player of the early 1900's died. At the time, Aston Villa were riding high at the top of Division Two and heading for promotion, but Burnley soundly beat them 3–0. And then, towards the end of the month, Tom Gardner, the English international half-back of Aston Villa signed for Burnley. The signing of Gardner seemed to be a turning point for Burnley; they had weathered eight difficult seasons in the Second Division with many playing problems and financial crises. Now the team had some fine experienced players like Robinson, Miller, Brocklebank, and now Gardner. There were several good prospects in the ranks like Taylor, Potts, Bray and Martindale; and there was money in the bank. As the 1937–38 season came to a close, with Burnley finishing sixth, their best League position since 1926–27, there was certainly a mood of optimism for the future at Turf Moor.

1938–39

There was only one signing of any note in the close season of

1938, and that was Jack Billingham, an outside-right, from Bristol City. The team which represented Burnley in the opening game was: Adams; Richmond and Chester; Gardner, Johnson and Smith; Taylor, Miller, Brocklebank, Fisher, Hornby.

Tom Gardner was an immediate favourite with the Burnley supporters; his blond hair and his prodigious throws which practically reached the goals, made him an outstanding personality with the team. Burnley beat Southampton 2–1, they drew at Coventry 1–1, they beat Notts Forest 2–1, and Fulham 2–0, and the locals began to whisper the word 'promotion' once again after many years of silence. But then the team went through a poor spell, which resulted in them only having ten points from their first nine games.

Burnley fans received a great blow when Billy Miller asked for a transfer in 1938. He had been extremely popular with the crowd at Turf Moor for his dazzling dribbles and body swerves, and his many tricks with the ball. Anyway, he was transferred to Tranmere Rovers, and in his first game, played against his old colleagues from Turf Moor. Burnley won the game 3–1, and George Bray completely held Miller.

The team was knocked out of the Cup in round three by Notts County, and despite their good start to the season, 1939 found the team in the bottom half of the League table. Jackie Billingham made his League debut, and three more players were signed on. First, James Clayton, a centre-forward, came from Aston Villa; then Burnley signed on a South African half-back, Steve Van Rensburg. But the most spectacular signing, in 1938–39, was when 19-year-old Billy Morris arrived from Llandudno, and immediately made his Second Division debut in the game against Norwich City. The team that lined up that day read: Adams; Robinson and Marshall; Gardner, Woodruff and Bray; Taylor, Morris, Billingham, Brocklebank and Hornby.

After 28 games, Burnley were just five points off the top, but they faded fast in the closing weeks, and finished in a very modest fourteenth position. By the end of the season, several young players like Bray, Marshall, Taylor, Morris and Billingham had become fairly regular first-team players, and now Burnley issued a statement, announcing their intention *not* to sell. Once again, the prospects looked good for the future, but Burnley's plans for the future were going to be delayed for quite a time.

1939–46

The main innovation of the new season was the introduction of numbered jerseys. They had first been seen at Turf Moor in the international trial of 1937, but they caused more than a ripple of interest when they were officially adopted by the League. Burnley drew their first game of the season, 1–1 at home to Coventry, and the team read: Adams; Robinson and Marshall; Gardner, Woodruff and Bray; Hays, Brocklebank, Clayton, Dryden and Hornby. Fred Taylor was injured in training, and Jack Hays came in for his debut on the right wing.

The same team lost the following week 2–0 at Birmingham, and then came the War! The home game due to be played against Newport County was cancelled, as were all the League games, and it was the end of organised League football for the next seven years. A fortnight later, a friendly game was played against nearby Accrington Stanley, but without the interest of League competition, and with menfolk already being called up, the attendance was a mere 2,817.

Various competitions were held during the war years, the Northern Regional League, the Northern League Championship, the Lancashire Cup, and the League War Cup. The team changed from match to match owing to players being unavailable, or on leave, and several players were attached to teams as 'guest players'.

In 1940–41, Burnley were beaten 1–0 in the Lancashire Cup Final by Manchester United. The United team included players like Carey, Rowley, Pearson and Mitten, and the beaten Burnley team read: Conway, Snowden, Mather, Gardner, Woodruff, Robinson, Coates, Brocklebank, Kippax, Hornby, Bright. Several players came into contact with the club over the war years, players like Jimmy Strong, Peter Kippax, Harold Rudman and Jack Chew. Other personalities who became great favourites with the crowd as guest players were Frank Soo of Stoke and Reg Attwell of West Ham United.

And so the Burnley team came to the last war-time season, 1945–46. In it, they were once again beaten 1–0 in the Lancashire Cup Final by Manchester United, and the usual team appeared looking like: Strong, Woodruff, Mather, Rudman, Johnson, Attwell, Chew, Morris, Jackson, Haigh and Hays. A Burnley player won the first international honour for the club for 12 years, when Billy Morris was chosen to play for Wales against Ireland in a 'Victory' international in 1946.

But now the war was over, and people were coming home again. Hopes for the future were high, and optimism swept the football world as the League clubs prepared to resume where they had left off in 1939. And nowhere was optimism higher than at Turf Moor.

SEVEN

BACK TO DIVISION ONE

PROBABLY THE most important newcomer to Turf Moor in 1945 was Cliff Britton, the ex-Everton and England left-half. He was appointed the club's manager in May, 1945, and assumed the position when he came out of the forces in September. Cliff Britton was to bring to Turf Moor new ideas in training, tactics and team strategy. These progressive ideas coupled with the experience at Turf Moor of men like trainers Billy Dougall and Ray Bennion, were to prove a splendid combination. At the club's annual meeting in June, 1946, Cliff Britton announced that the club had a 'promotion programme' and hoped to reach the First Division within three seasons.

1946–47

The club sold 1,300 season tickets for the new season, which was a Turf Moor record. The public practice match, held in August, 1946, was attended by over 10,000 people, and the teams were: Clarets: Strong; Woodruff, Mather; Reid, Johnson, Bray; Morris, Potts, Billingham, Hays and Hodgeon. Whites: Meadows; Butterfield, Marshall; Spencer, Brown, Loughran; Taylor, Knight, Harrison, Haigh and Hornby. The Whites won the game 2–0, Spencer and Hornby scoring the goals.

The season began in earnest the following Saturday, when 17,000 people, the best gate for eight years, turned out to see Burnley play Coventry City. The Burnley team that day read: Strong; Woodruff, Mather; Spencer, Brown, Bray; Chew, Morris, Billingham, Potts and Kippax, and Peter Kippax scored Burnley's goal in an uninspiring 1–1 draw.

The fixtures were the same as for the uncompleted 39–40 season, Coventry at home, followed by Birmingham away, and then Newport County at Turf Moor. The result in the Burnley–Coventry game had been the same as before, but the score at Birmingham was reversed with Burnley winning 2–0, instead of losing 2–0 as had been the case in 1939. The Burnley team was the same as had drawn the first game, and Harold Spencer and Jackie Billingham scored the goals that won the points. It is interesting to note that out of all the team, only Woodruff and Bray played in the corresponding games at the start of the 39–40 season.

The 'Clarets', (for the team had returned to their previous claret and blue strip, wearing a set of jerseys bought by supporters clothing coupons), made it five points out of a possible six when they beat Newport County the following Saturday. Chew and Billingham put Burnley two up, only for the Welsh team to equalise. Late in the game, Turner, the Newport goalkeeper, misjudged a speculative overhead kick by Gordon Haigh, and helped it in with his hand to give Burnley both points. But it was a poor performance, and Henry Rose described Burnley as 'ten comedians and amateur Peter Kippax'.

Both Jackie Chew and Billy Morris were injured in the Newport game, and Fred Taylor and Gordon Haigh formed a new right-wing partnership in the next match at home to West Brom. The new combination didn't come off, and the team as a whole gave a dreadful performance. 'Clarets made to look small', said the press as Burnley slid to a 2–0 home defeat. Two days later, with a new right-wing pair of Knight and Morris, Burnley played much better at Barnsley against the team at the top of the table, but they still lost 1–0. After two successive defeats, Burnley were causing their supporters to become restive.

But then came the turning point, when the Clarets visited St James' Park to take on fellow promotion candidates, Newcastle United. In their best performance to date, Burnley won 2–1 with goals by Potts and Billingham. The *Burnley Express* said of the game, 'on this display, Burnley have a side of promotion potentialities'. Then Burnley won again, beating Swansea Town at Turf Moor with a Ray Harrison goal. Despite the fact that Swansea were bottom of the table, it was only a freak goal which beat them, when a Swansea defender kicked the ball against Harrison and the ball rebounded into the net.

By this time, Barnsley were four points ahead of Burnley in the table, and a thrilling game at Turf Moor saw the two teams draw 2–2. Ray Harrison equalised an Alan Brown own goal, and then Robledo put the Yorkshire team ahead again. But late in the game, George Bray saved a point for the Clarets when he slammed the ball through a crowd of players. This result made the League table in early October read:

	Played	*Points*
Barnsley	9	15
Man. City	7	11
Newcastle Utd.	8	10
West Brom.	8	10
Burnley	8	10

A Peter Kippax goal earned Burnley a point in a 1–1 draw at Tottenham, and then the unbeaten run was extended to five games, when West Ham came north and lost 2–1. Reg Attwell, the West Ham half-back, had been a great favourite at Burnley during the war as a guest player, but in October 1946, he could only command a place in the West Ham reserve team. Jackie Billingham scored before West Ham equalised, and then Peter Kippax scored the winner from a twice taken penalty-kick. The run of success continued at Hillsborough, when the Clarets won 2–1, Chew and Billingham getting the all-important goals.

By now, the team was beginning to blend together with great success; Arthur Woodruff was proving an outstanding figure at right-back, Alan Brown was already stamping his leadership on the team, whilst Harry Potts was often described at the 'director-general' of the Burnley attack. The Lancashire team moved up into second place, a point behind Barnsley with a game in hand, when they beat Fulham 2–0 at Turf Moor. George Bray (penalty) and Jackie Billingham were the scorers.

But the most important news in Burnley that week was when the club signed Reg Attwell from West Ham 'for a substantial fee'. The arrival of Attwell, a stylish and cultured ball-player, caused great excitement in the town, for the fans well remembered him from his guesting days with the club.

There was a great exodus of Burnley supporters who made the trek over to Bury in November for the game at Gigg Lane. There they saw a real Lancashire 'derby' match with Burnley losing early on, going into a second-half lead, with goals by Billingham and Potts, and then conceding a point late in the game, when Bury came back to draw 2–2. This point put Burnley on top of Division Two, with just a third of the programme completed.

Reg Attwell made his debut on November 9 in the match at Turf Moor against Luton Town. Jack Billingham scored an important goal for the fifth successive game, as Burnley drew 1–1 and dropped a home point, which put them back in third place behind Manchester City and Birmingham City. A third consecutive draw came in the next game at Plymouth, when Billingham and Morris equalised after being two goals down. It was the team's tenth game without defeat, and one paper said: 'Burnley are all set for Division One after their display at Home Park. They have the strongest half-back line in Division Two'.

November 1946 was very wet, and every ground in the country was exceedingly heavy. Burnley made it a run of five successive draws with two goal-less results at home to Leicester and away to Chesterfield. Both games were played in heavy clinging mud, which only made it harder for other clubs to score against their now famous defence, which had conceded 17 goals in as many games.

Billingham, Potts and Kippax gave Burnley their best win so far, 3–0 against Millwall at Turf Moor, and then the following week, Burnley went to Bradford and won 1–0 with a goal by little Billy Morris.

A crowd of 30,000 people gathered at Turf Moor on the Saturday before Christmas to see the vital promotion clash between League leaders Manchester City and Burnley. George Bray missed a penalty in a hard fought game, and though Burnley took the honours, they dropped a point in a 0–0 draw. On Christmas Day 1946, Burnley entertained Notts Forest and won easily by 3–0 with goals by Jackie Chew (2) and Peter Kippax, but the following day in the return game, the Forest team beat Burnley 1–0. So ended the Clarets fine run of 16 games without defeat, with Notts Forest being the first team to score a goal against Burnley for six weeks!

At the start of 1947, the position in the top of the League was:

	Played	*Points*
Man. City	21	30
Birmingham	23	30
Burnley	22	29
Newcastle Utd.	22	28

The first game of the New Year was at Coventry, a team unbeaten at home till then. But just as Burnley's fine unbeaten run had been broken, so was Coventry's! A Billy Morris hat-trick gave the Clarets a fine 3–0 victory to strengthen their challenge to the top teams. The position at the top tightened when Birmingham, the current League leaders, came to Turf Moor and lost 1–0. The largest crowd yet, some 36,000, saw Harry Potts score the winner.

The third round of the F.A. Cup brought six-times winners Aston Villa to Second Division Burnley. Burnley had done well against other Second Division teams, but not many thought they would hold their own against top class opposition. Not only did they hold their own; they mowed the Villa down. 'BURNLEY'S BRILLIANCE DAZZLES THE VILLA' ran the headlines in the local paper. One newspaper said 'the ball went from man to man with machine-like precision'. Another commented: 'Burnley knocked out the famous Villa without frills or flounces—just by sheer methodical soccer played at top speed under rain and in mud'. Once again the highest attendance yet, 39,000 paying £3,472, saw Bill Morris score twice in the first half, Ray Harrison got two more in the second half, before Harry Potts made it five. In the last five minutes, Villa scored a consolation goal; it was only the second goal that the Clarets had conceded in ten games!

But more important than the Cup, was the battle to get out of Division Two, and this continued, when Burnley visited fellow promotion candidates, West Brom, and came away with a 1–1 draw, thanks to a Jackie Chew goal. January 24 brought the fourth round of the Cup, and Burnley's opponents at Turf Moor were fellow Second Divisioners, Coventry City. Once again the season's highest attendance was recorded when 39,796 saw the game, paying £3,500. Jackie Chew and Harry Potts scored the goals that saw Burnley into the fifth round, and one newspaper reporter said: 'Advancing on two fronts are Burnley, who take on all opposition in their facile stride these days'.

A 3–0 victory over promotion rivals Newcastle United made the position at the top of the League:

	Played	*Points*
Man. City	25	38
Burnley	26	36
Newcastle Utd.	27	34
Birmingham	25	32

'On snow-covered Turf Moor, Burnley played first-class workmanlike football, with no frills, no flounces, the complete "get on with the job" team. They are like a well drilled platoon, each man seems to know exactly what to do whatever situation the run of play throws up—a wonderfully well disciplined turn out. Newcastle's £50,000 eleven were pathetic by comparison.' Such was the verdict of the national press after the game, whilst another paper said: 'If ever a team looked capable of the double, it is Burnley—the team without a star, but every man a complete cog in a perfect piece of football machinery—the defence is just about as watertight as they are made'.

'CUP OR PROMOTION? OR BOTH?' asked the *Burnley Express*, and people throughout the country were beginning to sit up and take notice of the efficient performances by the team from North-East Lancashire. Harrison and Chew won two more points for the club when they scored the goals in the 2–0 victory at Swansea. On the same day, a young lad called Adamson, playing inside-left for the 'A' team scored four goals!

Clubs were now in the middle of one of the hardest winters on record, both for snow and frost. A 0–0 draw at Luton in the fifth round of the cup, was followed by a 3–0 victory in the replay at Turf Moor, Ray Harrison notching a hat-trick. About that time, Peter Kippax was selected twice for the Football League team.

A 0–0 draw against Tottenham, and a 2–0 victory over Sheffield Wednesday kept the Clarets up amongst the leading teams, and then came the sixth round of the F.A. Cup, and the hardest tie so far—First Division Middlesbrough, away. Thousands of Burnley fans made the journey by road and rail in Arctic conditions, only to find themselves locked out of the ground, filled by a record crowd for Ayresome Park (53,025). Former Burnley Chief Constable, Mr A. E. Edwards, then Chief Constable of Middlesbrough, climbed onto the wall surrounding the ground, and from his vantage point, he gave a running commentary to the thousands locked out. With the England captain George Hardwick, and England schemer Wilf Mannion in their ranks, the home team went ahead in the first half, but Billy Morris scored the equaliser to earn a replay the following week at Turf Moor.

A total of 49,244, the largest crowd at Turf Moor since the Arsenal Cup-tie ten years previously, paid record receipts for the Club of £4,124 to see the replay on March 4. In a tremendous battle, nothing was given away by either side and the final whistle blew with the score still 0–0. But 90 seconds into extra-time, Billy Morris again scored the vital goal, to put Burnley into the semi-finals for the first time since 1935. Both games against Middlesbrough were played in atrocious conditions due to the extreme weather, and in March, 1947, many games were called off, which necessitated them being played at the end of the season.

The draw for the semi-finals was: Burnley v Liverpool (at Blackburn) and Newcastle Utd v Charlton Athletic (at Leeds), and when tickets went on sale for the Blackburn game, a great queue formed outside Turf Moor from midnight the previous evening. Back in the League, the position now read:

	Played	*Points*
Man. City	28	43
Burnley	29	41
Birmingham	29	37
Newcastle Utd.	29	36

Burnley went to Luton and beat the 'Hatters' 3–1 in a blizzard, (Potts (2) and Harrison being the scorers). An off-form Burnley team struggled to beat Plymouth 2–1 at Turf Moor; Chew and Potts scoring after the team had been a goal down. Excitement was now at fever pitch in the town, as the club stood second in the League, and in the semi-final of the Cup. A crowd of 53,000 people, paying £11,000, saw the semi-final against Liverpool at Ewood Park. The game resulted in a 0–0 draw, but the highlight of the day was the battle between Burnley's captain, Alan Brown, who played a magnificent game, and the fine Liverpool centre-forward Albert Stubbins, who had recently cost the club a record £13,000 from Newcastle.

Now it was Easter, and Easter, 1947, proved to be one of the coldest and most bitter on record. Another two points were won on Good Friday, when a Peter Kippax goal helped to beat Southampton. The day afterwards was a memorable one recalled by many to this day, as Burnley met Chesterfield. An icy wind blew the length of Turf Moor, and conditions were perhaps as bad as they have ever been on the ground. Chesterfield scored first, but Harry Potts provided the equaliser. In the second half, Jack Hays had to go off with cramp, and then Jack Billingham collapsed and was carried off. Burnley finished the game with nine men, and at the final whistle, three Chesterfield players collapsed and had to be carried off and put in the bath to recover from the cold, boots, jerseys and all. Due to after effects of that game and several injuries as well, a much changed Burnley team travelled down to Southampton the following Monday, and thanks to a Jack Knight goal, the Clarets won 1–0. The position at the top of the League now stood as:

	Played	*Points*
Man. City	34	53
Burnley	34	50
Birmingham	35	44
Tottenham	35	41

Just before the semi-final replay with Liverpool, Arthur Woodruff was chosen for the Football League team, whilst Peter Kippax was selected to play for England against France.

The biggest crowd to see Burnley that season (72,000 paying £12,250) packed the Maine Road ground. Two of the Cup winning team, Bert Freeman and Billy Watson, were at Maine Road (along with Joe 'Andy' of the Championship side) to see the Clarets win through to their first ever Wembley Final. Against the best attack in the country, Burnley's defence held firm, and in both games, Liverpool's famed attack, Stubbins and all, failed to score. But at the other end, Ray Harrison sent the Burnley supporters wild when he pivoted round and slammed an unstoppable shot past Sidlow. Burnley were in the Cup Final for the first time since Halley, Boyle'n Watson!

But 'after the Lord Mayor's Show' . . . the following week, Burnley were beaten at home by Bradford 3–1 (Potts being the scorer). It was the first home defeat for the Clarets since the previous September, and it shook their hopes of promotion. It also shook the team's confidence as they prepared at Morecambe for the Final against Charlton (who had beaten Newcastle).

And so came the Final (only a fortnight after the semi-final, due to the replay). Before the Duke of Gloucester and 99,000 spectators, Burnley again played 90 minutes to a 0–0 draw. Although the Clarets had their chances, and Harry Potts hit the Charlton crossbar with a terrific shot, it looked as though they would repeat the victories over Middlesbrough and Liverpool, and win in extra time, for they had proved themselves apart from finishing, to be the better side. But out of the blue, Charlton's diminutive left winger Chris Duffy scored seven minutes from the end of extra time. Even after that, the Clarets almost equalised when a great header by Billy Morris just scraped over the bar with goalkeeper Sam Bartram nowhere near. The teams that day in April, 1947, were: Burnley: Strong; Woodruff, Mather; Attwell, Brown, Bray; Chew, Morris, Harrison, Potts, Kippax. Charlton: Bartram; Croker, Shreeve; Johnson, Phipps, Revell; Hurst, Dawson, Robinson, Welsh, Duffy.

During the game, the ball burst for the second consecutive Cup Final; extra time was played for only the fourth time, and the match was the first to be televised full length. Two days later, when the team returned to Burnley, they were given a rapturous welcome home by the townsfolk, which took the older supporters back to the time when Tommy Boyle had brought the Cup back to Burnley.

But now all eyes were on promotion; one objective had failed, but the more important one still lay ahead. The Saturday after Wembley, Burnley visited the already relegated Newport County and won 3–0, with goals from Potts, Morris and Hays. With six games to play, the position was:

	Played	*Points*
Man. City	36	55
Burnley	36	52
Birmingham	39	50
Tottenham	39	46

By now, the backlog of fixtures due to the freak weather conditions earlier in the year, meant that several teams were playing twice a week for weeks on end. Burnley and Manchester City both had six games to play (other teams in the League had eight and nine games left) and it was already May. On May 10, the two leading clubs met at Maine Road, and Burnley suffered their third defeat in four games, as Manchester City made certain of promotion, winning 1–0. The following Saturday, the Clarets went to Fulham, and again lost 1–0. Tension was gradually increasing at the Club, as supporters saw promotion slipping from their grasp. In the meantime, Birmingham had won one of their remaining games, and they went into second position above Burnley (who had three games in hand).

Another point came Burnley's way when they drew 1–1 at home to Bury, due to a Jackie Billingham goal. The week after, both Burnley and Birmingham won again; the Clarets 4–1 at Leicester, and Birmingham at Newport, to make the League position:

	Played	*Points*
Man. City	40	60
Birmingham	42	55
Burnley	40	55

And with Birmingham having the better goal average, it meant that Burnley had to gain a point from their last two games, which were both away from home! But one game was enough, for in their most convincing win of the season, Burnley beat West Ham at Upton Park 5–0 to clinch promotion. Chew, Morris, Potts (2) and Hays did the damage, and one national paper reported: 'It was a magnificent exhibition of splendid ball control. Such football compelled one to think that the Burnley team must be superior to two thirds of the First Division'. And just to make completely certain, the Clarets took another point at Millwall in the season's last match, when Billy Morris scored the equaliser in a 1–1 draw.

So came to an end, a season that would rank alongside those of 1914 and 1921 in the memories of Burnley supporters. The Burnley team had come very close to equalling West Bromwich Albion's unique record of winning the Cup and the Second Division Championship. They broke Barnsley's 1937 defensive record of conceding 34 goals, by only conceding 29. But most of all, for the third time in their history, they achieved promotion back to the First Division. This time, they were to stay there longer than ever before.

1947–48

Burnley's first match in Division One for seventeen years was played at Fratton Park, the home of Portsmouth on August 23, 1947. It took Harry Potts only two minutes to score the only goal of the game. The Burnley team that day read: Strong; Woodruff, Mather; Attwell, Brown Bray; Chew, Morris, Billingham, Potts and Hays.

The following week, Burnley entertained Derby County at Turf Moor. Derby included Billy Steel, for whom they had paid a record £15,500 that summer, but it was Raich Carter and Jackie Stamps who stunned the Turf Moor side, scoring twice in a minute to give Derby the points. Around that time, both Alan Brown and Arthur Woodruff were honoured by being chosen for the Football League side, whilst a 19-year-old player called Tom Cummings commenced training at Turf Moor in October, 1947.

The Clarets were really going well in November, when in consecutive games, they won 3–0 at Everton and 4–0 against Sunderland at Turf Moor. Famous names such as Ted Sagar and Jock Dodds were in the Everton side, but Burnley stormed to a convincing win in a tough game. The forward line that day read: Hays, Knight, Billingham, Potts and Kippax; and Billingham, Knight and Potts scored the goals. This win put Burnley six points behind leaders Arsenal and two behind second placed Preston. Two points from Sunderland put Burnley into second place, and diminutive Jackie Knight was the star that day. Burnley took the lead when Billingham headed in from a Chew corner, and the other goals came from Potts (2) and Knight. The League position at the end of 1947 was:

	Played	*Points*
Arsenal	23	35
Burnley	23	32
Preston	24	30
Derby County	24	28

The year 1948 began with a shock for the Clarets, for on January 1, they were well beaten 5–0 by Manchester United. Close on 60,000 packed into Maine Road that day, where United were playing their home games, due to war damage of their own ground. It was a bad performance by the Burnley team, and the first time for exactly two years since they had conceded five goals. Harry Potts missed a penalty, Alan Brown had his name taken, Arthur Woodruff was completely outpaced, and the team as a whole were utterly outclassed. United swung the ball about with devastating precision, and Jack Rowley got a hat-trick, whilst Charlie Mitten scored the other two.

The following week, Burnley were on the Wembley trail again, when they came up against lowly Swindon Town in the third round. Old-timers recalled 'the good old days', for Swindon's manager was the ex-Claret, Louis Page, who had himself played on the previous occasion that the two teams met in the Cup. This time, Burnley received an even greater shock than the Manchester United defeat. Over 34,000 saw the Third Division side score twice before half-time, and maintain their lead to win 2–0 at the final whistle. There could be no complaints for the better side won on the day, but the result still stands as one of the biggest cup upsets for Burnley of all time, ranking alongside the Hull City defeat of 1920–21.

On February 14, 1948, Burnley faced League leaders Arsenal at Highbury. If Burnley won, they would be four points behind with a game in hand; unfortunately they didn't! Arsenal ran out clear winners, 3–0, with goals from Don Roper and Ronnie Rooke (2). That game virtually decided the championship, for Burnley were the only team within striking distance, though Manchester United were coming up hard on the rails.

Three weeks later, Blackburn Rovers came to Turf Moor for the first time for nine years, and the last time for the next ten years! In 1947–48, Rovers were fighting an unsuccessful struggle against relegation, but still the 'old enemy' attracted a gate of 52,933 to Turf Moor for the local derby. The gate was second only as a League record for Turf Moor to the 53,133 that had turned out the previous October to see the Burnley v Blackpool Lancashire derby. Rovers won a valuable point in a 0–0 draw, but the result didn't help Burnley's hopes of honours. Two points out of a possible eight robbed Burnley of any chance of catching Arsenal, and the position in mid-March was:

	Played	*Points*
Arsenal	32	49
Preston	31	40
Burnley	31	39
Man. Utd.	30	36

Cliff Britton made several changes, bringing in Woodruff, Loughran, Harrison, Hornby and Haigh, and, as a result, both Grimsby Town and Stoke City conceded four goals at Turf Moor. Among the names beginning to become familiar in the 'A' team, at that time in 1948, were Tommy Cummings at centre-half, Doug Winton at outside-right and Jimmy Adamson inside-left.

By now Burnley's chances of finishing in second place were dimming, and the Clarets had to beat relegation-threatened Charlton to keep their hopes alive. But nothing went right in that third last match. Sam Bartram saved George Bray's penalty (there had been a spate of missed penalties by Burnley that season), and Charlton pulled off a shock 2–0 win, so escaping relegation. The Clarets came back in the next game to win 2–0 at Chelsea with Reg Attwell getting one of the goals in an unusual No. 10 jersey; and then a last match win against Huddersfield with goals by Bray and Harrison made sure of third position in the final League table. They were pipped on the post for the runners-up place by Manchester United who with a splendid run in 1948, climbed up from a mid-table position and won the F.A. Cup at Wembley. A fraction, 0.40 of a goal, separated Manchester United and Burnley at the end of the season, which had proved a very satisfying comeback to the First Division.

1948–49

Local boy, Fred Taylor, left the club at the end of the 1947–48 season whilst there were two interesting arrivals at Turf Moor in the close season of 1948. Ian Wilson, an outside-right, came from Preston North End, and John Aird, centre-forward or inside-forward, arrived from Jeanfield Swifts, the same Scottish junior club which had produced Jock Winton.

A crowd of 33,600 saw the first game of the new season at Turf Moor, when Manchester City were the visitors. Burnley's team that day was: Strong; Woodruff, Mather; Attwell, Brown, Bray; Chew, Morris, Billingham, Knight (J) and Hays, and Jackie Billingham's goal gave the Turf Moor team the two points. A sign of the times was that over 10,000 people saw the opening Central League game against Leeds United Reserves. After their first match success against

Manchester City, the team had a very indifferent spell; ten points came from the first twelve games, and the Clarets found themselves in the bottom six in Division One. And then to add to their problems, two of their stalwarts left the scene at Turf Moor. Manager Cliff Britton left Burnley and went to Everton, whilst captain Alan Brown was transferred to Notts County the following week.

The reorganised Burnley team after 'general' Alan Brown's departure looked like: Strong; Woodruff, Mather; Loughran, Johnson, Bray; Chew, Morris, Billingham, Potts, Wilson. Wilf Mannion had refused to re-sign for Middlesbrough at the start of the season, and Burnley made enquiries for him, but like the Doherty enquiries of 1936, they came to nothing! One new player who did sign for Burnley about that time was young 17-year-old goalkeeper Colin McDonald, and then in late October, Frank Hill, the ex-Arsenal player and Crewe manager, came to Turf Moor as Club Manager.

The centre-half position was proving a problem since Brown's departure, and after two and a half years at right-back, Arthur Woodruff found himself playing in the midfield role once again. Jackie Knight was transferred to Preston in part exchange for the Scottish International inside-forward, Andy McClaren, and following Frank Hill, centre-forward Alf 'Nobby' Clarke came to Burnley from Crewe. Then on December 18, 1948, 20-year-old Tommy Cummings was chosen to play for the first team against Manchester City at Maine Road. Burnley didn't win that day (they never had done at Maine Road!) but Tommy Cummings had an outstanding debut in the 2–2 draw.

The old team continued to break up in 1949, when in the first week of the new year, left-winger Peter Kippax left the club for Liverpool, whilst the oldest servant of the club, Bob Johnson, now in his 13th season with Burnley, was placed on the transfer list at his own request. Goals by newcomers McClaren and Clarke gave Burnley revenge over Cup Final victors Charlton in the third round in 1949. Tommy Cummings earned the local headlines when Burnley visited St James' Park . . . 'CUMMINGS EARNED HONOURS . . . HELD MILBURN'. The task of holding Jackie Milburn, England's speedy centre-forward, and taking a point from League leaders Newcastle United on their own ground, was one worthy of headlines in 1949.

Andy McClaren, who had not settled very well in the town asked for a transfer, and some months later, he went to Sheffield United. Jack Spencer made his debut at centre-forward in the fourth round Cup-tie at Rotherham, and in a hard game, he scored the winning goal. But later in the season he went down with cartilage trouble and missed many games. Full-back Jackie Butterfield had broken his leg in January, Ray Harrison was out suffering from boils, Harold Spencer and Gordon Haigh were others on the injured list. These injuries meant that the team was unsettled, and this was reflected both by the results and the fact that the side had six captains that season, Brown, Johnson, Potts, Bray, Loughran and Mather. There was disappointment in the town when Reg Attwell, after being chosen for the Football League team, was passed over by the England selectors. After their two fine seasons, the Clarets finished in a very modest fifteenth position. At the end of the season, the club's two longest serving players, Ronnie Hornby and Bob Johnson, were placed on the transfer list.

1949–50

The club made a great start to the new season, taking five points from the first three games. The team that faced Arsenal at Highbury in the first game was: Strong; Loughran, Mather; Attwell, Cummings, Martindale; Chew, Morris, Harrison, Potts and Hays, and Billy Morris scored the winning goal. They drew 2–2 in their next match at Turf Moor against Sunderland, and then the Clarets found themselves at the top of Division One with a 2–1 victory over Bolton. But their success was short-lived, and after eleven games, the club had slipped to third, four points behind leaders Wolves.

Jackie Billingham was transferred to Carlisle United, whilst George Knight, Jack Marshall and Jack Butterfield were all forced into an early retirement because of injuries. Meanwhile in a challenge match, Burnley Reserves, who had won the Central League championship for the first time the previous season, beat a Rest of the Central League team 2–1. Roy Stephenson and Reg Attwell scored for Burnley, whilst a Liverpool player called Les Shannon scored for the Rest. Not very long afterwards, Shannon was signed by Burnley for a fee of about £6,000, and about the same time, another of the Cup Final team, Ray Harrison, went to Doncaster Rovers.

At the end of the year, the club had slipped several places in the League, though they were still only four points behind leaders Liverpool. In the third round of the Cup, Burnley visited Notts County (plus Tommy Lawton) and won easily 4–1, with Tommy Cummings containing the ex-Burnley and England centre-forward well. Attwell, Potts, Wilson and Spencer were the scorers. In the fourth round, Burnley came up against Port Vale. Though the Clarets won the tie 2–1 at the Turf, the team suffered several injuries in a tough match. Hays sustained a broken nose, Mather had tendon trouble, whilst Spencer, Potts and Attwell were all badly bruised. However, after these two victories against lower clubs, Burnley went out of the competition when they were beaten 2–0 at Highbury, by the eventual winners, Arsenal.

Meanwhile in the League, the Clarets were finding things hard going. They didn't win a League game between December 24, when they won at Bolton 1–0, and March 18, when they beat Huddersfield Town by the only goal at Turf Moor. And despite this bad run, with seven games to play, Burnley were still only seven points off the top team Manchester United; with any sort of consistency, the team could surely have been League champions in 1949–50.

Bill Hayes, a veteran Irish International left-back, came from Huddersfield, and maybe because of this, stalwart Harold Mather was placed on the transfer list at his own request. He didn't leave the club, but one player who did was left-winger Ian Wilson, who went to Leicester. Burnley were searching for an inside-forward, and at one point were on the verge of signing Dennis Wilshaw from Wolverhampton, but the player declined to come to Burnley. Good player though Wilshaw was, perhaps it was a good thing that he didn't sign! The club continued their search, and came back from Northern Ireland with a player called Jimmy McIlroy!

McIlroy made his debut the following week at Turf Moor in front of 8,646 people in the Central League game against Chesterfield Reserves. The date was March 25, 1950, and though the young Irishman played a superb game, it is doubtful if many people there realised how great a player he was to become. Jimmy McIlroy was only one of several young players coming through the ranks in 1950; Les Shannon had made his debut earlier in the season, whilst Jock Aird and Roy Stephenson appeared for the first time in Division One over Easter 1950. Another player made his debut in the Reserves in the last match of the season away to Sheffield United, goalkeeper Colin McDonald. The forward line playing for Burnley Reserves that afternoon was interesting: Shannon, McIlroy, Adamson, Morris and Chew. Other players who were beginning to take the public eye in the Reserve and 'A' teams were Tony Hapgood, Billy Holden, Terry Lyons and Bobby Seith.

The first team continued to average a point a match, getting seven points from their last seven games, and strangely, they still only finished seven points behind the eventual champions, Portsmouth. Burnley's weakness was undoubtedly their attack, for whilst there were only two better defences in the First Division (Portsmouth and Blackpool), there were only two worse attacks (Manchester City and Birmingham City) and they were both relegated!

1950–51

The Turf Moor side commenced the new season with a game at home against Cup-winners Arsenal, led by Player of the Year, Joe Mercer. The Burnley team that day was: Strong; Woodruff, Mather; Martindale, Cummings, Bray; Chew, Morris, Clarke, Potts, Stephenson. Arsenal had not been beaten at Turf Moor since 1926–27 and true to form they won once again 1–0.

Another name which was to become familiar at Turf Moor, Billy Holden, made his debut on September 2 in the home game against Middlesbrough. Meanwhile, young Tommy Cummings played for the Football League team, and was selected as reserve for the England team. But as Burnley's young players were improving, so one old favourite of the Turf Moor crowd bid farewell for the time being to the local scene. Harry Potts, who had first signed on for the club in 1937, had been asking for a transfer for some time, and in October, 1950, his request was granted. Several clubs enquired about his services, but eventually he was transferred to Everton for a Burnley record fee of around £20,000.

The week after Harry Potts' departure to Goodison Park, 18-year-old Jimmy McIlroy made his League debut for the club, away at Sunderland. Several times from that day onward, the young Irishman hit the headlines in his first season, for his outstanding promise, whilst at the same time 'Big Bill' Holden was also establishing himself locally with many superb goals.

After 17 games, Burnley were nine points behind the League leaders, Arsenal. The weak point in Burnley's play was their away record; it was now December, and they hadn't won away since August 26. On December 16, they visited Highbury to play the leaders Arsenal. The 'Gunners' were undefeated at home, and they were the only team to have beaten the Clarets at Turf Moor that season. But that day, it was Burnley who provided the surprise result, when they won 1–0, the winner coming from Billy Holden. Several players had cause to remember the game, as they finished the match injured, and as a result of hard tackling, Attwell, Holden, McIlroy and Cummings all bore wounds from the Highbury battle.

The New Year saw Burnley making another fine away performance against the new League leaders, Middlesbrough. Three goals down after 25 minutes, Burnley came back with goals by Chew, Morris and McIlroy to draw 3–3. By now, McIlroy and Holden had both soundly established themselves as first team players. But other fine players were coming 'through the ranks' in 1951. In January, Aird, Shannon, Adamson and Stephenson were all regular Reserve team players, Winton and Seith were in the 'A' team, whilst a young player called Albert Cheesebrough, was beginning to make a name for himself in the 'B' team.

After McIlroy's debut, the next young Burnley player to make his initial first team appearance was Jimmy Adamson, who appeared in the 1–1 draw at Burnden Park, Bolton (Feb 10, 1951), whilst Roy Stephenson became a regular performer in the first team from March, 1951, when he played in the Manchester United game. That season certainly saw an influx of young talent into the senior team ranks, for the forward line at the close of the season sometimes read: Stephenson, Samuels, Holden, McIlroy, Lyons. But March, 1951, was a memorable time for two Burnley veterans too. Goalkeeper Jimmy Strong completed 200 consecutive League appearances, whilst trainer Billy Dougall celebrated 25 years since he had first arrived at Turf Moor.

1951–52

Burnley began the sixth post-war season away to Charlton Athletic. The Lancashire team lost 1–0, and they turned out as: Strong; Woodruff, Aird; Adamson, Cummings, Attwell; Stephenson, Morris, Holden, McIlroy, Shannon.

Jack Hays was put on the transfer list at his own request, and the same week, Terry Lyons, recognised as the fastest man on the club's books, went to Bradford. The left-winger saga continued on the last day of August, when the Turf Moor club paid their highest ever fee of about £25,000 for Billy Elliott, the Bradford Park Avenue left-winger. Elliott made his first appearance the following Saturday, in the away game at Middlesbrough. Tony Hapgood, son of the Arsenal and England full-back Eddie Hapgood, also made his first team debut that day, but even with their two newcomers, Burnley still lost 5–0!

After a very poor start, Burnley beat West Brom 6–1 at Turf Moor. It was the club's highest score since before the War, and Billy Morris scored four of the goals. But the week after, Burnley were on the receiving end again, when they were tanned 7–1 at Newcastle (George Robledo getting 4). That week, Jack Hays went to Bury, whilst Jimmy McIlroy was chosen for Ireland. Because Billy Holden was injured, Elliott played centre-forward, and then later, McIlroy was tried in the position. And at the same time, the 'old-school' of Chew and Morris were having a fine spell on the right wing; so well was Morris playing, that he was chosen once again to play for his native Wales.

Tommy Cummings hit the headlines in November, when he scored the equaliser against Wolves, but after 18 games, Burnley were only five points off the bottom club, Fulham. Billy Elliott scored his first Burnley goal and made two others in the fine 3–1 win at Huddersfield, and Tommy Cummings scored again, (but this time an own goal!). After being on the injured list McIlroy

PROMOTED. The Burnley team that won promotion and reached the F.A. Cup Final, 1947. Reg Attwell, Arthur Woodruff, Jimmy Strong, Harold Mather, George Bray; Jackie Chew, Billy Morris, Alan Brown, Ray Harrison, Harry Potts, Peter Kippax

JIMMY ROBSON, Burnley's inside left, who scored many vital goals in the 1959–60 Championship season and ADAM BLACKLAW, goalkeeper, member of the same Championship team

BURNLEY IN EUROPE. Gordon Harris (far left) drives home an unstoppable shot past the Hamburg goalkeeper in the European Cup tie in Germany, 1961

RESERVE DOUBLE. The Burnley Reserve team that in 1962 won the double of the Central League title and the Lancashire Senior Cup

returned to the first team as an outside-right, and he had a lengthy spell in that position. The forward line at the time: McIlroy, Morris, Holden, Shannon, Elliott. That Christmas was the occasion of the infamous Elliott-Cunningham incident in the Burnley-Preston game at Turf Moor, when Preston won 2–0.

Despite their uncertain League position, Burnley began 1952 well, with a fine 7–1 victory over Middlesbrough. This was the club's highest score since they had beaten Reading 8–1 in 1930–31, 21 years previously. Holden (3), Morris (3) and Shannon were the Burnley scorers that memorable day. Tommy Cummings was now the club captain in place of George Bray who was in the Reserves.

The Clarets met Third Division North team Hartlepools United in the Cup, and won a close game 1–0. In the fourth round, they were drawn at home again, this time against Coventry City. Goals from Holden and Elliott gave the Clarets a 2–0 win over the Coventry team.

Burnley prepared for their fifth round tie with Liverpool; the club purchased a smart new change strip, navy blue jerseys with white collars and cuffs, and on the previous Sunday morning there was a great queue for tickets. In a fine game, Burnley had a great 2–0 win with goals by Morris and Shannon. This put the Clarets in the sixth round, and they were drawn against Blackburn Rovers, who were then in the Second Division. In front of a great crowd at Ewood, Chew scored first, but Nightingale equalised right on half-time. In the second half, amateur Bill Holmes and Glover scored further goals to give the Rovers a deserved 3–1 victory.

Jimmy Strong had had a bad spell, and he joined McIlroy, Woodruff, Pilkington and Stephenson in the Reserves, Joe McNulty taking his place in the first team goal against Aston Villa. It proved to be a particularly tragic game for Burnley, because as well as losing, Billy Holden broke his leg, whilst Morris and McNulty were both badly injured. The next week, Alf Clarke came in place of Holden, Jimmy McIlroy resumed in place of Morris, whilst Jimmy Strong came back once again; 11,618 shivered on the Turf Moor terraces that day when Burnley entertained Sunderland—the smallest gate since the war.

The 17-year-old Albert Cheesebrough made his first team debut at outside-right at Old Trafford, but Manchester United had an easy 6–1 victory. Cheesebrough was the first Burnley boy to play for the Clarets since Peter Kippax. After the 6–1 defeat at Old Trafford, came another 4–1 beating at Stamford Bridge, and so a very moderate season came to a close, with Burnley in fourteenth position. But it was going to be a long time, thirteen years, before the Clarets finished in the bottom half again.

EIGHT

JOURNEY TO THE TOP AGAIN

1952–53

There were several departures from the Turf Moor scene during the close season of 1952. Joe McNulty went to Sheffield United, Alf Clarke signed for Oldham, and Arthur Woodruff went to Workington. Meanwhile, Joe Brown, a left-half for Middlesbrough came to Turf Moor, and Billy Holden was back after his broken leg had kept him out at the close of the previous season.

The Clarets lost the opening game at Turf Moor, 1–0 to Middlesbrough. The team was: Strong; Aird, Mather; Adamson, Cummings, Attwell; Cheesebrough, Morris, Holden, Shannon and Elliott. After this home defeat, Jackie Chew and Jimmy McIlroy came in for Cheesebrough and Morris for the second game against Stoke, which Burnley won 3–2. Then came wins against West Brom (away), Stoke (away), Newcastle (home) and Manchester City (home) to give Burnley 10 out of 12 points, and put them at the top of the First Division.

A rumour that Spurs had offered £50,000 for McIlroy and Elliott was denied at Turf Moor. Two 0–0 draws at Manchester City and Cardiff City kept Burnley at the top. The Cardiff City game had a special significance for Jimmy Strong, for in playing at Ninian Park, it meant that he completed a personal record of having played on every ground in the four divisions. The famed Derek Dooley made his first Division One appearance at Turf Moor for Sheffield Wednesday, and scored the equaliser in a 1–1 draw.

Meanwhile, Billy Elliott was injured whilst playing for the Football League, and 19-year-old Brian Pilkington made his debut. The game was against Tottenham, and young Pilkington was facing the England defender, Alf Ramsey. However, after young Pilkington had made the Burnley goal, Spurs came back to win 2–1 in the last minute. A poor run put Burnley into a mid-table position; when they beat Manchester United 3–1, it was the Clarets' first victory for seven games (McIlroy 2 and Holden scored the decisive goals). About that time, both McIlroy and Elliott played again for their countries.

In November, 1952, Burnley bought Desmond Thompson, a goal-keeper, from York City and Jock Winton made his debut in the right-back position against leaders, Wolves. In the following game, Reg Attwell failed to turn up against Arsenal; Chew went to left-half, and Billy Morris played on the right wing. That game, which resulted in a 1–1 draw, proved to be the last first team appearance for two fine servants of the Burnley club, Jimmy Strong and Billy Morris. The week afterwards, Des Thompson made his first team debut against Middlesbrough.

A good sequence of ten games and only one defeat saw Burnley heading for the top again, as they entered 1953. They kept within two points of the top by beating the League leaders West Brom 5–0, Les Shannon scoring a hat-trick. Meanwhile in the Cup, Burnley drew 1–1 at Portsmouth, and won the replay 3–1 to enter round four. They were drawn against Sunderland at home, and once again, large queues formed outside Turf Moor when the tickets went on sale. The largest crowd of the season, 53,213 saw Burnley win 2–0. But Arsenal became the first team to beat Burnley for three months, when they won the fifth round Cup-tie at Turf Moor 2–0. The League position now read:

	Played	*Points*
West Brom. A.	28	35
Burnley	27	34
Wolves	29	34

Then the Clarets beat Spurs, and as a result they went to the top of the League. A victory at Derby kept them there, but when Portsmouth beat the Clarets 2–1 in the last minute, the club began to falter. In the end, though changes were made in the team and Roy Stephenson and Joe Brown were introduced to the team, Burnley still lost touch with the leaders, and finished in sixth position, six points behind champions Arsenal.

1953–54

The great surprise of the 1953 close season was the transfer of international left-winger Billy Elliott, who had become a great favourite with the Turf Moor crowd. Elliott went to Sunderland, and as a replacement, Burnley signed Billy Gray from Chelsea.

In the first game of the season at Turf Moor, Hancocks of Wolves scored the season's first goal in the first minute, but the Clarets came back to win 4–1. The Burnley team that day was: Thompson; Aird, Winton; Adamson, Cummings, Rudman; Gray, McIlroy, Holden, Shannon, Pilkington. Another player made his debut in October, when Bobby Seith came into the team for the first time in the game at Old Trafford, which the Clarets won 2–1.

Des Thompson faced his brother George, who kept goal for Preston in the games played over Christmas, in which each club had a 2–1 home win. In the third round of the F.A. Cup, Burnley had been drawn at home against Manchester United. 'This Cup-tie could be a stylish classic' said the *Burnley Express*, and the reporter turned out to be quite a prophet! Two Burnley goals in the first three minutes, two all after six minutes, with Burnley going on to win 5–3, made it a game that is still recalled to this day. The Clarets were in the fourth round again, but this time they were beaten by Newcastle by a penalty goal at St James' Park.

The same week as they lost to Newcastle, Burnley signed Johnny Walton, an English Amateur international inside-forward from Bury. Billy Holden was injured once again, and Jock Winton played centre-forward against Newcastle. He was according to the paper, 'an outstanding success', though Burnley went down, 3–1. Then a third win over Manchester United put the Burnley club in fourth place with just eleven games to play. Soon afterwards, Burnley beat Arsenal 2–1, for their first victory against the 'Gunners' at Turf Moor since 1926! But four points from their last seven games, nearly all against relegation threatened teams, destroyed any chance of getting among the talent money.

Due to financial problems, Burnley announced that they were prepared to sell several of their players, mentioning Mather, Attwell and Stephenson among others. Colin McDonald was given his first opportunity in the Burnley goal in April, 1954, in the away match at Aston Villa, but with no blame attached to McDonald, it turned out to be the Claret's worst defeat of the season, 5–1.

1954–55

Jimmy Strong, Jackie Chew, Joe Brown, were all placed on the transfer list at the end of the 1953–54 season, but the biggest surprise was when the club's manager, Frank Hill, decided to move to nearby Preston. Turf Moor itself saw a major change, when the new £20,000 stand on the long side of the ground was opened.

The only important arrival on the playing staff was Peter McKay, a centre-forward signed from Dundee United. He came with quite a goal-scoring reputation, having scored 202 goals in his previous 237 matches. He didn't play in the first team immediately, as the side that faced Cardiff in the first game read: McDonald; Aird, Mather; Adamson, Cummings, Seith; Gray, McIlroy, Holden, Shannon, Pilkington.

The first team only scored two goals in their first four games, whilst the Reserves were scoring a dozen in their first three outings (McKay getting 8 of them!). Because of this, McKay made his first team debut in the game against Everton; Shannon moving back to left-half, where he proved an instant success, and McKay coming in at inside-left, next to Bill Holden. But the biggest move of the new season came not on the playing field, but in the offices, when Alan Brown, ex-centre-half and captain of Burnley, returned to the club as manager.

Burnley met Billy Elliott once again, when he played against his old club for Sunderland in a Roker Park Cup-tie. Ironically, it was Elliott who scored the only goal just five minutes from the end to knock the Clarets out of the competition. Des Thompson, having lost his place in the first team, was placed on the transfer list at his own request, whilst Johnny Walton became a regular first team player about the same time. One of the major events of the New Year was when the old Burnley favourite, Tommy Lawton, returned to Turf Moor for his first League game since he had left Burnley in the thirties. He returned with his current club, Arsenal, but he didn't get many opportunities to show his old fans the sort of things they remembered of him, and Burnley won 3–0.

A major Turf Moor personality 'Butch' Mather, left the club to become player-coach at nearby Nelson. He was the last of the Wembley team to leave the playing staff, though Alan Brown (manager), George Bray (A team coach) and Billy Morris (B team) were still with the club, and Harold Rudman, who had been with the club at the time of their promotion, was still playing (in fact better than ever).

As rumours were being denied regarding the possible transfer of Billy Holden, who had lost his first team place, so in March, 1955, the club signed right-winger Doug Newlands from Aberdeen. Meanwhile, the current outside-right, Billy Gray, was forming a fine partnership with the established Jimmy McIlroy, whilst Johnny Walton was also becoming a favourite with the Turf Moor crowd. Once again, Burnley were hovering around the top of the table towards the end of the season. Several points had been thrown away, but because of the inconsistency of other clubs, the Clarets found themselves just four points from the top with only seven games to play. However, a poor run in, in which the team only gained three points from six games, saw Burnley finish tenth in a season when with any consistency, they could well have been champions. Two players made their League debut that April, David Smith at right-back, and Doug Newlands came in for the last game. Peter McKay finished with 36 goals for the Reserves, whilst a Burnley Colts team at the end of the season included two young unknowns called Lawson and Robson.

1955–56

The new season began with a splendid 1–0 victory at White Hart

Lane. Burnley's winning team was: McDonald; Rudman, Winton; Adamson, Cummings, Shannon; Gray, McIlroy, Holden, Walton, Pilkington. But the team fell from grace the week afterwards, when they lost at home to Blackpool. After this defeat, McIlroy moved to the centre-forward berth, with Stephenson and Cheesebrough on either side, but they still lost again at home, this time to Everton. Another away point came at Blackpool, before there was another change at centre-forward. This time, it was Peter McKay who was reintroduced for the home game against Luton. He had played twice the previous season, but neither occasion had provided suitable conditions for his type of on-the-ground football. This time, however, the diminutive centre-forward 'came good' and scored a hat-trick in his team's 3–1 win. The forward line that day was surely one of the smallest ever to play for any Football League team, Gray (5ft 6in), McIlroy (5ft 8in), McKay (5ft 6in), Cheesebrough (5ft 7in), Pilkington (5ft 6in) with 'Mac' towering over the others—all 5ft 8in of him!

McKay scored the winning goal the next week against Birmingham City, and then he chalked up another two in the 2–2 draw against First Vienna. Unfortunately in this friendly game, the new idol of the crowd was injured, and without him the club lost their next game against West Brom. Probably because of the form of McKay and the reduced first team chances of Billy Holden, Blackpool expressed their interest in 'Big Bill', but Burnley turned down their offer.

McKay returned to the team, and scored against Huddersfield, and again the following week in the 2–2 draw at Cardiff, and again in the 2–0 victory over Bolton Wanderers. This win put the Clarets just four points behind Manchester United at the top, with a game in hand. A 2–0 victory over Aston Villa, with McKay getting both goals helped Burnley's cause, and then the Turf Moor team brought home a point from Roker Park with a fine 4–4 draw. McKay scored yet again, but Jimmy McIlroy was badly injured in this game. At the time Sunderland were League leaders, and this result put Burnley just two points behind them. McIlroy suffered a damaged ankle ligament and missed several games, but in the meantime, the young Scots centre-forward went on his merry way, scoring a hat-trick against Portsmouth.

Bill Holden asked for a transfer, and then a win at Highbury made the Division One table:

	Played	*Points*
Blackpool	18	24
Man. Utd.	19	24
Burnley	18	23
Sunderland	17	23

Now with McIlroy absent, the forward line was even smaller! Gray, Stephenson, McKay, Cheesebrough, Pilkington. Albert Cheesebrough was now the tallest at 5ft 7in.

In December, 1955, Bill Holden followed other ex-Turf Moor heroes, like Bob Kelly and Billy Elliott, when he was transferred to Sunderland. That Christmas proved a bad one for the Clarets' title hopes, for Preston performed the double over them. Then came the New Year and the F.A. Cup-ties which were to prove even more memorable than usual.

To begin with Burnley visited Gigg Lane, Bury, on a very foggy January afternoon. They were two goals up at half-time, playing in atrocious visibility, but Bury came back to equalise soon in the second half. Then after 65 minutes, the referee called the game off, much to the relief of all concerned. The following Tuesday, the Clarets won the replay 1–0 to face Chelsea in the fourth round. By the time the home tie with Chelsea came round, McIlroy was back in the team after his ankle injury. Peter McKay scored for Burnley, but with just five minutes to go, Parsons equalised to take the two teams to a replay the week afterwards. That Wednesday, Tommy Cummings played his first game at right-back, whilst Brian Miller made his first team debut, coming in at left-half. Both left-wingers scored, Brian Pilkington equalising Frank Blunstone's earlier goal, and after extra time, the scores were still level. The teams tossed for choice of grounds, and Burnley won, choosing St Andrew's, Birmingham.

The teams met at Birmingham the following Monday, and Peter Sillett put the Pensioners ahead. But McKay scored for the Clarets before Roy Bentley made it 2–1 for Chelsea. Once again Burnley drew level with a Jimmy McIlroy goal, and once again the teams went to extra time. Chelsea won the choice of grounds this time, and they plumped for Highbury. But the fourth game between the two teams only resulted in a 0–0 draw. And so to a fifth game, a record for the Turf Moor team. But in this fourth replay, played at White Hart Lane, Chelsea won through 2–0.

After this marathon Cup-tie, the remainder of the season was rather an anti-climax, as Burnley gradually slid down the League table. (Incidentally, some weeks after the Burnley–Chelsea weekly serial, the clubs met again in the League, and Burnley won easily 5–0, with Pilkington scoring a hat-trick!) Peter McKay established a new post-war goal-scoring record for the club, when he finished with 24 goals in 34 games.

1956–57

In the first game of the new season, Burnley and Chelsea met for the seventh time in six months! Goals from Cheesebrough and

McIlroy gave the home side victory, and Burnley's full team read: McDonald; Cummings, Winton; Seith, Adamson, Shannon; Gray, McIlroy, McKay, Cheesebrough, Pilkington. A fortnight later, John Angus made his first team debut (Sept 1 v Everton), only three days after his first Central League appearance.

Whilst McIlroy was playing for Ireland in October, another youngster, 17-year-old Jimmy Robson made his debut, against Blackpool. In December, Colin McDonald sustained a cracked ankle bone in the away game at Chelsea, and Jock Winton deputised for the remainder of the game. 'Mac' had until that time played in 96 consecutive games, and in his absence, 19-year-old Adam Blacklaw made his debut on a foggy December afternoon in the game against Cardiff which the Clarets won 6–2.

The 1956–57 season was certainly one for debuts, for, in 1957, there came one of the most sensational debuts of all time. Burnley were drawn at home against lowly Chesterfield, and manager Alan Brown gambled by playing 17-year-old Ian Lawson. The gamble paid off handsomely, for young Ian scored four goals in his team's 7–0 win.

In the fourth round of the F.A. Cup, mid-table Burnley were drawn at home against non-League giant-killers, New Brighton. About that time, Peter McKay, who had lost his place to Ian Lawson, was transferred to St Mirren in his native Scotland. The successful run by New Brighton was devastatingly halted in a 9–0 trouncing at Turf Moor. Again Lawson was in the forefront of the scoring with three, McIlroy scored 3, and Pilkington, Cheesebrough and Newlands made up the total. It was the highest Burnley score since the Crystal Palace Cup-tie in 1909, and it could have been their highest of all time, if Doug Winton hadn't missed a penalty!

In a hard-fought fifth round tie at Leeds Road, Burnley won through to the last eight with a 2–1 victory over Huddersfield Town. The sixth round saw the Clarets at home to their old rivals Aston Villa. After Burnley had gone into the lead, and looked set for the semi-final, Peter McParland, who more than once proved to be a 'thorn in the flesh' for Burnley, scored the equaliser and earned a replay at Villa Park. He scored again the following Wednesday, as Burnley went down 2–0 in the replay, played in heavy mud. Another centre-forward made his appearance in the Burnley colours that day, Alan Shackleton.

The only thing that was holding the club back in 1956–57 was a very poor away record. When Burnley beat Luton 2–0 at Luton in March, it was the team's first away victory since October. In contrast, the club was still unbeaten at Turf Moor. However, they lost at home for the first time, 3–1 to Manchester United, on Good Friday, 1957. And the next day, they went down again at Turf

Moor, this time 3–0 to Manchester City who were bottom of the League. But despite these dropped points, and their very poor away record, Burnley still finished seventh in the League. During the close season, Billy Gray was transferred to Notts Forest, mainly because Doug Newlands was established in the first team, and young John Connelly had made his first-team debut towards the end of the season, showing great promise.

1957–58

Facing Portsmouth at Fratton Park in the first game, the Clarets came away with a goal-less draw. The team that day read: McDonald; Angus, Winton; Seith, Adamson, Shannon; Newlands, McIlroy, Shackleton, Cheesebrough and Pilkington.

Manager Alan Brown left Turf Moor to follow Holden and Elliott to Roker Park, Sunderland, and another familiar Claret, Roy 'Stevie' Stephenson had been transferred to Blackburn. During the early months of the 1957–58 season, Burnley scored and conceded a fair number of goals. In the space of three days, they conceded 13 goals (0–7 at Notts Forest, and 1–6 at Chelsea) whilst in their next few home games, Burnley beat Sunderland 6–0 (Newlands 2, Shannon 2, Pointer and Cheesebrough) and Leicester City 7–3 (Cheesebrough 3, McIlroy 3 and Pointer). Ray Pointer had been promoted from the 'A' team to the senior team in a very short time, in an attempt to find a goal-scoring centre-forward. The Leicester City game provided the Burnley fans with the highest aggregate of goals in a League game at Turf Moor since Burnley had beaten Loughborough 9–3 in 1897–98!

On the ground itself, floodlight pylons were being erected, and they were switched on at a friendly game staged between Burnley and Blackburn Rovers (then in Division Two). The following Saturday after the Blackburn game, lights were used at Turf Moor in a League game for the first time (v Portsmouth, December 21, 1957).

The Clarets played a friendly game against the Polish team, L.K.S., and won easily 6–0. This made a total of 22 goals in four home matches (6 v Sunderland, 3 v Aston Villa, 7 v Leicester and 6 v Lodz in a friendly). But the club were still in a mid-table position, as 17 points in 17 games developed into 25 points from 25 games. In the F.A. Cup, Burnley beat the bottom team of Division Two, Swansea 4–2 at Turf Moor. In the fourth round, they were drawn against another Second Division team, not much higher than Swansea in the League, Bristol Rovers. At Eastville, Bristol were winning 1–0 at half-time, but goals by Connelly and Pointer put the Clarets on the way to Wembley, until Les Shannon put through his own goal to give the Bristol team a second chance at Turf Moor. In the replay the following Tuesday, Burnley had a shock. McIlroy put his team ahead, but Rovers equalised. Ray Pointer scored a second, but once again the Rovers drew level. And then with just ten minutes to go, Ward scored the winner for the Bristol team!

Billy Dougall unfortunately had to relinquish the manager's post due to ill health, and later he was appointed the club physiotherapist.

February 1958 was dominated by the Munich air disaster, and soon afterwards, Burnley were involved in a bit of unpopular publicity when Bob Lord made a statement to the fact that there was no hope of Manchester United obtaining any players from Burnley; Brian Pilkington especially, was not for sale at any price. February also saw the arrival of a new manager to take the helm of the football club, the old favourite of the Burnley crowd, Harry Potts. After a coaching appointment at Wolverhampton and the manager's job at Shrewsbury, Potts moved north back to his old club at Turf Moor.

The practically new post-Munich Manchester United side made their appearance at Turf Moor in March, and right from the first minute clash of Gregg and Shackleton, the game was marred with bad feeling. Mark 'Pancho' Pearson was sent off, as much as an example as anything, and several other players were fortunate not to be 'booked'. Burnley won the game 3–0, but after the match there was trouble behind the scenes between players and officials, which all added to future Burnley–United rivalry.

The team finished sixth in their highest position for six seasons.

1958–59

The new season began with a most memorable game at Turf Moor against Manchester City. Three up at half-time, Burnley seemed set for a high score, but City came back in the second half to win 4–3. The Burnley team that day was: McDonald; Cummings, Winton; Seith, Adamson, Shannon; Newlands, McIlroy, Pointer, Cheesebrough and Pilkington. After a second defeat at Arsenal 3–0, John Connelly came in for Newlands, whilst Jimmy Robson replaced Cheesebrough. Not for the first nor the last time, there were rumours in the local and national press that McIlroy was leaving the club, but they were without substance, and were firmly denied by both club and player.

The New Year came with Burnley in their usual mid-table position, having achieved 24 points from 24 games. Andy Lochhead came for a trial with Burnley from Renfrew Juniors. He was just 17, and he was so unknown that when he made his Reserve team debut in January, 1959, the local paper called him 'Lockhart'. Another 17-year-old to sign for Burnley early that year was Alex Elder, who came from Jimmy McIlroy's old club Glentoran.

Burnley met their old colleague Billy Holden in the F.A. Cup in 1959, when the Clarets visited Stockport County, where they won 3–1. In the fourth round, Burnley were drawn at Ewood Park. After Peter Dobing had put the Rovers ahead, McIlroy and Robson scored the goals that put Burnley into the next round, Robson's winner coming just two minutes from time. In the fifth round, a Jimmy Adamson goal was enough to beat Portsmouth, and round six saw the Lancashire team down to visit their bogey ground, Villa Park.

However, Burnley earned a 0–0 draw, and the following Tuesday night, the clubs met again at Turf Moor to fight for a semi-final place. It proved to be Villa's night, for despite the fact that they were bottom of the League, they won 2–0, thanks to two McParland specials. Doug Winton, who had played in nearly 200 League games, was transferred to Aston Villa, and Adam Blacklaw came back into the team in place of Colin McDonald, whilst 'Mac', now England's regular goalkeeper, was playing in Dublin for the Football League. Tragically that night in Dublin, McDonald broke his leg and never again played for Burnley. But at the time, neither the player nor the club were to know that.

Twenty points, and only one defeat in the last 13 games, took the team up the League table, and at the close they finished in a very commendable seventh position. The major factor in Burnley's improvement was the form of Ray Pointer, who broke the club's post-war goal-scoring record with 27 goals.

In June, Albert Cheesebrough went to Leicester for £20,000, whilst Doug Newlands was transferred to Stoke City for £10,000.

1959–60

In a pre-season friendly game, Burnley visited Glentoran and beat the Irish team 8–1, Jimmy Robson scoring four. Looking back, perhaps it was the overture of greater things to come.

The League programme began in splendid style for the Clarets. In the first game the team went to Leeds and won 3–2. Pilkington, Connelly and Pointer were the scorers, and the Burnley team read: Blacklaw; Angus, Cummings; Seith, Miller, Adamson; Connelly, McIlroy, Pointer, Robson and Pilkington. Three days afterwards, 29,192 fans at Turf Moor went home in praise of a superb team performance, as Burnley beat Everton 5–2. After two successive victories, the hopes of Burnley supporters were high, and when John Connelly scored after three minutes in the next home game against West Ham, the team seemed to be on the victory path again. But Burnley faded, and West Ham came back to win easily 3–1.

Undeterred, the Burnley team went to Goodison Park, and a superb performance by Adam Blacklaw, and two goals from Ray Pointer were enough to give the Clarets a fine 2–1 victory over Everton. Once again, John Connelly scored very early on in the away game at Chelsea, but yet again the Clarets faded and were well beaten 4–1. It seemed as if the team were going to lose again when Preston were winning well into the second half in a September night match at Turf Moor. But Ray Pointer equalised after 71 minutes, and with just six minutes to go, Jimmy Robson gave his team the points, both goals coming from Connelly centres.

There was a repeat performance the next Saturday at Turf Moor, when Bobby Robson put West Brom in the lead, only for Burnley to hit back in the second half with goals by Jimmy Robson and Pilkington. But Burnley went to their third defeat at Deepdale when they were beaten 1–0. Unfortunately, both McIlroy and Seith suffered bad injuries that night, but the game was most memorable for Burnley fans because Alex Elder made his League debut against the great Tom Finney.

Skipper Jimmy Adamson played his 300th League game for his club when he led the Clarets out against Newcastle United at St James's Park. It was a great day for the lanky 'Geordie', for after Tait had scored first, Burnley turned on their usual second half recovery to win 3–1. By this time, the performances of the Burnley team were beginning to attract attention, and Pointer, McIlroy and Connelly gave them another 3–1 win, this time at Turf Moor against struggling Birmingham. This win put Burnley in the top four along with the 'big guns':

	Played	*Points*
Spurs	10	15
Arsenal	10	14
Wolves	10	14
Burnley	10	14

The next match was the most important one so far, v Tottenham at White Hart Lane. Because of the Scotland–Ireland international match, Burnley were without their 'general' McIlroy, but Spurs were without Blanchflower, McKay and Brown who were all involved in the international too. Terry Medwin scored in the first half, but 'Dusty' Miller scored an all important goal late in the second half to grab a vital point.

Burnley's strange habit of scoring first, but allowing their opponents to win comfortably, continued against Blackpool. Jimmy Robson put the Clarets ahead against the 'Seasiders' who were near the foot of the table, but a Dave Durie hat-trick set Blackpool well on the way to their 4–1 victory. And then another Lancashire derby defeat saw Burnley slip to seventh position. This time, it was at Ewood Park, and Burnley's forward line had to undergo drastic changes, due to Connelly playing his first game for England and Robson being injured. Brian Pilkington played at outside-right for the first time since 1953, and Gordon Harris came in for only his third game on the left wing. 'Mac' moved to inside-left, and Billy White played at inside-right. Only Ray Pointer retained his position. 'Pilky' scored and Brian Douglas contributed an own goal, but even this did not save Burnley going down again. Despite the skilful efforts of the players, it seemed that the club were beginning to slip down the League table.

But another Lancashire 'derby' proved third time lucky for Burnley, for a great game against Manchester City at Turf Moor resulted in an exciting 4–3 win for Burnley. It was during this game that Ray Pointer, on one occasion, went crashing against the stone wall behind the cricket field end goal. But typical of Pointer's courage and skill, he came back onto the pitch after a short time with no loss of speed or effort.

Again Pointer scored in the 1–1 draw away to bottom club Luton Town, and the end of October saw the Clarets lying four points behind Spurs. It was perhaps a hint of things to come when Burnley beat the Wolves, who were then next to the top, 4–1. 'Indeed, this was a famous victory', ran the headlines in the local press, and their performance that day ranked with the best that season. A superb McIlroy display, coupled with goals from Ray Pointer (2), Jimmy Robson and John Connelly, put Burnley fifth, just two points behind the Spurs.

A Jimmy Robson special helped the Clarets to share the points with Sheffield Wednesday, and now three points separated the top seven teams in the League table. On November 21, Burnley entertained Notts Forest at Turf Moor. It may be that Forest were not so much entertained as the crowd, for the Clarets ran out 8–0 victors that day. Billy Gray was captain for the day for the Forest, but the crowd's cheers were reserved for Jimmy Robson who scored five goals. Forest set out to shadow McIlroy wherever he went, but in doing so they tended to ignore Robson and Pointer, who took advantage of the fact. Ray Pointer (2) and Brian Pilkington added to Jimmy Robson's five, which was the best individual Burnley scoring feat since Louis Page's six. The League table now stood:

	Played	*Points*
West Ham	18	25
Preston N. E.	18	25
Spurs	18	24
Burnley	18	23

But after the Lord Mayor's Show! The team went up to London to meet Fulham, who were also in the championship race, and lost 1–0. Adam Blacklaw played a brilliant game, but nothing really went right for the Clarets that day, with Tony Macedo also having a fine afternoon keeping out the Burnley forwards.

The team seemed to be reserving their goal-scoring exploits for the Turf Moor crowd (16 in the last three home games). Once again the team turned it on for their fans when they met Bolton Wanderers on December 5, winning 4–0. Pointer, Connelly and McIlroy (2) were the scorers, and one of them was from a penalty, after 'Mac' had previously missed two for Ireland!

Bobby Seith played his 200th game for the first team in the next match against Arsenal, and it proved to be Burnley's greatest ever performance at Highbury. Early in the first half, McIlroy was injured, and soon afterwards, the Gunners went two goals ahead. At half time, it must have seemed grim for Burnley, two down with their Irish inspiration badly injured. But in the second half, McIlroy and Adamson turned on their full genius with 'Mighty' Miller driving his forwards on and on. On one occasion, as big Brian charged into the penalty area, he was brought down and the Clarets were awarded a penalty. The injured McIlroy couldn't take the kick, and young John Angus declined, so captain Jimmy Adamson took it and scored. From this moment, Adamson joined the forwards, and soon after, John Connelly made the score 2–2 with the Claret's fiftieth goal of the season. John Connelly went on to score a hat-trick inside 12 minutes, and Arsenal finished up a well-beaten team. Said one newspaper after the game: 'McIlroy did enough on one leg to make observers wonder to what depths of humiliation Arsenal would have sank if he had been able to bewilder them on two!'

When Leeds United came to Turf Moor the next Saturday, they were bottom of the League. By the time they left Burnley, they had climbed away from the foot, thanks to an early Christmas present of two points from the home club. Billy White replaced the injured McIlroy, and Leeds provided the surprise result of the day by winning 1–0. This set-back made the position at the top:

	Played	*Points*
Spurs	22	30
Preston N. E.	22	29
Wolves	22	28
Burnley	22	27

Burnley and Manchester United met twice over Christmas 1959. Ian Lawson replaced White at inside-forward, and he celebrated his recall by scoring along with Jimmy Robson, to give Burnley a 2–1 win at Old Trafford on Boxing Day. But in the return game, two days later, United scored first through Dennis Viollet, before 'Robbo' equalised. But in the second half, Viollet scored again, and then Albert Scanlon (2) gave United an easy 4–1 victory.

The Clarets now had the inconsistent form of having won their last two away games, whilst losing their last two home games! Ian Lawson came in again for the not quite fit McIlroy in the next game, away to West Ham United, another team who were well up with the leaders in Division One, and once again, the Clarets hit the headlines in the metropolis by winning 5–2.

But now the F.A. Cup had come around again, and Burnley were drawn to play Lincoln City at Sincil Bank. On a very cold January afternoon, Burnley held the Lincoln fans spellbound in the first half, but they were only able to score one goal through Ray Pointer. In the second half, Lincoln equalised and the ground almost erupted. In the end, Burnley were very glad to leave Lincoln with the promise of a replay the following Tuesday. For the replay, McIlroy returned in place of Ian Lawson, and in a much improved team performance, Burnley won through to the fourth round with goals from 'Mac' (penalty) and 'Pilky'.

Once more, Ian Lawson returned to the side to meet Chelsea, and two goals from 'Robbo' ensured a 2–1 Burnley victory, despite Brian Pilkington being badly injured in the very icy conditions. These two points put Burnley second in the table, their highest position so far:

	Played	*Points*
Spurs	26	36
Burnley	26	33
Preston N. E.	26	31
Wolves	26	31

Gordon Harris came in, in place of the injured Pilkington for the goal-less draw at West Brom, whilst Colin McDonald made his first Turf Moor appearance for the Reserves since his injury. A full strength Burnley team went to Swansea for the fourth round, and after a dour 0–0 struggle in the Vetch Field mud, Burnley came back to win 2–1 in the replay. North Eastern 'exiles' Pointer and Robson both scored in the 2–1 victory over Newcastle United at the Turf, which kept the Clarets in second place. Now the championship was developing into a three-horse race between Spurs, Burnley and Wolves.

Back at full strength, the team, backed by thousands of fans, travelled to Valley Parade to meet Third Division Bradford City in the Cup. At half-time, the score was still 0–0, but then gradually the City team took the initiative with a two goal lead. A sensational turn-up seemed on the cards, even when John Connelly made it 2–1 with ten minutes to play. Still the City team cheered on by their excited fans held their ground until the last minute of injury time, when with practically the entire Burnley team up in the Bradford area, Connelly shot through the ruck of players to save the day and earn another replay.

On a memorable night in February, 1960, the largest gate of the season, some 52,850, crowded into Turf Moor, with perhaps almost as many never getting into the ground. They saw another fine performance by Burnley as the team ran out 5–0 winners. Unfortunately, both Seith and Robson were injured and their places were filled by Tommy Cummings and Ian Lawson for the next match at Burnden Park; Bolton, who were not so far behind the Clarets in the table, achieved revenge for their earlier 4–0 beating at Turf Moor, by winning this time 2–1. John Connelly scored his nineteenth goal of the season, (Robson had 18, and Pointer 17).

'One of the most important matches we have staged at Turf Moor for many years', was how manager Harry Potts described the next match at Turf Moor, when League leaders, Tottenham were the visitors. (At the time, Spurs were five points ahead, but Burnley had two games in hand.) As usual, the meeting of these two fine teams was an epic struggle, and at the close of a splendid game, Burnley emerged 2–0 winners.

The following two games were also at Turf Moor, and both were all-ticket matches. Both games were against the 'old enemy' Blackburn Rovers, who were not so very far behind the Clarets in the League table, and had been drawn at Turf Moor, in the sixth round of the Cup. Prices, even in 1960 were only 2s for the Ground, and 3s for the Enclosure, but, for the following week, prices were increased by a shilling all round.

The Cup-tie rehearsal proved to be a very dull game, which Burnley won 1–0 thanks to a Jimmy Robson goal. But the week after was anything but dull when 51,501 people packed into the Turf, paying a ground record receipt total of £10,148. They saw a first half closely fought but with Burnley coming very close to scoring on several occasions. In the second half, the game swung completely in the Claret's favour, as Pilkington, Pointer and then Connelly scored to put the team 3–0 ahead. With a quarter of an hour to go, Burnley were well on the way to the double . . . third in the League, and almost in the semi-final. Then Alex Elder stopped a Rovers shot, and the ball spun up and hit his arm. The whistle blew, and the referee pointed to the penalty spot, adjudging the Burnley defender to have handled the ball. Fans argue the point to this day, but there was no argument about the way Douglas slotted home the penalty kick. Suddenly, the Rovers sensed they were back in the game. With ten minutes to go, it was now all Blackburn, and Peter Dobing stopped all Burnley hearts as he made the score 3–2. And then with just four minutes to go, and the Burnley defence fighting desperately to keep the Rovers out, Mick McGrath made the come-back complete as he hit the equaliser, via a goalpost. And so the game ended 3–3, with Rovers achieving a remarkable fight-back.

The replay the following Wednesday was notable, said one paper, only for the fact of 'Burnley's worst display of the season'. Nevertheless, they managed one way or another to contain the Rovers to 0–0 at full-time. But goals by Dobing and McCleod in extra-time set the seal on a Rover's victory, as Burnley bid goodbye to the Cup once again.

But now it was back to 'the job in hand', the League championship. Ian Lawson returned for the injured McIlroy, as the Clarets took two valuable points from Arsenal 3–2 and as the season entered its final quarter, the position at the top read:

	Played	*Points*
Spurs	34	46
Wolves	34	43
Burnley	32	42

Then came a critical match against Wolves at Molineux! For this game, as John Angus had 'flu, Tommy Cummings came back into the first team at right-back. Besides being just three points behind Spurs, Wolves were also in the Cup semi-final, and had every chance of the famed 'double'. Certainly, that night in March, any spectator at Molineux must have favoured them, for the Wolves ran riot against the Clarets winning to the tune of 6–1. Despite a Ray Pointer consolation goal, the night belonged to Wolverhampton, and it was said afterwards that the Burnley team were so dazed by it all, that some players came off not knowing the correct score! Things seemed no better, the next Saturday at Turf Moor, when visitors Sheffield Wed went into a two goal lead, but John Connelly and Jimmy McIlroy's 'magical' penalty which had England goalkeeper Ron Springett spell-bound, brought the scores level. Sheffield scored again, but 'Dusty' Miller made the final score 3–3 with only two minutes to play.

But Burnley were beginning to slip a little behind in the title race.

Then came a bombshell in the Turf Moor camp! Bobby Seith asked for a transfer! He had played in 27 of the 34 games that season and was very much a part of the basic first team. But in the game against Notts Forest, Seith was dropped in place of Tommy Cummings (Adamson moving over to right-half), and the Scottish player took exception to this action. It seemed that he had felt unsettled for some time, and now he decided that he must move on. Meanwhile, against a struggling Forest team including ex-Claret Billy Gray, Burnley won 1–0. The next week, another old favourite of the Turf Moor crowd, Albert Cheesebrough, now with Leicester City, returned to the ground for the first time since his transfer. Leicester, too, like Forest, were fighting for their First Division lives when they came to Burnley on Good Friday 1960. But a John Connelly goal was enough to send them home still in the bottom half-dozen. Unfortunately, Connelly was badly injured during the match, and he was unable to take any further part in Burnley's games that season.

On Easter Saturday, Trevor Meredith made his home debut for the team on the right wing against the team destined that year to be relegated, Luton Town. There were six games remaining, and this was one of the only two home fixtures. The team took the opportunity to reassure their fans that they were still in with a chance of the title with a fine display in which Meredith, McIlroy, Cummings and Elder took the honours. Goals by Robson, Pointer and another penalty which McIlroy 'ghosted' past England goalie Ron Baynham gave the Clarets a comfortable 3–0 win. But the effort to clinch their third Easter victory came to grief at Filbert Street on Easter Monday, when Leicester gained revenge for the Good Friday defeat by winning 2–1. Now Burnley were in with a possible, rather than a probable chance of the championship. And Adam Blacklaw was injured!

On April 23, Burnley went to Bloomfield Road, Blackpool, accompanied by a vast following of fans. On the same day, Wolves who were now three points ahead of Tottenham and Burnley, were at home to Tottenham in a match in which they could almost clinch the title. At this late and vital stage in the programme, a very nervous Jimmy Furnell made his League debut in place of the injured Blacklaw. Once again, Trevor Meredith, who was already a great favourite with the club's followers, scored the vital goal, as Burnley brought away a point in a 1–1 draw. But down at Molineux, Spurs reopened the title race, as they beat Wolves 3–1. The position now read:

	Played	*Points*
Wolves	41	52
Tottenham	41	51
Burnley	39	50

The title was now within Burnley's grasp, and even more so the following Wednesday, when they went to St Andrew's to play the rearranged game against Birmingham City who desperately needed points to avoid relegation. Ray Pointer had a goal disallowed, Meredith was brought down from behind in the penalty area but with no whistle blown, before Brian Pilkington scored his memorable goal with only nine minutes remaining.

This victory put the Clarets in second place (strangely they were the only team in the title-fight, not to have occupied top place at some time during the season). The last Saturday of the season saw Burnley at home for the last time to Fulham; Wolves were away to Chelsea; whilst Spurs entertained Blackpool. There was no score at Turf Moor, as the scores in the other vital games began to filter through on the half-time scoreboard: Chelsea 1 Wolves 0, Tottenham 2 Blackpool 0, then Chelsea 1 Wolves 2, and still no score at Burnley! The game finished a very disappointing 0–0 draw at Turf Moor, and anxiously, the crowd waited the final results from London. Chelsea 1 Wolves 3; Tottenham 3 Blackpool 0.

With Burnley having one game to play, and Wolves and Spurs having completed their fixtures, Burnley were back in third position, a point behind Wolves, level with Spurs, and both teams had a superior goal average to the Clarets. The only chance of Burnley taking the title was to win their last match, away to Manchester City! The following Monday Burnley fans began arriving in Manchester for the crucial game before lunch, and the game was an evening match! And when shops and factories closed at tea-time, all roads led to Manchester. The gates were closed and thousands who had made the journey were locked outside when the teams kicked off. When Brian Pilkington scored, Burnley fans were all ready to receive the trophy, but little Joe Hayes scored a fine equaliser. And then came Burnley's winning goal from 'reserve' Trevor Meredith. With the final minutes ticking away, Pilkington lying just off the pitch injured, McIlroy holding onto the ball at the corner flag and the ref looking at his watch, the tension was unbearable. The entire Wolves team were spectators at the game, and a fair number of Wolves fans added their distinctive amber and black colours to the scene. But when the whistle blew for full-time, with Burnley having won 2–1, the only colour to be seen all over the ground was claret and blue as the joyous Burnley supporters invaded the pitch.

Special trains stopped at every station on the way home that night; people came out onto the streets as the Burnley coach came through on its way home; cars and coaches pulled to one side to allow the coach through, and thousands of people were ready to receive the players at the Town Hall on their arrival back in town. Burnley were champions once again!

NINE

UPS AND DOWNS

SOON AFTER the Maine Road triumph, and the capture of the League Championship trophy, the club went to the U.S.A. to compete in the New York Tournament. This was the first competition of its kind and leading clubs from England, Scotland, Europe and South America were invited to compete. Even before Burnley won the title, they had accepted the invitation from America, and along with Nice, Glenavon, Kilmarnock, Bangu (Brazil), Red Star (Yugoslavia), Sampdoria (Italy), Sporting Club of Portugal, Rapid (Austria), Norrkoping (Sweden) and Bayern Munich (Germany), they set off to the United States with high hopes of strengthening the soccer cause in the country. Very little went right for the tournament from the start. Grounds were unsuited; the humid summer weather heavily taxed the players; there was trouble over hotels and accommodation; there were scenes on and off the field, which were blown up by the press into almost international incidents, and in the end, the players and officials who had set out with such high hopes, were glad to get home.

1960–61

Season 1960–61 was to prove the most ambitious in the club's history, for now instead of clubs aiming for the famous 'double' they were now able to compete for the triple-honour of League, F.A. Cup, and the newly instituted League Cup. And on top of everything, the League Champions now represented the country in the already famous European Cup. And if all that wasn't enough, the Claret's first game of the new season was for the F.A. Charity Shield! The game at Turf Moor against the Cup-holders, Wolverhampton Wanderers, whom only Burnley had stopped from winning the 'double' three months previously, proved to be a fine game. The result was a 2–2 draw (Miller and Connelly) and both clubs held the trophy for six months.

Burnley's team in the first game when they faced Arsenal at Turf Moor was: Blacklaw; Angus, Elder; Adamson, Cummings, Miller; Connelly, McIlroy, Pointer, Robson and Pilkington. Goals by Connelly (2) and Pointer gave the new Champions a fine 3–2 start. Then came a setback. In their second game at Maine Road, where they had clinched the title the previous season, City managed to equalise a Robson goal; then on a waterlogged pitch, John Connelly was injured, and City scored a late winner. The following week, Manchester City came to Turf Moor and registered the double over the Champions. A brilliant display of inside-forward play from Law, Hannah and Hayes gave City a 3–1 win and left most people present convinced that on that form City were potential champions themselves.

Four days later and 10,000 of a crowd less, the champions suffered another blow to their prestige, when they went down at home again to Cardiff. But then, with four successive victories, the tide turned and altogether 16 points were gained from the next nine games. After 14 games, the Clarets were third behind Spurs and Sheffield Wednesday, but Spurs were still unbeaten and storming on to the double. In four games against Fulham, Manchester United, Blackburn and Chelsea, the Clarets scored 20 goals, but the best was yet to come! Wolves came to Turf Moor and were thrashed 5–3, and then Burnley went to Bolton and repeated the 5–3 score.

But by this time, in November, the team was getting involved in the Cup competitions, notably the European Cup. After a bye in round one, Burnley were drawn against the French champions, Rheims, including players like Kopa and Fontaine. A crowd of 36,742 people, including hundreds of French fans, saw the Burnley team play like true champions as they beat the French champions, 2–0 with goals by Jimmy Robson and Jimmy McIlroy. However, it was far from being a one-way game, and only a superb game by Adam Blacklaw ensured that the Clarets took a two goal lead to France for the return game.

Meanwhile, away from the European Cup, the Champions were drawn against Third Division Brentford in the League Cup. There was more than a ripple of protest when Burnley announced their team for the game; out of the eleven, only Marshall, Meredith, Lochhead and Harris had appeared in the first team that season, and as the eleven team changes were broadcast over the Brentford loudspeaker, a chorus of booing greeted each name. Anyway, after all the jeers had ceased, Burnley 'Reserves' came away with a 1–1 draw. In the replay, the Clarets won through to round four by the skin of their teeth, 2–1.

Hundreds of Burnley fans travelled to France for the European Cup second leg, but it was the French spectators who stole the show and practically ruined the match that night. Firework rockets shot from the stands into the Burnley defence, and torch-lights flashed into Blacklaw's eyes as he went for the ball, were only two of the extra hazards that the Claret's had to contend with that night. Another frustration was the constant stealing of ground at the taking of free-kicks. On one such occasion, manager Harry Potts raced onto the field to register his protest, an action for which he was to pay dearly later. The French team, Rheims, won 3–2 that night, but thanks to another sterling display from Adam Blacklaw, Burnley held out to win 4–3 on aggregate.

Four days after the fireworks in France, the Clarets returned to London to play Tottenham. It was last season's Champions v the current League leaders, only beaten once in twenty games. Burnley began at a cracking pace, and should have had at least three goals early on in the game. But instead, it was Spurs who scored first, and then again, and again, and again! When the news came through to the Reserve match at Turf Moor that afternoon, that the Clarets were 4–0 down, local fans feared even worse to come. What we didn't realise was that Jimmy Adamson and Co were playing what was later described as 'the game of a lifetime' and 'one of the greatest in England's soccer history'. With the White Hart Lane crowd roaring for more goals against the champions, the Clarets fought back into the game. Incredibly goals by Robson, Pointer and Connelly (2) brought them level, and with the score 4–4, both sides came close to winning. Said one reporter: 'It was a brilliant football exhibition that will long be remembered by all who witnessed it. Indeed one doubts if there will ever be another better'.

After the Wolves' five and the Bolton five and the Tottenham four, the Clarets scored another three in beating Leicester, before going to Highbury and winning 5–2 there. But the title midway through the season was really already won, for now Spurs were ten points ahead of any other club.

Chasing Spurs in the League, involved in Europe, contending in the new League Cup, Burnley also joined in the Wembley trail when they met Bournemouth in the F.A. Cup. A 1–0 win saw them through to round four, where after a 3–3 draw, Burnley met Brighton in a replay at Turf Moor. A 2–0 win saw them facing Swansea, who had provided difficult opposition the previous year. This time, however, a 4–0 victory for the Turf Moor team gained Burnley a place in the last eight for the third season running.

On January 18, 1961, Burnley competed in the third round of the European Cup, when they played the German champions, Hamburg, complete with the legendary Ewe Seeler. Once again, Burnley turned on their many talents with a fine team performance by everyone, from goalkeeper Adam Blacklaw, now an established favourite in the Burnley side, to left-winger Brian Pilkington, who scored two fine goals. Jimmy Robson scored a third, and the final result was 3–1 for the Clarets. Going from one Cup match to another, Burnley came up against Second Division Southampton in the League Cup and beat them away, 4–2. The semi-final draw paired Burnley off with Aston Villa.

March 4 was the date of yet another great performance from Adam Blacklaw, when as on so many other occasions it was only he who kept the score down. This time the opponents were Sheffield Wednesday, and the occasion was the 0–0 draw in the sixth round Cup-tie at Hillsborough. The following Tuesday, the largest gate of the season, 49,118, packed into Turf Moor to see the Clarets win the sixth round and overcome Sheffield Wednesday with goals by McIlroy and Robson.

Looking back now, 1960–61 seems to have been a season of one sensation piled upon another. Four days after entering the F.A. Cup semi-final for the first time since 1947, the team to play Chelsea in Saturday's League game was announced. It read: Furnell; Smith, Marshall; Walker, Cummings, Scott; Meredith, Lawson, Lochhead, Fenton and Harris. It was very much the Reserve team playing a first team fixture once again, for only Cummings and Harris had played the previous game against Sheffield Wednesday. The reason for so many reserve players being picked, stated the management, was the number of injuries sustained the previous week. And in a quite amazing game, the gallant second string almost brought off the result of the season, when they drew 4–4 with Chelsea. Harris (2) and Lochhead (2) scored for the Clarets and only a very late goal by the inimitable Jimmy Greaves gained a point for Chelsea. Nevertheless, the club was fined £1,000 for fielding a weak team.

And so Burnley came to the most critical week of the season; Hamburg away in the European Cup quarter-finals, and Spurs at Villa Park in the F.A. Cup semi-finals. But 71,000 jubilant Germans saw an unstoppable Hamburg team power their way to a 4–1 lead. Jimmy McIlroy hit the post in the last minute, but Hamburg held out to beat Burnley 5–4 on aggregate.

After this disappointment, it was back to Villa Park and their great rivals, Tottenham. Burnley had only won five times at Villa Park in their entire history. They didn't make it six on the occasion of the semi-final, for despite a disallowed Jimmy Robson effort, and a vain appeal for a penalty when Henry appeared to handle, and an incident when Brown seemed to slip and take the ball over the goal-line, Burnley were knocked out of the Cup, 3–0 by Tottenham, who were carrying all before them.

The year 1961 had not quite matched 1960 for results and success, for in addition to losing interest in the European Cup and the F.A. Cup, the Clarets did not win a League game at Turf Moor until the last week in March; now there was only the League Cup to play for, in which Burnley were due to meet Aston Villa in the semi-final. Meanwhile, a great favourite of the Turf Moor crowd had left the scene—Brian Pilkington. Though he had scored two vital goals in the first leg against Hamburg, the Germans were surprised to learn that Burnley had transferred 'Pilky' to Bolton Wanderers prior to the second game. And ten years to the day of his League debut for Burnley, Brian Pilkington returned to Turf Moor with his new club, Bolton. In that game, Burnley scored their 92nd goal of the season, a new club record, and the same week, they drew 1–1 with Aston Villa in the League Cup, thanks to a Brian Miller goal.

The 1961 new champions, Tottenham, visited Turf Moor to play 1960 champions, Burnley, and seemed to have earned their new accolade when they were two up early on. But in the second half, Burnley regained their own championship form and goals by McIlroy, Robson and Harris (2) gave the Clarets a fine win and some consolation for the F.A. Cup disappointment. The team were losing 2–0 once again the week after, when they visited Villa Park for the second leg of the League Cup semi-final, but a splendid recovery inspired by goals from McIlroy and Robson gave them a 2–2 draw and a replay at Old Trafford.

Later in the season though, the Clarets were beaten in the League Cup semi-final replay, 2–1 by Aston Villa. And so this momentous season drew to a close. Burnley's record was, fourth in the League Table, European Cup quarter-finalists, F.A. Cup and League Cup semi-finalists. So near, yet so far. The following season, they were going to go farther and get even nearer!

1961–62

The team began with a good 2–2 draw at Arsenal. The Burnley side that day, in August, 1961, read: Blacklaw; Joyce, Elder; Adamson, Cummings, Miller; Connelly, McIlroy, Pointer, Robson and Harris. Alf Ramsey brought newly promoted Ipswich to Turf Moor the next Tuesday, and everyone there that night will remember the power of big Ted Phillips' shooting. Despite his crackerjack shots which gave him two goals and Adam Blacklaw a nervous evening, Burnley came out 4–3 winners.

After a 3–1 victory over Bolton, when Ian Towers made his debut, the Clarets travelled to East Anglia to play the return game against Ipswich. This time, Ipswich (including Roy Stephenson) gained full revenge by hammering the Clarets, 6–2. Victories against Manchester City and Leicester City then took Burnley to the top of Division One for the first time since they had won the title, eighteen months previously.

The following day, five Burnley players, Connelly, Angus, Harris, Miller and Pointer, were among the 22 named in the England party for the Luxemburg match. As if to celebrate, the team visited St Andrew's and thrashed Birmingham City, 6–2. After the six at Birmingham, came another six at Leicester, and another splendid success at Craven Cottage, when they beat Fulham 5–3.

Before the game against Tottenham at White Hart Lane, the team went to Folkestone for special training. Two Ray Pointer 'specials' seemed to have the Clarets on the way to another remarkable White Hart Lane performance, but Spurs came back to win 4–2. This made the top of the table positions:

	Played	*Points*
Burnley	12	19
West Ham	13	17
Tottenham	13	16
Man. United	12	15

There was a set-back to the club's championship hopes when Burnley were beaten at Turf Moor for the first time for ten months, when Arsenal won 2–0 in mid-December. This was also the first game that Burnley had failed to score in that season. But it was a rare occasion that winter. Four at Old Trafford, four against Sheffield Wednesday, six in the Third Round Cup-tie against Q.P.R., another six the following week against Manchester City, and seven more against poor Birmingham City, all came in the space of two months. After one such performance, one paper ran the headlines: 'BURNLEY THE MAGNIFICENT! ON THIS FORM IT'S THE CHAMPIONSHIP, AND NO MISTAKE!'

The position at the start of 1962 read:

	Played	*Points*
Burnley	22	32
Tottenham	24	31
Everton	24	30
West Ham Utd.	24	29

These were great days for the Irish. Alex Elder scored his first goal for Burnley in the Cup-tie against Queen's Park Rangers, whilst Jimmy 'Mac' was making football reporters search for new superlatives after a sequence of magnificent performances. Meanwhile, Willie Irvine scored 10 in two games for the 'A' team.

There was almost a turn-up in the fourth round of the F.A. Cup when Second Division Leyton Orient were winning at Turf Moor, 1–0, but with just seven minutes to play, Gordon Harris crashed home a left-foot pile-driver to force a replay. Again in the replay, Leyton took the initiative, and Adam Blacklaw proved to be the hero of the hour. The winner came when big Brian Miller raced upfield to head home a John Connelly corner. A total of 50,514 spectators packed into the Burnley ground on February 17 for the Burnley–Everton Cup-tie. Bobby Collins sent the many Everton fans wild by putting his side ahead with a wonderful shot, and at half-time, Everton led 1–0. Only one minute of the second half had passed when Burnley were level. 'Dusty' Miller moved on to a Jimmy 'Mac' pass, and from fully 30 yards, he scored with a terrific shot. John Connelly put the Clarets ahead, and eight minutes later, Jimmy Robson made the result certain with a third goal.

The sixth round draw saw Burnley at Bramhall Lane, the home of Sheffield United. Sheffield were weakened by an injury to Gerry Summers, but they held out until Ray Pointer headed home an Alex Elder centre for the winner. The Clarets were in the semi-final again!

The semi-final draw promised a possible Burnley v Rovers match, but Fulham beat Blackburn in the sixth round to prevent a real Lancashire derby match. And so it was to be Burnley v Fulham at Villa Park.

On March 24, 1962, Burnley were top of Division One, Burnley Reserves were top of the Central League, and Burnley 'A' were top of the Lancashire League. At the same time, the club was in the semi-final of the F.A. Cup, whilst the Reserves were in the semi-final of the Lancashire Senior Cup. Altogether, five trophies were now well within the club's grasp. All seemed well, when Burnley won a League game at Villa Park for the first time in 12 years, to make the positions in Division One:

	Played	*Points*
Burnley	32	46
Ipswich	34	44
Tottenham	34	40

Came the big day, and in the first half, hampered by a blinding snowstorm, the Clarets trailed 1–0. Though Fulham were battling against relegation, and Burnley were heading for the championship, the Londoners had their chances to put Burnley out. Once again, it was Adam Blacklaw who stood alone keeping the Fulham forwards at bay, and then John Connelly put the scores level with a great shot. Nine days later at Filbert Street, Leicester, the two teams met again. 'Robbo' put the Clarets ahead in the first half, and then scored a second with ten minutes to play, following a wonderful move by Jimmy 'Mac'. Fulham scored one just before the close, but it was Burnley's night, and they were back at Wembley for the first time for fifteen years. In the F.A. Cup Final, Burnley were to meet Tottenham Hotspur. It was 1960's Champions versus

1961's Double winners, and it was billed nationally as 'The Final of the Century'.

Meanwhile, in the League, Ipswich had closed the gap at the top, though Burnley had three games in hand.

	Played	*Points*
Burnley	34	48
Ipswich	37	48
Tottenham	36	43

But things were beginning to go wrong now for the Clarets. Playing without McIlroy, Adamson and Miller, they went down 3–1 at home to Manchester United. Tommy Cummings scored his first goal for ten years, when Burnley beat Blackpool 2–0. Burnley and Ipswich were still level, but the Clarets had lost the advantage of two of their games in hand.

	Played	*Points*
Burnley	38	51
Ipswich	39	51
Tottenham	38	46

The Reserves clinched the Central League title, but the first team dropped two vital points to Sheffield United, 2–0, and another at Blackpool, 1–1. Now Ipswich were at the top, but the initiative still rested with Burnley. If they won their final three games, they had won the double. But they didn't win any of them!

	Played	*Points*
Ipswich	41	54
Burnley	40	52
Tottenham	40	48

Chelsea, who were already doomed to relegation, came to Turf Moor and drew 1–1. The gloom that hung over Burnley that afternoon had to be experienced to be believed. The nightmare of March and April was coming true in front of us all. We stood and waited for the result to come through from the Ipswich v Aston Villa game, half-knowing what it would be. We were right. Ipswich had won, and were Champions.

The last League match of the season made no difference, and five days before the F.A. Cup Final, Burnley were trounced by Sheffield Wednesday. In the last ten games, all played in April, the Clarets had won only one, and scored only six times; it was little wonder that they conceded the title to Ipswich. Though to this day, supporters still look back and wonder how it ever happened!

And so to Wembley, with 15,000 fortunate Burnley fans who had managed to get tickets. The League championship disappointment was put to the back of local minds, and optimism soared again when Jimmy Adamson was chosen as Footballer of the Year, whilst Jimmy McIlroy came second in the same poll.

But optimism was flattened by a Jimmy Greaves goal which put Tottenham ahead after only three minutes. Despite Burnley's efforts, the half-time score was still 0–1, but things looked brighter when Jimmy Robson banged home the equaliser five minutes after the restart. Hardly had the Lancashire fans finished cheering, before Bobby Smith rushed in to put the Spurs ahead again. The second half was a battle as the Burnley side fought to get back on level terms, but ten minutes from the end, tragedy struck for the Clarets. Adam Blacklaw appeared to be fouled, the ball ran loose, and Tommy Cummings was hit on the arm by the ball as it was going goalwards. It was a penalty, and Danny Blanchflower settled the game when he stroked the ball past Adam Blacklaw to make the score 3–1.

Many people viewed the season as a complete failure, but to finish runners-up in the two major national competitions, and be within three games of accomplishing the double was certainly a magnificent failure. Some consolation for the senior team's disappointments was gained when the Reserves achieved their 'double', when they added the Lancashire Senior Cup to their Central League title.

1962–63

Once again, there was great local optimism at the start of the new season, as the club started off again on their League campaign. There was, however, quite a setback, when Everton came to Turf Moor for the first match and won 3–1! The Burnley team that day, read: Blacklaw; Angus, Elder; Joyce, Cummings, Miller; Connelly, McIlroy, Pointer, Robson and Harris.

With several injuries hampering the club's progress, (Jimmy Adamson had had to miss the first game, and then Ray Pointer was injured) there were quite a few team changes in the early part of the season. One of the major moves was to introduce Andy Lochhead at centre-forward, so that the forward line began to appear: Connelly, Pointer, Lochhead, McIlroy and Harris. A John Connelly hat-trick gave the new-look Clarets a fine 5–2 win at Old Trafford, whilst Jimmy Adamson returned for the twelfth game, which resulted in a grand 3–2 victory at Ewood. The top of the League table now read:

	Played	*Points*
Tottenham	18	27
Everton	18	27
Burnley	18	25

Over 44,000 people came to Turf Moor later that month to see the great Clarets v Spurs clash, which the home team won 2–1. And to add to the rivalry between these two great teams, for the third season running, they were drawn to play each other in the F.A. Cup, this time in the third round at White Hart Lane.

But severe frost and heavy snow led to the cancellation of many games in the New Year, including the star Cup-tie, Spurs v Burnley. When the game was eventually played, it resulted in a magnificent performance from the Lancashire club, as they stormed to a convincing 3–0 victory. Goals by Harris, Connelly, and of course, Lochhead, saw Burnley into round four; whilst Spurs came in for some heavy criticism for the tough manner in which they had played the game.

In the following week, Burnley came up against Liverpool in round four, and thanks to a John Connelly goal, the Clarets managed to force a draw, 1–1, and earn a replay the next Wednesday at Anfield. Once again, snow and ice intervened, and altogether that replay was called off five times! By February, Burnley had had seven League games cancelled, and they still hadn't got around to playing Liverpool in the Cup replay.

Is there anyone in Burnley who cannot remember the events of that week in late February, 1963? First came the Anfield game, and with the scores level at 1–1, and late into extra-time, it seemed that the Clarets had won a well-earned draw. But with the referee looking at his watch and the crowd moving slowly away, Adam Blacklaw kicked the ball against St John, pulled him down in a desperate attempt to stop the Liverpool player scoring from the rebound, and Moran cracked home the resultant penalty kick. Stood in the middle of the Kop that night, it was unbelievable. The crowd stood and cheered and sang for nearly an hour after the players had left the field, and one half-expected Shankley's men to come back on the field for a bow!

Burnley were out of the Cup with a last-minute sensation, but it was nothing compared to the shock that hit the town the next day, when Jimmy McIlroy was placed on the transfer list. 'I couldn't believe it,' said 'Mac'. Letters of protest poured into the local press, petitions were begun, expressions of protest were daubed on walls in the town, as supporters objected to the transfer of their idol of over a decade.

A cartoon in the local paper summed up feelings in the town: 'What a shock! It's unbelievable! My eyes are deceiving me! I never thought it could happen! What was it? Had the Kierby fallen down? Was the Town Hall up for sale? Had Burnley Cricket Club signed up Morecambe and Wise as joint professionals for the 1963 season? Or had Ena Sharples joined Mrs Dale in retirement?'

'WHY—BURNLEY HAD PUT JIMMY McILROY ON THE TRANSFER LIST!!'

The club gave their reason for the action. They said that they felt Jimmy McIlroy was not maintaining the consistency of ability which he was able to command. It was said that he was not giving the club the wholehearted effort which was expected from him.

His fans disagreed. They recalled the recent performances of their idol, notably in the 4–0 beating of Sheffield Wednesday, when the paper said: 'Despite the ice rink surface, this was a vintage McIlroy who gave a performance his fans won't forget for a long time, highlighted by that magnificent burst, four minutes from time, which led to Pointer scoring the final goal. Who said McIlroy is finished?'

However, the club and a fair number of the supporters agreed to differ, and went their separate ways. But whatever side one takes, the affair certainly put the club in a bad light, and many people have never been to Turf Moor since.

On March 2, Burnley played their first League game of 1963, and their first game for 13 years without the services of Jimmy McIlroy on their playing staff (he had gone to Stoke City for £25,000). The Clarets went down 1–0 at Bramhall Lane, and the week after, they drew 1–1 at home against West Ham. It was the smallest gate at Turf Moor for two seasons, and more than 2,000 less than at any game that season.

The next Burnley 'fixture' to leave Turf Moor was Tommy Cummings, who closed his playing career and relinquished his office as Chairman of the P.F.A., when he took over the manager's seat at Mansfield. Both McIlroy and Cummings had made well over 400 appearances for the senior side, and the Burnley team seemed strange without their names included. Three other regular faces, Adam Blacklaw, John Angus and Alex Elder created a club record when they appeared together for 65 consecutive games as Burnley's defence, and the sequence was only broken when Elder had to miss a game when he was chosen for his native Ireland.

The departure of established personalities in the Claret's team gave the opportunity for several of Burnley's talented youngsters to make their debut. Arthur Bellamy played his first game, and scored in the fine 5–2 victory at Maine Road; Willie Morgan made his debut against Sheffield Wednesday; Brian O'Neil was another to make his first appearance, a week later against West Brom; whilst Willie Irvine made his first appearance in the final away game at Arsenal, and like Bellamy, he scored in his first game, an excellent 3–2 victory at Highbury.

With Reserves of this calibre, and others like Walter Joyce, Harry Thomson, Freddie Smith and Jimmy Robson, it was little wonder that the Burnley Reserves topped the Central League for the second consecutive season. Whilst despite all the McIlroy hubbub, the club still managed to finish the season in a creditable position —third. They had been in the top four clubs in the country for four seasons now.

1963–64

There were several setbacks for the Clarets at the start of the new campaign. Ian Towers was transfer-listed at his own request, Alex Elder broke his ankle in training, whilst Ray Pointer was still unavailable since his injury the previous April. Burnley visited Ipswich in the first game, and were beaten 3–1. The team that afternoon read: Blacklaw; Angus, Joyce; Adamson, Talbut, Miller; Connelly, Lochhead, Irvine, Robson and Harris. Soon, Andy Lochhead and Willie Irvine had joined Ray Pointer on the injured list, and so Jimmy Robson found himself deputising in the centre-forward position. Arthur Bellamy scored a hat-trick in the team's very fine victory at Goodison Park. Burnley's 4–3 win was Everton's first defeat at home for two years. But all in all, it was a very average start to the new season, with just ten points won from nine games. Brian O'Neil came in for the injured Adamson, whilst another debut was that of young Johnny Price. Price, all 5ft 3in in his size five boots, came in on the right wing against West Ham at Upton Park.

On November 2, Burnley went to Stoke, and for the first time came face to face with their old colleague, Jimmy McIlroy. After being three goals down, the Clarets came back to draw 4–4 in a memorable game.

Ray Pointer returned to the side after a nine-months lay-off, but regulars like Elder, Angus and Connelly were still absent, and with Adamson still being out of the team, Brian Miller was now the captain. Alex Elder returned to the team for his first game that season in the December match against Sheffield Wednesday.

Christmas 1963 saw the Clarets' best performance since the Goodison Park success, when they beat Manchester United, Charlton, Crerand, Quixall and all, 6–1, at Turf Moor. The team that memorable day was: Blacklaw; Angus, Elder; O'Neil, Talbut, Miller; Morgan, Pointer, Lochhead, Harris and Towers. However, pride comes before a fall, and it was a different story the following day, when United turned the tables at Old Trafford, winning 5–1!

Eighteen-year-old Frank Casper scored Rotherham's equaliser in the 1–1 draw in the third round Cup-tie at Turf Moor, but the Lancashire side won through 3–2 in the replay. Then the Clarets moved into the last sixteen, with a 2–1 win over Newport County.

Willie Morgan was the star of the afternoon, and old hero Bob Kelly who was present at the match, described him as a 'great prospect'.

There was quite a stir at the announcement of the Burnley team to play Huddersfield in the fifth round. Skipper Brian Miller was dropped, and Jimmy Adamson returned. Robson and Towers were also replaced by Pointer and Harris, and Harry Potts' sweeping changes came good, as Burnley strolled to an easy 3–0 win. But West Ham, who went on to beat Preston in the Final, put paid to Burnley's hopes when they won 3–2 at Upton Park.

Utility defender Walter Joyce was transferred to Blackburn, but the most sensational week of the season was the last one. During that week, England winger John Connelly was transferred to Manchester United, and this local sensation was followed by the win of the season, 7–2, against reigning champions, Tottenham. Sammy Todd made his League debut in that game, and Gordon Harris scored two in the first 15 minutes. Spurs never recovered from this setback, and further goals by Willie Irvine (2), Brian O'Neil (2) and Andy Lochhead sealed the issue. On the same day, Ray Pointer was finishing the season with a bang, scoring five in the Reserve team's 7–0 beating of Manchester City Reserves.

Once again, the average gates dropped by 5,000, and this was surely the main reason why Burnley were compelled to sell John Connelly, a decision which caused more controversy among Burnley fans.

1964–65

The big talking point during the close season was Alex Elder. He was wanting a rise in wages, and because of the dispute, he was requesting a move from Burnley. Despite the trouble, Alex played in the opening game at Turf Moor against Blackpool. The team read: Blacklaw; Angus, Elder; O'Neil, Talbut, Miller; Morgan, Lochhead, Irvine, Harris and Towers. The game resulted in a 2–2 draw, but the saddest fact was that only 15,775 saw the season's first match.

After two months, Alex Elder signed on again for the club. Meanwhile, the team had played their first six games without a win. It was only after they had drawn four and lost four, that the Clarets gained a success against West Ham. At that time, the foot of the League read:

	Played	*Points*
Burnley	9	6
Birmingham	8	4
Aston Villa	9	4
Wolves	9	3

F.A. CUP FINAL AT WEMBLEY, 1962. Jimmy Adamson, Burnley's captain introduces his team to the Duke of Edinburgh

BURNLEY'S ONLY GOAL. Jimmy Robson scores in the 1962 F.A. Cup Final. This was the one hundredth goal scored in Wembley Finals

THE LEGENDARY JIMMY MCILROY IN ACTION in the 1958 game against Manchester City

JIMMY ADAMSON, player, coach and manager at Turf Moor for over 25 years, pictured in 1973

FULL BACK JOHN ANGUS, one of Burnley's longest serving players with over 500 League and Cup games to his credit from 1960 to 1970

The best result of the season so far occurred when Andy Lochhead, getting a hat-trick, helped his team to a 4–2 victory over Blackpool at Bloomfield Road. Ralph Coates made his first team debut in December against Sheffield United, and then four goals from Willie Irvine in the two Christmas games against Fulham helped Burnley to a Christmas double.

After a 1–1 draw at Turf Moor, Burnley beat Brentford 2–0 in the F.A. Cup. This was followed by another 1–1 result at Elm Road, before the Clarets beat Reading to go into the last sixteen again. In the fifth round, Burnley were drawn to meet Manchester United at Old Trafford. As often happens the two clubs were due to meet the previous week in a League match, and United won the 'Cup rehearsal' 3–2, on a day when Les Latcham made his League debut on the left wing.

Naturally, United were favourites to win the Cup match on their own ground, but, with reserves in the side, and against all the odds, Burnley were one goal in the lead (Andy Lochhead) with just five minutes to play. When George Best lost his boot it seemed to help Burnley's cause, but it was really the beginning of the end! Best picked up his boot, and after an amazing run through the Claret's defence, he crossed the ball for Dennis Law to equalise. Suddenly, the game was transformed, and it was Burnley who were fighting for their lives. It was practically the last minute, when George Best, still boot in hand, gathered the ball and with his stockinged foot, he passed to the unmarked Paddy Crerand. Crerand's 25-yard shot deceived Adam Blacklaw, and slipped in by the far post, to the horror of the Burnley defence. The Stretford End crowd went wild, the referee blew his whistle, and Burnley were out of the Cup, beaten by 2–1, and a stockinged foot!

There was trouble on the field at Elland Road not long afterwards, when the referee had to speak to all twenty-two players during the Leeds v Burnley game, which Leeds won 5–1. Adam Blacklaw was one of the several players injured in this game, and his absence the following week brought to an end his run of 194 consecutive team appearances. Harry Thomson made his debut after waiting three years in the Reserves. In his very first game against Leicester City, the young Scot saved a penalty, whilst Ralph Coates scored his first League goal in that same Filbert St game. Meanwhile, leading scorer, Irvine, was chasing Ray Pointer's post-war goal-scoring record, but his effort was to prove unsuccessful.

A mixture of youth (Coates, Kinsella, Price, etc.) and experience (Blacklaw and Pointer) gave the Clarets a 2–0 win over Southport in the Lancashire Senior Cup Final; it was the fourth time in six seasons that the trophy had come to Turf Moor. Once again,

Burnley reserved their highest score for their final game, at Turf Moor against Chelsea. Andy Lochhead scored five in the Claret's 6–2 win, and in so doing, he joined Page, Anderson and Robson as the only Burnley players to score five or more in a League match.

There was a further big drop in gates, and to help compensate for this loss of income, Jimmy Robson was transferred to Blackpool in March 1965 for £10,000.

1965–66

Adam Blacklaw put in a transfer request at the start of the new season, as he couldn't stand Reserve team football; Jimmy Adamson was now on the staff as coach; whilst Ray Pointer was transferred to Bury in Division Two.

In the season's first game, Burnley came away with a 1–1 draw from Stamford Bridge. The Clarets team that day was: Thomson; Angus, Elder; O'Neil, Talbut, Miller; Morgan, Lochhead, Irvine, Bellamy and Coates. This result was followed by a victory over Blackpool, a 2–2 draw against Arsenal, and a 3–1 win at Blackpool. It was the best ever post-war start by the club until Everton beat them 1–0! But after further victories against Manchester United, Northampton and West Brom, the position at the head of the table read:

	Played	*Points*
Sheffield Utd.	11	15
Burnley	10	14
Liverpool	10	14
Leeds Utd.	10	14

All was going well until October 9! On that day, the 'old enemy', Blackburn Rovers came to Turf Moor. At the time, the Clarets were unbeaten at home, and high among the League leaders, while the Rovers were stranded at the foot of the table, still looking for their first away win. At Turf Moor, they got it, with interest! The 4–1 result for Blackburn raised their hopes of escaping relegation, and shattered the Burnley hopes of honours.

But the team came back with further victories over Leicester, Sheffield United, West Ham and Sunderland, so that the League position in late November read:

	Played	*Points*
Burnley	16	23
Liverpool	16	22
Leeds Utd.	16	22
West Brom.	17	21

The New Year got off to a bad start with the usual feud between Burnley and Blackburn; though the Clarets won 2–0, Willie Morgan was sent off. Ian Towers began 1966 by signing for

Oldham Athletic, and the same week, Gordon Harris made his international debut for England, in the game against Poland. Andy Lochhead scored five in one match yet again, this time in the F.A. Cup third round replay against Bournemouth, as the Lancashire club swept to a 7–0 victory. Once again, the Cup draw paired Tottenham and Burnley, at White Hart Lane. Willie Irvine sent Burnley's hopes soaring by scoring in the first 40 seconds, and it seemed unbelievable when he scored a second after only four minutes. Spurs fought back to get on level terms with two goals by Alan Gilzean before Willie Irvine put the Clarets on top once more by completing his hat-trick. However, there were signs of relief for Spurs when, with twenty minutes left, they equalised for a second time, and Burnley had every reason to feel cheated when Gilzean scored the winner from fully twenty yards; just two minutes from the final whistle!

Two points gained in five League games robbed the Clarets of any chance of catching up on champions-to-be Liverpool, but Willie Irvine got his name in the record books when he scored his 28th goal in the game against Aston Villa, and so at long last broke Ray Pointer's club record.

Again, the season closed in a spectacular fashion. A 15-year-old prospect called David Thomas signed on as a schoolboy associate with the club, but attention then switched from the future to the present, when rivals for the runners-up position, Leeds United, came to Turf Moor. Again, the game proved to be a disgrace as players fought with one another, and once more, the referee called all the players together to lay the law down. But the lasting memory of this match is the winning goal, scored for Leeds by Burnley captain Alex Elder. With the score at 0–0, Elder gathered the ball near the left-hand corner flag, and from a very narrow angle, he lobbed the ball back to goalkeeper Blacklaw. Unfortunately the goalkeeper had come out of his goal, and from an almost impossible angle, Elder sent the ball soaring over Adam Blacklaw's arms into the far corner of the net. It was a truly amazing goal. It would have been a superb shot from a Leeds player; from the Burnley captain, it was incredible. But it proved to be the winning goal, and as a result Leeds managed to clinch the runners-up position behind Liverpool.

Once again, and for the fifth time in seven seasons, the Lancashire Cup came to Burnley when the Clarets beat Barrow 4–0 in the Final. But by now, it was nowhere near the achievement that it was when the club first gained the trophy in 1889. One interesting fact was that Brian Pilkington, the ex-Claret player, played in the Barrow team that night.

1966–67

By finishing third in the League the previous season, the club had qualified for the European Cities Fairs Cup; the first time since 1960–61 that Burnley had competed in a European competition. It was going to be another memorable season.

The season began in fine style as Burnley trounced Sheffield United 4–0 at Turf Moor. Harris scored a hat-trick and Irvine got the other. The team which started out on the new campaign was Blacklaw; Angus, Elder; O'Neil, Miller, Todd; Morgan, Lochhead, Irvine, Harris and Coates. That side constituted a club record by containing seven full international players, Blacklaw, Angus, Elder, Miller, Todd, Irvine and Harris. Len Kinsella made his League debut in the 3–0 win over Fulham, and altogether seven points were won from the first four games.

David Thomas had already progressed through the 'A' and 'B' teams, and he played at outside-left for the Reserves against Bury. By doing so, he became the youngest player ever to play for the Reserves, beating Tommy Lawton's thirty year old record by a few days. Sadly there was a repetition of the law of the jungle scenes when Leeds United came to Burnley, with violence both on and off the pitch. A 1–1 draw helped the Clarets to remain unbeaten and stay at the top of the table.

	Played	*Points*
Burnley	7	10
Sheff. Wed.	7	10
Chelsea	7	10
Spurs	7	10

It was then, as League leaders, that Burnley went to Stuttgart to represent England in the European Fairs Cup. Irvine scored after 17 minutes, only for the German team to equalise. Near the end, Brian O'Neil was sent off and as a result missed the return match the following week. However, in between the two games, Burnley lost their unbeaten record when they were defeated 4–1 at Old Trafford. There was quite a surprise, locally, when the news leaked out that Burnley had offered £40,000 for their old player John Connelly, but the international winger decided against returning to Turf Moor and instead he went from Manchester United to Blackburn Rovers. Andy Lochhead and Ralph Coates scored the winning goals in the return match against Stuttgart, and in the next round, Burnley found themselves drawn against Lausanne Sports of Switzerland.

Ralph Coates, now an England Under-23 international, was regularly grabbing the headlines, such as in the 5–2 drubbing of Leicester City; 'COATES—THE EXECUTIONER IN GREAT TEAM DISPLAY'. The Clarets made a further step forward in the European competition when they beat the Swiss team 3–1 in Switzerland and again 5–0 at Turf Moor. By this stage Burnley had gradually slid down the League table to a modest eighth position.

Back in Europe, Burnley the unfashionable Lancashire team were drawn in the last sixteen against A.C. Napoli, the millionaire-backed team from Italy. Napoli included players like the famed Sivori and Altafini, whilst their 50,000 season ticket holders included Sophia Loren. This Anglo-Italian Cup clash excited much anticipation in Burnley, and many fans began to make preparations to journey to Italy.

Another regular first-teamer, John Talbut, was transferred to West Brom, but he was back in Burnley the following Saturday when West Brom visited Turf Moor. It proved a sad return, because inside four minutes, John had headed into his own goal, and his old team went on to win 5–1.

But the Claret's League form was very inconsistent, and only the week before the Naples game, bottom club Newcastle United came to Turf Moor, and won their first away victory of the season, 2–0. Burnley's European hopes increased with a convincing 3–0 win over the Italians at Turf Moor, despite the expected passionate Neopolitan scenes, which included the sending off of Panzanato. About this time, rumours began to grow concerning the future at Turf Moor of players like Morgan and Irvine, but they were officially denied by the club. Indeed Willie Irvine was recalled from the Reserves for the Cup-tie against Everton at Goodison Park. It was a dramatic come-back for Willie, who scored to put his team ahead, but later in the game he broke his leg, and Burnley slid to defeat.

And so to Naples for the return match. If there had been drama in the first leg at Burnley, the scenes in Italy were almost beyond description. Passions flared both on and off the field, and there were several extremely frightening scenes in what came to be known as 'the battle of Naples'. As for the result, the Clarets came away with a 0–0 draw, thanks almost entirely to goalkeeper Harry Thomson who had a magnificent game. Not for the first time, he saved a penalty, and his performance was compared with that of Blacklaw at Rheims, six years earlier.

Now the unfancied, unfashionables from Turf Moor found themselves in the last eight, facing Eintracht of Germany, and optimism was high when Burnley, thanks to a Brian Miller goal, came away from Germany with a 1–1 draw in the first leg. But on April 18, 1967, the Claret's hopes of glory foundered when they failed miserably at home to Eintracht, 2–0.

Whilst Burnley had been involved in the European Fairs Cup,

Arthur Bellamy had been out of soccer with a broken leg, young Michael Docherty, son of a famous father, had joined the club, aged 16, and Naples had been fined £1,000 for their behaviour in the Cup game. After Eintracht had beaten the Clarets, Alex Elder was dropped 'on a matter of discipline', and he pondered his future with the club. Another stalwart, Brian Miller, unknowingly played his final game for the first team. It was against Aston Villa that Brian badly wrenched his knee, and the following week Dave Merrington took over.

After the 4–1 defeat by Arsenal at Turf Moor, Burnley travelled to Sheffield Wednesday for their final away fixture of the season, and were trounced 7–0. It was Burnley's biggest defeat for ten seasons. Once more Harry Thomson saved a penalty; he had faced five in first team games, and he had saved the lot! In the last match of 1966–67, David Thomas made his debut in the senior team—the youngest ever Burnley player to appear in Division One. At the end of the season, the Clarets finished fourteenth in the League, their lowest position for 15 years, and there were rumours that they were about to buy players, but in contrast the club announced that they were prepared to sell Adam Blacklaw and Alex Elder.

1967–68

Just before the new season kick-off, Alex Elder went to Stoke City, and Adam Blacklaw to nearby Blackburn, whilst Frank Casper had been signed during the close season from Rotherham. Burnley began with a good 2–1 win over newly promoted Coventry City, and Frank Casper scored on his debut. With Miller having retired, and Irvine making his come-back after a broken leg, the team read : Thomson; Angus, Latcham; O'Neil, Merrington, Todd; Morgan, Bellamy, Irvine, Harris and Casper.

When Martin Chivers failed to score for Southampton with a penalty, it made a record of seven out of eight penalties stopped by Harry Thomson. (Only Alan Ball had succeeded in scoring from the spot).

It was a time of transition at Turf Moor. After Casper, 19-year-old Colin Waldron of Chelsea arrived on the scene, whilst another youngster, Steve Kindon, signed on as professional in December. After Blacklaw and Elder, club captain Gordon Harris was the next player to move, when he was transferred to Sunderland for £70,000. The team was changing, and the ground was changing too. Work began on the new cricket field and stand, and for some time to come there were only three sides for spectators at Turf Moor.

The year 1968 saw new happenings in football; there were more suspensions and fines on players, and more violence off the pitch too. Willie Irvine was the next regular to join the transfer list, and Martin Dobson, quite an unknown, made his first team debut. By now, Burnley had become a very mid-table outfit, as the big city teams, United, City, Leeds, Everton and Liverpool took over at the top. But away from Division One, the prospects looked brighter for Burnley than for most other clubs, because of their youth policy. In 1967–68, it certainly paid dividends, as Burnley's Youth team beat Manchester United, Manchester City, Sheffield United and Everton to reach the Final of the F.A. Youth Cup. In the Final they were beaten in the first leg at Coventry, 2–1, but a 2–0 victory in the second leg at Turf Moor gave them the F.A. Youth Cup for the first time in their history. The team that represented Burnley was: McEvoy; Jones, Cliff; Docherty, Wrigley, West; Hartley, Probert, Brown, Thomas and Kindon.

Andy Lochhead became only the sixth player in the club's history to score a century of League goals. He followed in the footsteps of Bert Freeman, George Beel, Louis Page, Jimmy McIlroy and Ray Pointer.

But the general decline continued; five points won over Easter saved the club from relegation. The team was turning in some dreadful performances, and the 2–0 home defeat by Sheffield United, who were themselves about to be relegated was described as the club's worst show in 21 seasons in the First Division. Gates fell and sometimes they were even under the 10,000 mark.

1968–69

Transfer fees were rising rapidly, and when Willie Morgan asked for a transfer just before the start of the new season, several clubs showed interest. Leeds United made a bid of £75,000, but eventually Morgan went to Old Trafford for the £117,000 fee which United paid. The Government-inspired Chester Report described Burnley Football Club as 'a phenomenon explicable only in terms of superb management'. They were now the only Lancashire club in Division One outside the city clubs, but the fight for survival was going to get much harder.

The opening game of 1968–69 saw the Clarets come away with a point after a 2–2 draw with Nottingham Forest. The team that day read: Thomson; Angus, Latcham; O'Neil, Waldron, Merrington; Coates, Lochhead, Casper, Bellamy, Thomas. The future at Turf Moor, suggested by the large transfer fee for Willie Morgan, was underlined by the attendances at the first games that season. Burnley, who had not so long before commanded gates of 30,000, 40,000, and even occasionally 50,000 people, had a total of only 26,000 to watch the first two games against Newcastle and Southampton. The team managed to hold their own at home most games, but their away record was appalling. Steve Kindon made his debut at West Ham (0–5), and a fortnight later a return visit to London resulted in Spurs winning 7–0.

Burnley met Grimsby Town in the League Cup, and soon afterwards the Clarets signed Doug Collins from that club. What defence Burnley had in 1968 was dominated by Brian O'Neil, who scored a memorable goal in the closing minutes to give Burnley the points against Manchester United. The Collins signing was made necessary by Arthur Bellamy being injured again, this time with a broken arm, whilst at the back, John Angus was in hospital with leg trouble.

The Burnley team was christened the 'babes' when Colin Waldron, the youngest skipper in the country, was appointed club captain, and the team he led out against West Ham United read: Thomson; Smith, Latcham; Todd, Waldron, Blant; Thomas, Murray, Casper, Dobson, Kindon. The youngsters gave a grand performance as they beat West Ham, Moore, Hurst and all, 3–1, and gained ample revenge for the earlier beating at Upton Park. Ralph Coates came in for Sammy Todd, as the young Clarets repeated the formula in a 3–1 win at Stoke. In the League Cup, the Clarets made another step forward beating Leicester City 4–0. But then came the big test, when League leaders, Leeds United, who had only lost one game so far, came to Turf Moor. But the young Clarets team sent the leaders home with their tail between their legs as Burnley won easily 5–1. Jim Thomson was bought from Chelsea for a record fee for Burnley of £40,000, as the Clarets raced to their fifth successive victory, once again Leicester City. Colin Waldron and Alan Clarke clashed, and were both sent off.

Victory number six came when the Clarets beat Crystal Palace 2–0 in the League Cup, and inside a 25-day spell, the club recorded their seventh consecutive win, when they defeated Ipswich 1–0. Queens Park Rangers were the next victims going under 2–0 at Loftus Road. Of course, the run had to end sometime, and the most successful sequence since 1913 ended when Wolves took a point from Turf Moor, 1–1.

Despite this wonderful run, there was little prospect of League honours for Burnley due to so many lost points early in the season. But the club was still very much involved in the League Cup, and they had now reached the semi-final stage. In the two-leg semi-final, the Clarets were drawn against Third Division Swindon Town. Against all the odds, Swindon came to Turf Moor and won 2–1! But Burnley turned the tables in the second leg, and won 2–1 at Swindon. Changes continued to take place in the Burnley first team: veteran Andy Lochhead, the club's leading goalscorer in the sixties was transferred to Leicester for £70,000, whilst, in December, Mick Docherty made his first team debut. By then, the first team looked like: Thomson; Merrington, Latcham; Docherty, Thomas, Blant; Collins, Dobson, Casper, Todd and Kindon.

Then came the Swindon–Burnley semi-final replay at the Hawthorns, and it seemed as if Swindon were about to upset the odds again when Smith put them ahead after nine minutes. But in the very last minute, David Thomas equalised to take the game into extra time. And then in the first minute of extra time, Frank Casper seemed to administer the final blow when he put the Clarets ahead, 2–1. But it was not to be Wembley for Burnley, as first of all Arthur Bellamy put through his own goal to level the scores, and then, later on, Noble scored the winner for Swindon.

After the League Cup K.O. by Swindon, came an F.A. Cup K.O. by Liverpool. League form was very erratic. Seven goals were conceded to Manchester City, six at Leeds, four at Coventry, and five at Southampton. Sometimes the form was too bad to be true, and in the end the only team who had a worse defence record were Queen's Park Rangers (who finished bottom!).

1969–70

'It won't be easy, but the Clarets can win the fight for survival', said Keith McNee in the *Burnley Express* at the start of the new season. His words summed up the general atmosphere in Burnley; survival, rather than success. At the end of the previous season, Harry Thomson had been dismissed by the club, and new man Peter Mellor took his place as goalkeeper.

The first game was at newly promoted Derby County, and resulted in a 0–0 draw, with Frank Casper missing a penalty. The team that day was: Mellor; Angus, Latcham; O'Neil, Waldron, Todd; Thomas, Coates, Casper, Docherty and Kindon. It proved to be a very indifferent start to the new season as the club gained just three points from the first eight games. Occasionally, there was a fine result, like Liverpool 3 Burnley 3, when the Clarets after being two down came back to be ahead 3–2, but conceded an equaliser just ten minutes from time. After eight games, Burnley had still only won once, the main reason being that goals were proving difficult to come by. After 17 games, the team were only five points off the foot of the table.

Ralph Coates, who was being strongly tipped to play for England, was easily the outstanding player, despite his team's disappointing performances. Several players seemed to become restless, and Blant, Murray and Kinsella went on the transfer list at their own request. Towards Christmas 1969, the Clarets were fielding their youngest ever team in the First Division: Mellor (22), Nulty (20), Latcham (26), Docherty (19), Merrington (24), O'Neil (25), Coates (23), Thomas (19), Murray (21), Dobson (21) and Kindon (18).

If ever the writing was on the wall it was Boxing Day 1969, when Burnley were well beaten 5–1 at home by Liverpool. In February, 1970, there was a change in the 'back-room boys' as Jimmy Adamson took over as team manager, and Harry Potts moved over to become general manager.

Dave Merrington was now the club captain; John Murray went to Blackpool; Steve Kindon scored a hat-trick in Burnley's best win for over six years (5–0 v Notts Forest); Leighton James signed professional forms for the club. But what the team lacked it seemed, was experience, an 'old head' to bring a steadying and calming influence to the obvious talent that was contained in the young Burnley side. In the end, the season petered out to its usual anti-climax, with the club finishing in fourteenth position for the fourth consecutive season.

1970–71

After several run-of-the-mill seasons, there was renewed optimism in town, especially when Jimmy Adamson prophesied that Burnley would prove to be 'The Team of the Seventies'. However, things got off to a bad start even before the kick-off, when full-back Peter Jones broke a leg in training, goalkeeper Peter Mellor badly injured his shoulder, and captain Martin Dobson broke his leg in a pre-season friendly at Middlesbrough. In place of the injured Mellor, Burnley signed the ex-England and Blackpool goalkeeper Tony Waiters, from his coaching position at Liverpool. The team to represent Burnley in the opening game was: Waiters; Angus, Latcham, Bellamy, Waldron; Thomson, Thomas; Coates, Nulty, Collins and Kindon, and in a home game against Liverpool, the 'team of the seventies' began by losing 2–1. 'GRIM START STUNS FANS' ran the local headline—but events were going to get a lot grimmer.

Things didn't seem too bad when the Clarets went to Goodison Park the week afterwards, and snatched a 1–1 draw. Colin Waldron starred in defence, and as in the Liverpool game, Dave Thomas scored Burnley's goal. And then came another useful point, when the Clarets came away from Maine Road, Manchester, with a 0–0 draw.

Coupled with the several injuries, Burnley had as difficult a sequence of matches to begin a new season as any team could ever have had. The prospect of facing Liverpool, Everton (Champions), Manchester City, Manchester United, Leeds United and Chelsea (Cup holders) in rapid succession didn't ease the minds of the

Clarets fans. When United came to Turf Moor and won 2–0, Burnley found themselves next to the bottom with just two points from four games. Leeds United, with four wins in four games, came to Burnley and trounced the Clarets 3–0. There was such a big difference between the teams that day that it was obvious to all present that Leeds were going to have another great season ahead of them, while, in contrast, Burnley had a struggle on their hands. Their record now read five games without a win, and only two goals scored.

A goal-less draw against Chelsea at Turf Moor brought a little hope, but now Burnley were in the position of being grateful for solitary points won at home. 'We are *not* thinking of buying', said Jimmy Adamson, and, indeed, they sold, when Len Kinsella went to Carlisle for £10,000. Even Ipswich Town who were at the bottom of the table and hadn't won a game, trounced the Clarets 3–0.

A succession of Cup games didn't bring much happiness to anyone around Turf Moor. After managing a draw against Fourth Division Rochdale in the Lancashire Cup, the Clarets lost the replay 1–0. Against Third Division Aston Villa in the League Cup, Burnley went down 2–0, and letters began to pour into the local press. The team *did* actually win a game against Scottish side Hearts in the newly instituted Texaco Cup, but their success was short-lived as the Scottish team easily won the second leg, and so the Clarets were knocked out of that competition as well!

Rumours were rife that Ralph Coates was wanting a transfer, but these tales were stoutly denied. Another home defeat, this time 2–1 to Arsenal, landed Burnley firmly at the foot of the League table for the first time for many seasons.

	Played	*Points*
Blackpool	8	5
Ipswich	8	4
Burnley	8	3

Defeat at Derby was followed by defeat by Wolves and then the Clarets were beaten at West Ham. (This was also the first victory of the season for the Hammers, so even the other struggling teams were beating Burnley now.) Besides Jones, Mellor and Dobson, several other players had been on and off the injured list, including Merrington, Kindon, Coates, Casper, Collins, Latcham, Thomas and West. Another point came Burnley's way against Coventry, but this was rapidly followed by defeats at Liverpool and Southampton. (Brian O'Neil, who had been transferred, was playing a great part in the Saints rise up the League table.)

Never had Burnley's League position looked so desperate:

	Played	Points
Derby	14	11
Blackpool	14	8
Burnley	14	4

It was the club's worst start since the 1889–90 season, when they had not won until their eighteenth game. But in 1970, the Clarets eventually won in their fifteenth game, 2–1, against Crystal Palace. 'We will not go down now', smiled Jimmy Adamson, but there was a long, long way to go. More than a third of the season was over, and the Clarets were going adrift of the other teams in the relegation struggle. Further defeats by Spurs and Huddersfield didn't help matters either!

The team seemed to be getting younger with each match. Ex-Youth team members Eddie Cliff, Peter Jones and Alan West, had now joined their Cup-winning colleagues Dave Thomas, Steve Kindon, Mick Docherty and Eric Probert in the first team. Martin Dobson and Peter Mellor made their long-awaited return to first team football, and along with them came another promising youngster, Leighton James. A second win over fellow strugglers Nottingham Forest brought the Clarets within four points of getting off the bottom of the table

	Played	Points
Notts Forest	18	12
Blackpool	18	8
Burnley	18	8

Two points were dropped at Newcastle, but two valuable points were gained by draws against West Brom and at Stoke. This brought Blackpool and Burnley within three points of Notts Forest, and the 1–1 draw played out between the two bottom teams on Boxing Day at Bloomfield Road made the League table even more hopeful.

	Played	Points
Notts Forest	22	13
Blackpool	23	12
Burnley	23	11

That position at the end of 1970 was the nearest that the Clarets came that season to escaping from the bottom two. The second half of the season was to prove slightly more successful than the beginning (it could hardly have been worse!), but other teams near the foot of the table, Notts Forest, West Ham, and even Manchester United, were to show greatly improved form, and so widen the gap.

Burnley's first win came in October, the second in November and the third in February. They were well spread out and events to be cherished.

Second Division Oxford United sent the Clarets reeling out of the F.A. Cup, the first time since 1958, when Bristol Rovers had beaten them, that Burnley had been defeated in the Cup by a team from a lower division. A slight wave of hopefulness ran through the town when the team had a sequence of six draws in seven games, which made the League table :

	Played	*Points*
Notts Forest	24	17
West Ham	24	15
Blackpool	25	14
Burnley	25	13

'NOW TIME IS RUNNING OUT FOR CLARETS' ran the local headlines when they went down 1–0 at the Hawthorns. Meanwhile, West Ham were improving, and when they won away at Coventry, the Burnley football writer's comment sank to 'OUTLOOK WORSE THAN EVER FOR CLARETS'. The next blow came when the team went down to fellow strugglers, Nottingham Forest, which meant that Burnley had only won two out of 28 League games so far that season! 'THIS COULD BE THE BEGINNING OF THE END OF BURNLEY'S FIRST DIVISION DAYS' was the gloomy view of the *Burnley Express*. Amazingly, the Clarets drew 1–1 at Stoke, but to be fair, Stoke had half a dozen reserves playing, and now the position was so bad that the odd point made little difference. 'NOW THE END IS NEAR' commented the local press, like a relative half anticipating the death of a loved one. The players were going on to the pitch frightened of losing, the supporters were numbed and dismayed by it all, and national newspapers were holding inquiries as to how a team with Burnley's potential and natural talent should be at the foot of the Division. It seemed as if Burnley's youth policy had rebounded back at them; there were now too many youngsters in the team, and a shortage of 'old-heads' to guide them.

And then! The Clarets went and recorded their first away win, and at the same time their one and only 'double' of the season, when they beat Crystal Palace 2–0.

There were strong rumours that the club were about to buy players like John Hickton of Middlesbrough and Derek Dougan of Wolverhampton, but once again the Clarets looked towards youth for help, when they signed Paul Fletcher from Bolton Wanderers for a Burnley record transfer fee. But Paul's debut was unmemorable as Brian O'Neil and company came to Turf Moor and Southampton won 1–0.

Thanks to a Colin Waldron effort, the team won their fourth game of the season, 1–0 at Huddersfield, and Burnley found themselves off the foot of the table for the first time in months.

	Played	*Points*
Notts Forest	31	23
West Ham Utd.	32	22
Burnley	32	19
Blackpool	32	16

'TEN GAMES LEFT AND TOTTENHAM MUST BE BEATEN' said the *Burnley Express*, but they weren't! Spurs went away with a 0–0 draw. Another home point was dropped and another nail hammered into the Claret's coffin, as Burnley drew 2–2 with Ipswich. It was typical of the whole season when Colin Waldron missed a penalty, and in case anyone thinks we are being unfair, it was the team's seventh penalty miss in ten successive spot kicks!

West Ham won at Everton, and now the table read:

	Played	*Points*
Ipswich	34	27
West Ham	34	25
Burnley	34	21
Blackpool	34	17

What last remnants of respectability the Burnley fans were clinging to, were torn away when struggling Burnley went to Elland Road to meet top of the table Leeds United. The papers said at the time that it was like amateurs taking on professionals, boys tackling men, as Burnley bowed under, 4–0. Alan Clarke scored all four, and never had the gap between the all conquering city clubs and the rapidly declining town clubs, such as Burnley, looked wider.

Easter brought new hope. Paul Fletcher scored his first goal for his new club in the 1–0 victory over bottom club Blackpool, and then came another 1–0 win over fellow-strugglers, West Ham United. But it was all a flash in the Turf Moor pan, as Coventry City trounced the Clarets 3–0, and recorded Burnley's nineteenth League defeat in eight months.

'I accept the whole blame', said Jimmy Adamson as the inevitable ending to the whole nightmare season happened. Burnley F.C. were relegated to the Second Division. And there was nothing last minute about it either; goal average didn't enter into it. Burnley went to Highbury to take on championship-chasing Arsenal, with both teams needing to win their last four games desperately, for entirely opposing reasons. Arsenal won that night 1–0, and the Clarets slipped into Division Two, still with three games to play.

	Played	*Points*
Ipswich	39	32
West Ham Utd.	39	31
Burnley	39	25
Blackpool	39	19

Jimmy Adamson's pre-season promise that Burnley would be 'the Team of the Seventies' seemed all the sadder now.

Turf Moor bid farewell to the First Division, when Burnley went down to Derby County, 2–1; strangely, the Clarets recorded another away victory when they beat Chelsea 1–0 in the penultimate game, and in the season's final match, Wolves beat Burnley 1-0 at Molineux.

After 24 years and 1,008 games, Burnley were back in Division Two. And on the season's performances, there could be little argument! The same week, the inevitable happened again, when the transfer deal of Ralph Coates to Tottenham for £190,000 went through. To many Burnley fans who had hopes of an immediate return to Division One, it was a more bitter blow than relegation. Whilst sadly, the majority of people in Burnley were past caring!

TEN

WE ARE THE CHAMPIONS!

1971–72

Seeing the so-called 'Team of the Seventies' down in the Second Division, one didn't know whether to laugh or cry. Most people just tried to forget the claim, and face up to the realities of the Clarets tackling teams like Oxford, Watford and Carlisle. 'We have gone down, and it has been accepted', said Jimmy Adamson at the annual shareholders meeting. 'We shall fight back, and our target is promotion as soon as possible.' Several players were given free transfers, including former club captain, Dave Merrington who went to Bristol City, whilst Les Latcham moved to Plymouth Argyle.

The team to face Cardiff City at Ninian Park in the first game read: Waiters; Angus, Wilson, Bellamy, Waldron; Dobson, Thomas; West, Fletcher, Casper, Kindon and Dave Thomas starred in the 2–2 draw.

It was the season of the big 'clean-up football campaign' by referees, and in the League Cup-tie at Coventry, Arthur Bellamy was booked for the third time in 11 days. Besides this 'hat-trick', Kindon, Dobson, West and Waldron had also found their names in the book within the first six games! Leighton James came in for the injured Kindon against Coventry, when Burnley won 1–0. In the next League game, he scored two against Fulham, as Kindon came back as substitute. Frank Casper made a great start to the season, scoring against Luton, Preston and Cardiff, getting the winner at Coventry, and hitting a gem of a goal against Oxford. Arthur Bellamy, despite his bookings, was having a new lease of life, as he hit a hat-trick against Orient, and the winner against Q.P.R. (When the Clarets scored six against Orient, it was their highest score for seven seasons). Now the Clarets were second in the League, but ex-Claret Alan Brown (manager) and Billy Elliott (trainer) returned to Turf Moor with their team, Sunderland, and upset the promotion plans by winning 1–0 (though Waldron missed a penalty).

But big Colin made amends the next week with a fine king-pin

NAMES IN 1973. (*above left*) Skipper Martin Dobson, given a free transfer by Bolton, but in 1973 an indispensable member of the Burnley team. (*right*) Burnley's costliest player, £60,000 Paul Fletcher, came to Turf Moor from Bolton Wanderers and played an important part in the Clarets' promotion success of 1972–73. (*below*) "Taffy" Leighton James, Burnley's Welsh International forward, at full stretch in the 1973 game against Q.P.R.

FOUR POST-WAR PROBABLES (see page 189). (*above left*) Macdonald, one of the finest goalkeepers ever at Turf Moor, an England regular whose career was tragically cut short. (*right*) Coates, the idol of the Turf Moor crowd in the late 1960s. (*below left*) Cummings, who replaced Alan Brown in 1948, and played in the first team for the next fifteen seasons. (*right*) Elliott, Burnley's English International left winger who created a great impression during his short stay at Turf Moor

performance in the 1–1 draw in the League Cup-tie at Old Trafford. It was a good team performance, but the greater interest, locally, was in the League, where Norwich were gradually easing away from the other clubs in Division Two (after 12 games, they were already 5 points ahead of Burnley in sixth place). United came to Turf Moor for the League Cup replay, and after a keenly fought first half, Bobby Charlton scored the winner late on. United were fortunate not to concede a penalty soon afterwards, and as Peter Mellor still claimed he had been pushed as United scored the equaliser in the first tie, Burnley naturally felt 'robbed'.

Leighton James, when still four months short of his nineteenth birthday, became the youngest Burnley player ever to win an international cap when he played for Wales v Czechoslovakia (Elder and Irvine were 19 when they had first played for Ireland). In mid-November, Jeff Parton, aged 18, made his debut in goal in place of Peter Mellor. (He was the youngest goalkeeper since the days of Jerry Dawson.) Meantime, Tony Waiters had been on the transfer list since September, and later in the season left to become coach at Coventry.

The bottom club Watford, trained by ex-Claret Mick Buxton, shocked Burnley by a 2–1 win, and another defeat at home to struggling Swindon underlined the fact that it wasn't going to be promotion at the first attempt. Ex-Burnley players, Fred Smith, Colin Blant and 34-year-old Ray Pointer all turned out in the Pompey team which beat their old colleagues 3–1 at Turf Moor. The Clarets were now ten points off the top, and only nine places from the bottom. So much for promotion!

Struggling Huddersfield came to Turf Moor in the F.A. Cup, but they proved too good for the Clarets, winning 1–0. The defence was very much at fault, and the local paper suggested that it must be one of the most suspect and easily penetrated in the Football League. (Only the six teams at the bottom of the League had conceded more goals than Burnley). Something had to be done and quickly. And it was. Within a week, Burnley had paid £50,000 for goalkeeper Alan Stevenson from Chesterfield, with Peter Mellor going to Fulham later for £25,000.

But it wasn't a happy debut for goalkeeper Alan as Burnley went down at Orient, 1–0. Frustration was beginning to well up in the town. Relegation had been hard to accept by the fans, and now it seemed that promotion was only a distant dream. The team were losing more often than they were winning, and when Burnley went under 2–0 at home to Hull City, the fans began to demonstrate with shouts of 'Adamson out, Adamson out'. Now there was talk of Division Three, following the likes of Accrington, Bolton and

Blackburn. Supporters were disappointed when two points were lost against Luton, and when there were two more defeats over Easter at Bloomfield Road and Roker Park, frustration boiled over into anger. Jimmy Adamson needed a police escort after the 4–2 defeat at Blackpool. 'Resign, resign, resign!' shouted the fans, for now the team were only six points off relegation!

Then just as the Burnley world seemed to be coming apart came a revival. On Easter Tuesday at Charlton, the Clarets refound their form and beat the home team 3–1, thus helping to relegate them. Then came another three goals against already doomed Watford. But one swallow, or even two, doesn't make a summer, and the fans were unconvinced. Only 8,663, Burnley's lowest gate since the war, came to see the Watford game. When Eric Probert scored a gem at the County Ground to give Burnley two points at the expense of Swindon, it was their third consecutive victory, but there was no chance of promotion. High flying Millwall came to Turf Moor, and Burnley helped to keep them in the Second Division with a great 2–0 win. By now, little Billy Ingham was appearing regularly in the first team, and when Waldron was suspended, 17-year-old Billy Rodaway made his first team debut. The season ended on a high note with two more victories against Preston and Portsmouth.

Success followed success as first the club won the Lancashire Cup for the ninth time since the war, beating Manchester United 3–0, and then the following week Burnley's youth team won a five nations' International Youth Festival at Washington, Co. Durham. The squad of young Claret stars that raised local hopes for the future was: Parton, Falconer, Wilson, Flavell, McNamara, Rodaway, Morris, Brennan, Hankin, Flynn, Jones, Finn, Lewis, Milloy and Cook.

1972–73

Changes galore greeted the new season at Turf Moor. First to go was left-winger, Steve Kindon, who went to Wolves for £100,000. After 18 years in claret and blue and 438 League games, John Angus retired at 33. In his place in the back four came experienced English international, Keith Newton, released by Everton on a free transfer. Another of the senior professionals with the club, Arthur Bellamy, was transferred to Chesterfield. But the biggest news came in July, when Harry Potts and Burnley Football Club parted company, after more than twenty-five years association.

Eric Probert was injured in a pre-season friendly at Blackpool, and the team that faced Carlisle United at home in the first game read: Stevenson; Docherty, Newton, Dobson, Waldron; Thomson, Ingham; Casper, Fletcher, Thomas and James. 'We can go up,' said manager Jimmy Adamson before the start of the season, but the opening began with a tinge of disappointment, when the Clarets could only draw 2–2 with Carlisle after being twice behind. It was a somewhat shaky start. The gate, too, gave cause for concern, being only 9,804 and the lowest opening attendance at Turf Moor since the war.

Burnley met up with Peter Mellor at Fulham the next week and came away with another draw, 1–1. Newly promoted Aston Villa, came to Turf Moor, along with veteran ex-Claret Andy Lochhead. Villa were already leading the Division, whilst the Clarets were unbeaten in their last eight games. There was a good crowd, and TV was there to record the occasion. They saw the best soccer that season as the Clarets powered to a 3–1 half-time lead with Frank Casper putting the result beyond all doubt in the second half. Proud Preston were beaten the following Tuesday evening, which pushed Burnley into second place in the League table. The game was most memorable for a superb individual goal from over 20 yards by Dave Thomas. (He had been transfer listed but his appearances and goals were proving popular with local fans.) At the end of the game, the crowd once more gave Burnley a standing ovation.

Portsmouth were also among the early promotion contenders, but Burnley were the first team to beat them, winning 2–0 at Fratton Park, again with a Dave Thomas special. The club were now top of Division Two, and Jimmy Adamson was named Manager of the Month, a far different state of affairs from the 'Adamson Out' shouts six months before! A second half blitz from Leeds United shot the Clarets out of the League Cup, but already in the season, promotion was the main target.

Two more unbeaten teams clashed at Turf Moor, when Burnley (unbeaten in 11 games) met Q.P.R. (unbeaten in 17 games). Both teams extended their fine records another notch by drawing 1–1, and then another draw came in the Hull City game at Boothferry Park. Several members of the team were now playing better than they had done for some time; Doug Collins back in the number 10 jersey was making a very definite impression upon his colleagues, whilst Keith Newton was proving an outstanding asset at full back. Every game seemed to be getting harder, and it was only three minutes from time when Frank Casper scored the vital equaliser against Orient at Brisbane Road. Another near thing happened in the game at Turf Moor the next Saturday against Blackpool. Down 4–0 at one time, Blackpool pulled one back, and then two more in the last ten minutes which had the Burnley fans anxiously whistling for the final whistle. But still they all count, and after the excitement was over, the Clarets were well up there just behind the leaders, and still unbeaten. A 0–0 draw at home to Middlesbrough proved a disappointment to the Clarets fans, who came expecting victory. But it seemed as if the best performances were being reserved for the away games, and a point was gained in the 2–2 draw away to Luton. A classic downward header from Martin Dobson gave Burnley the points in the 2–1 home victory over Swindon.

	Played	*Points*
Sheff. Wed.	13	18
Burnley	12	17
Aston Villa	11	16

Well over 1,000 Burnley fans made the trip to Hillsboro' to see the top scoring League leaders, Sheffield Wednesday, play the only unbeaten team in the Football League—Burnley. It was in the eyes of many supporters *the* performance of the season as the Clarets gained a splendid 1–0 victory, with a Leighton James special that eventually became one of the goals of the season on TV. Dave Thomas was still transfer listed, and in mid-October, this troubled star left the club to go to of all places, Queens Park Rangers, who by now were among Burnley's main rivals for promotion. A reported £165,000 was paid for the talented 21-year-old, and many Burnley folk were sad to see their favourite player leave the club. And while everyone was still talking about Dave Thomas, it was his old room mate Paul Fletcher who scored a great hat-trick in the 3–0 win over Cardiff City at Turf Moor. Fletcher quietened the restless Thomas fans the next week with another important goal in the draw at Millwall.

The record was now 21 unbeaten League games, but still the average crowd at Turf Moor was only 13,000 to watch the most successful team in the country. Martin Dobson ended his Middlesbrough jinx with an 87th minute header to gain a point at Ayresome Park. Totally against the run of play, Colin Waldron scored first, but Middlesbrough hit back, one, two, three to go into a well deserved lead in front of their delirious fans. It was nearly 4–1 when John Hickton was deprived of getting a fourth only by a brilliant save by Alan Stevenson. Paul Fletcher made the score 3–2 with less than ten minutes to go, and then came 'Dobbo's' remarkable equaliser. So it was 23 League games without defeat, and the old record of Halley, Boyle'n Watson was beginning to seem highly suspect.

But pride comes before a fall. Incredibly, it was Orient, third from the bottom of the Division, without an away win to their name, who came to Turf Moor and beat the unbeatables, 2–1! Now the League position read:

	Played	*Points*
Burnley	18	25
QPR	18	23
Luton	18	22
Aston Villa	18	22

If doubts had been expressed after the Orient set-back, they were more than erased by four successive victories by the up and coming Clarets. First it was Brighton, then Notts Forest, Sunderland and Bristol City. Colin Waldron was playing at his peak, 'Dobbo' seemed to be in among the goalscorers every other week, 'Taffy' James was by now a regular Welsh international, and goalkeeper Alan Stevenson was proving one of the best ever Burnley buys.

Burnley had never beaten Oxford in League or Cup, and they failed again in December when the ever-improving United team took a point home from Turf Moor.

Harry Potts was back in football as manager of Blackpool, and by a strange twist of fate, his first game was against his old colleagues from Burnley in the Boxing Day fixture at Bloomfield Road. The game turned out as Blackpool papers later described it to be at 'gloomfield Road' for Blackpool. Frank Casper was the 'goal man' with a goal in each half and he had a fine game with Martin Dobson playing a real skipper's part. Burnley's Lancashire rivals finished the game with only nine men, Tully and Alcock being sent off in the second half.

The Clarets were still finding it easier to win points away from home than they could at Turf Moor. When they could only draw 2–2 with Fulham, and a fortunate draw at that, it meant the club had recorded four successive victories away, but only one win in the previous four games at Turf Moor. Indeed, over the season till then, Burnley had won more points away than at home.

If the victory against Sheffield Wednesday had raised hopes of promotion, and the win at Blackpool had confirmed these hopes, then the Aston Villa result surpassed all our dreams and aspirations. Over the years, was there ever a bigger graveyard of Claret hopes than Villa Park? But not this time! This was surely Burnley's finest ever performance at Villa Park, as goals by Keith Newton, Geoff Nulty and Billy Ingham convinced everyone present that surely Burnley were on their way back to Division One. 'WHO CAN STOP BURNLEY NOW?' asked the *Burnley Express.*

The following week saw the League leaders in Division One, Liverpool, visit Turf Moor to play the Second Division leaders in the third round of the Cup. The older generation recalled the first Cup meeting of the clubs in the 1914 Cup Final, whilst the younger ones remembered that ten years before, Jimmy McIlroy had played his last game as a Burnley player in a cup-tie against Liverpool. The biggest gathering of the season, some 35,730 people crushed into Turf Moor to witness yet another excellent performance by the rising Clarets. Both sides had their chances but neither team scored, and like ten years earlier, the cup-tie went to a reply at Anfield. A 56,000-crowd saw another great game, but Burnley were second best that night to the future League Champions, Liverpool. The Reds won 3–0, but the man of the match was once again Alan Stevenson. He had two saves in particular from Cormack and Lawler that stay in the memory, in a performance that had the Kop groaning in despair and roaring in appreciation at the same time.

Now, as before, all attentions were turned to the job in hand, promotion. The key game was against Q.P.R. and the Claret's unique unbeaten away record took a dive in the Loftus Road mud. Sixteen League games away from home without a defeat came to an end as the Rangers worked their way to a deserved 2–0 win. Burnley gave a dreadful first-half display the week afterwards, too, but came back to beat lowly Huddersfield 2–1. Again the following week, the Clarets seemed to be making uphill work of beating Hull City at Turf Moor, but in the second half the promotion pacemakers really showed what they were capable of, racing to a 4–1 win. At one time it seemed as if the forwards were queueing up to pepper the Hull City goalmouth. Said one paper, 'The Tigers were given a real mauling'. It was an expertly headed goal by Martin Dobson that put Burnley ahead at Carlisle but the Cumbrian team fought back for a late equaliser. But for a superb save from Alan Stevenson it could even have been 2–1. But one wonders if Alan Stevenson ever had a finer hour than in the home game against Bristol City. At times, only he and the woodwork stood between Bristol springing a surprise win against the Clarets. As it was the League leaders managed to salvage a point from a slightly disappointing home display.

Paul Fletcher scored in the first five minutes at the County Ground, Swindon, and after a stout rearguard action for the remainder of the match, the result was another two points in the bag for Burnley. Two defeats in 31 League matches had made the position at the top:

	Played	*Points*
Burnley	31	45
QPR	32	44
Fulham	31	36
Aston Villa	31	36

And just when everyone was saying that promotion was cut and dried, the Clarets lost at home to Derek Dooley's lads from Sheffield Wednesday. Still on the fringe of the promotion stakes, Wednesday held the Turf Moor side in the first half, and won in the second half, thanks to a headed goal by David Sunley. 'We have lost a battle, but we haven't lost the war yet!' said Jimmy Adamson. The attendance that afternoon was the season's best League gate at Turf Moor till then, some 16,927, but many who had come expecting to see success went home disappointed.

Two points came from struggling Cardiff, and then came a nostalgic reunion with ex-Claret Ray Pointer who was captain for the day of his team Portsmouth. But after the sentiment, it was back to business, with Burnley putting on the most scintillating 45 minutes seen for a long time at Turf Moor. With the Burnley fans roaring 'the lads' along, Nulty, Casper (2) and Fletcher responded with four goals to remember with pleasure. In the second half, Pompey came out to keep the score down to a respectable level, but the cheers at the end were all for Burnley, now just seven points off promotion. Two of those seven points came at Turf Moor four days later, when despite an early Millwall goal, Messrs Dobson and Nulty did the trick to make it 2–1 at the final whistle.

But one of the biggest upsets of the season came on the last day in March, when mid-table Nottingham Forest inflicted the heaviest League defeat of the year on the Clarets, 3–0 at Nottingham. There could be no arguments, Forest were the better team on the day and fully deserved their convincing victory.

Strangely enough, despite the incredible run of success which had only seen four defeats in 42 League games, there were still some local moaners . . . people who said the Clarets weren't good enough to go up, and if they did go up, they were not good enough to stay up. There's nowt so queer as folk! They deserved to watch a team like Preston who hadn't won since Christmas and looked bound for Division Three! Another of the teams in the relegation battle were Huddersfield Town, and it was a crucial game for both sides when the clubs met at Leeds Road the week before Easter 1973. Thousands of Burnley fans made the journey across the Pennines to see the lads from Lancashire. It wasn't the luckiest of days for Burnley when Mick Docherty was taken off on a stretcher early in the game with a bad knee injury. But Billy Ingham, coming on as usual as substitute, again proved his versatility, playing in the 'Doc's' position at full-back. Frank Casper and Paul Fletcher scored Burnley's goals in the 2–0 victory that almost doomed Huddersfield and set Burnley off on the victory road again.

The best League gate at Turf Moor that season rolled up the following Monday to witness one of the most memorable occasions in the Claret's long history. The opponents were Sunderland, who under new manager Bob Stokoe had won through to the F.A. Cup Final at Wembley. The tension spoiled what could have been a fine game. Five players were booked as Sunderland battled to the end for the two points which would have kept their faint promotion hopes alive. But the night belonged to Burnley. Paul Fletcher hooked a shot over the advancing Montgomery halfway through the first half, but still the tension remained in the game as the Clarets fans waited for the final whistle. Just before the end, Fletcher again sent the ball wide of the Sunderland goalkeeper to put everything beyond doubt. And Burnley were back in Division One! A lap of honour by the team, public salutes on the pitch by manager Adamson, singing fans and champagne in the dressing-room marked a historic evening in the story of Burnley F.C. 'My Finest Hour' said Chairman Bob Lord, as the club once again put the town on the football map.

Another important win came on Good Friday at Oxford who themselves were in with good chances of talent money. The rock hard pitch made football difficult, but a cool piece of marksmanship by Frank Casper put the Clarets ahead just before half-time, and a Billy Ingham header made sure of the points in the second half.

Easter Saturday saw the League leaders, Burnley, at home to bottom team Brighton, almost certainly doomed to drop back into Division Three. However, in the first half, Brighton more than held their own, and smarter finishing would surely have seen them ahead, but a soft goal from Leighton James, an end to end move finished off by Frank Casper, and another from skipper 'Dobbo' from a narrow angle gave Burnley their ninth goal, their fourth win and their eighth point within eight days. Two games remained and three points were needed to secure the Second Division title from challengers Queen's Park Rangers, who themselves had also confirmed their promotion place.

Easter Tuesday marked a giant step towards the title, as the Clarets turned on another superb display of attacking soccer against Luton Town. A burst of three goals in the space of ten minutes from Burnley had the 'Hatters' gasping. Leighton James, now back in his early season goalscoring form crashed in an unstoppable shot; Jim Thomas scored his first goal of the season, and Doug Collins scored his second of the season. Late in the game, 17-year-old Ray Hankin came on as substitute for his first taste of League football. As the players left the pitch after their last home game, the crowd gave the all-conquering Clarets a tremendous ovation, and not for the first time, the players responded by saluting the thousands of faithful fans.

Now the national press were raising their glasses and their hats to the East Lancashire team, whilst local papers were publishing promotion souvenirs. The players were the toast of the town as

Burnley prepared to celebrate their first major success since the title win of 1959–60. But it all had to be done yet. A point was essential at Deepdale in the final game of the season, and to make it even harder, Preston also needed a point to stay in Division Two after a desperate relegation battle since Christmas. However, there would be no 'old pals act' assured Jimmy Adamson, as anticipation mounted in the town. Not since the Clarets had had to win at Maine Road in the last match of 1959–60 had an away game aroused so much interest in the town. By one o'clock on the Saturday, there was a 100-yard queue at the turnstiles, whilst stand seats had been booked up for a week. The game promised everything, but of course there was too much at stake for both teams to make the match a classic. Backed on by a tremendous following, Burnley were well held in the first half by a desperate Preston team who fought for every ball in their last chance to survive. And Burnley paid the price of being overstretched; as their defence was caught completely out of position just before half-time, Preston went one goal ahead! And so were Queen's Park Rangers in their game at half-time. There were anxious visions of the title slipping at the last moment.

Thirty-seven minutes of the 1972–73 season remained when big Colin Waldron sent in a shot from fully 30 yards on the Burnley left flank which screamed through the packed defence and past helpless Alan Kelly into the top corner of the Preston net. 'Goal of the month? It must have been the goal of the season!', said Waldron afterwards. Now it was the Clarets who were putting on the pressure, and most of the last half hour was spent in the Preston half. But the game gradually deteriorated as Burnley players began time wasting and Preston players happily stood on watching. Burnley needed the point. Preston needed the point. After early hopes of victory, fans of both teams resigned themselves to settling for a point. And that was how it finished, 1–1, with everyone going home happy. Burnley were Champions and Preston were safe.

There were as many suggestions, whispered and shouted, of the game being fixed as there had been in 1897–98, when Burnley and Stoke had both required a point, and got it. But as long as the system is such, accusations will continue to be levelled over similar results.

'We are the Champions!', sang the players, the fans and the local press. For the first time for a decade, Burnley had more than a little to shout about. And they did! The fans hailed the Champions on May 1 when a testimonial match for long servant John Angus was held on Turf Moor. Four teams of Clarets, veterans, like Jimmy McIlroy, Brian Miller and Tommy Cummings, recently

G*

transferred Clarets like Ralph Coates, Steve Kindon and Dave Thomas, and up and coming Clarets like Bryan Flynn, Terry Pashley and Bobby Flavell brought back memories and raised future hopes at Turf Moor. But the applause and the honours of the season belonged not to those of the past, nor the future, but the stars and stalwarts of 1972–73. Alan Stevenson, Mick Docherty, Billy Ingham, Keith Newton, Martin Dobson, Colin Waldron, Jim Thomson, Geoff Nulty, Frank Casper, Paul Fletcher, Doug Collins and Leighton James.

The following week, at a civic reception held to honour the Champions, Chairman Bob Lord pledged that the club would not be content just to be members of the First Division. 'This team is quite capable of winning further honours,' said 'Lord' Bob. 'But in the meantime, " We are the Champions !" '.

ELEVEN

THE TEAM OF THE SEVENTIES?

WE SET ourselves an impossible task when we tried to compress over 90 years into about 200 pages; we could have filled an encyclopaedia with the stories and the legends, the facts and the fiction of Burnley F.C. Because of the limits of time and space, we have omitted a hundred times more than we have included.

We haven't mentioned the collier who was sentenced to a month's imprisonment for throwing a piece of clinker at an opposing player at Turf Moor in 1897; how Charlie Bates was unable to play one Saturday because his legs were badly chafed through wearing extra tight shorts the previous week! Or the time when the wind was so strong on the Turf that a Jerry Dawson goal-kick went off behind his goal for a corner! What about Lawrence the Derby goalkeeper sorting out Joe 'Andy', or the occasion when a Barnsley forward brought the whole Bee Hole end goalposts crashing down when he collided with them? Who can forget Tommy Cummings' 75-yard run when he scored against Newcastle, or Harry Thomson's goal against Chorley in the Lancashire Cup straight from his own penalty area, or . . . a thousand and more incidents that sadly have had to be left out of this book?

A book could have been devoted to the rivalry between Burnley and the Rovers, 'the old enemy', but we wanted to tell the story of the Clarets and not any ordinary Third Division team! ('And it's no nay, never, will we play Blackburn Rovers, no never again!')

Chapters could have been given to the Club's talent-scouting system, the conveyor belt of talent, and the 'football farm' at Gawthorpe, something quite unique in British football. There is a scouting system which has been the envy of League clubs for two decades. Headed by ex-Chesterfield centre-half Dave Blakey, the network covers the country and involves hundreds of people, known and unknown. And once at Burnley, a young player comes into contact with a training staff second to none, with men like Brian Miller, George Bray and Joe Brown, all ex-Clarets, with a wealth of knowledge and experience at their command. Closely linked with these men—and another key figure in the promotion season—is one of the least known of them all, physiotherapist, Jimmy Holland.

Over the years, the Club have had some tremendous service from hundreds of faithful behind the scenes workers. One can go back to the first Board of Directors which included stalwarts like Edwin Whitehead a local cotton manufacturer, Sam Thomas a mineral water manufacturer and Dick Wadge, a builder. They were followed by men of the calibre of Johnny Catlow, Jimmy Harrison and Harry Windle. The twenties saw W. E. Bracewell and E. Tate, the thirties owed a great deal to Tom Clegg and his colleagues, the forties to E. D. Kay and W. Hopkinson, and where would we be today without Bob Lord?

The first Secretary, Harry Bradshaw, was succeeded by Mr E. Mangnall who bore the whole financial responsibility during the early years of the century. Another Secretary who served the club well was Spence Whittaker, who met with a tragic death in 1910. Whilst on his way to London to register a player, Mr Whittaker fell out of the train and was killed instantly. John Haworth then took over the role of Club Secretary, and he in turn was followed by men like Albert Pickles, Alf Boland, Henry Smith and the current Secretary, Albert Maddox.

British football owes an unpayable debt to one of the sons of Burnley, Charles E. Sutcliffe. He was the 'law-giver' of association football, and for many years he worked out the League fixtures. President of the Football League, the Players' Benevolent Fund was begun in his memory. And he came from Burnley! Think, too, of another of soccer's grand old gentlemen, Jimmy Hogan. He played for Burnley 70 years ago and still lives near the Turf Moor ground. In between times he travelled the European continent, teaching the Swedes, the Austrians, the Germans and another half dozen countries how to play football. When Puskas led the 1953 Hungarians to victory at Wembley, he said, 'We owe it all to Jimmy Hogan'. A Burnley lad, Jimmy Hogan is just the same age as Burnley Football Club, now both in their 92nd year. We salute them both!

I have concentrated without apology on the players and the games of the last 91 years; that is why we haven't dwelt on the 'backroom boys' over the years. If you want to see something that does justice to these loyal servants of Burnley Football Club, these unnamed, unnumbered, unknown workers and benefactors over the years, visit Turf Moor next Saturday, and look around you.

I did set out to include a chapter on Turf Moor itself, but there was such a story there that it threatened to become another book altogether. Alas there wasn't space to record the first floodlit match in 1891, when the light was provided by 16 Wells lights, burning over 140 gallons of creosote oil in the game. The ball was constantly changed, and each new one had a fresh coat of white paint! And what about the old Star Stand which stood opposite the Brunshaw Road site until 1913. That stand cost the club £80! And how many of the real old timers remember the slope on Turf Moor? Imagine the team that won the toss choosing to play with the wind, the rain, and 'down the hill!'

And what about the lifeblood of professional football—the fans? There are those faithful thousands who used to walk to nearby towns for away games; those who have queued (remember the Cup-tie ticket queues in the early 1950's, right up on the Ridge); those who have shouted on 'the lads', notably 'The Voice', Bobby Driver, and those who to this day travel the country and spend a fortune on following the Clarets. Maybe it is because in these days of sprawling cities and impersonal communities, Burnley is still 'our town' and the Clarets are 'our team'.

Like every other football fan, I have my own opinions about different players. Whilst writing this story, many people have asked whom I believe to be the best players of all. Originally, I wrote a chapter about their qualities, but now I've condensed it into twenty lines. Four teams who are in my view, the best of a tremendous bunch. Two pre-war, and two post-war.

PRE-WAR PROBABLES. Dawson; McCluggage and Waterfield; Halley, Boyle and Watson; Bruton, Kelly, Freeman, Cross and Page.
PRE-WAR POSSIBLES. Hillman; Smelt and Taylor; Crabtree, Hill and Leake; Nesbitt, Miller, Anderson, Beel and Mosscrop.

Not a bad choice for someone who never saw any of them play! And post-war? Well, here's where I come into my own, because I've seen them all and can recall them like well loved friends.

POST-WAR PROBABLES. McDonald; Angus and Elder; Adamson, Cummings and Shannon; Connelly, McIlroy, Pointer, Coates and Elliott.
POST-WAR POSSIBLES. Blacklaw; Woodruff and Mather; Attwell, Brown and Bray; Chew, Morris, Holden, Harris and Pilkington.

And having chosen those teams, I wonder which would win if they met? I can't help remembering what happened in 1883 when the Improbables beat the Probables, 8–3!

But enough of past glories. Again we raise our glasses to the players who have brought success in the 1970s, and we look forward to future triumphs from what could well prove to be, in the words of Jimmy Adamson, 'The team of the Seventies'. Since that claim was made, Mellor, Waiters, Angus, Latcham, Bellamy, Merrington, Thomas, Coates and Kindon have all left the club. Stevenson, Newton and Fletcher have arrived at Turf Moor, whilst James and Ingham have graduated from the ranks. It would have been difficult for the management or the fans to imagine the Clarets achieving success without so many of the players who have left Turf Moor recently. But they did succeed, beyond our wildest imagination!

The season 1970–71 was a sad one for Lancashire; Burnley and Blackpool were relegated from Division One; Blackburn and Bolton from Division Two, Bury went down from Division Three, whilst Barrow failed to gain re-election in Division Four. What a change, two years later, in 1972–73 when Lancashire won all four titles, Liverpool the First, Burnley the Second, Bolton the Third and Southport the Fourth. Watch out the rest of the country, Lancashire is back at the top, and it could be that Burnley, 'the Team of the Seventies' will be leading the way.

Remember what Bob Lord said at the civic dinner given in honour of the 1973 Champions? 'This team is quite capable of winning further honours.' It wouldn't be the first time this century that Bob Lord has been able to tell the football world, 'I told you so!'

APPENDIX I

FACTS AND FIGURES

High scoring League and Cup games

1885–86	Darwen Old Wanderers 11 Burnley 0	(F.A. Cup Round 1)
1889–90	Wolves 9 Burnley 1	(Division 1)
1891–92	Burnley 9 Darwen 0	(Division 1)
1897–98	Burnley 9 Loughborough 3	(Division 2)
1903–04	Burnley 8 Keswick 0	(F.A. Cup Round 1)
1908–09	Burnley 9 Crystal Palace 0	(F.A. Cup Round 2)
1922–23	Burnley 8 Notts Forest 2	(Division 1)
1925–26	Aston Villa 10 Burnley 0	(Division 1)
1925–26	Bury 8 Burnley 1	(Division 1)
1925–26	Manchester City 8 Burnley 3	(Division 1)
1928–29	Liverpool 8 Burnley 0	(Division 1)
1928–29	Sheffield Utd 10 Burnley 0	(Division 1)
1929–30	Blackburn Rovers 8 Burnley 3	(Division 1)
1930–31	Burnley 8 Reading 1	(Division 2)
1930–31	Spurs 8 Burnley 1	(Division 2)
1956–57	Burnley 9 New Brighton 0	(F.A. Cup Round 4)
1959–60	Burnley 8 Notts Forest 0	(Division 1)
1967–68	West Brom 8 Burnley 1	(Division 1)

Longest winning sequence

Burnley had ten successive victories in 1912–13. The sequence began on November 16, 1912, when they beat Fulham. The ten consecutive League games were: Fulham, home, 5–1; Barnsley, away, 4–1; Bradford, home, 5–1; Wolves, away, 2–0; Leicester Fosse, home, 5–1; Stockport County, away, 1–0; Blackpool, home, 4–0; Glossop, away, 3–1; Clapton Orient, home, 5–0; Lincoln City, away, 3–1. The run ended when they were beaten at home by Notts Forest on January 25, 1913, by 5–3.

Longest unbeaten sequence

Between September 6, 1920, and March 26, 1921, Burnley played 30 consecutive League games without defeat.

Best home unbeaten sequence

Between March 20, 1911 (lost 3–1 to Bolton), and January 25, 1913 (lost 5–3 to Notts Forest), Burnley were unbeaten in 34 consecutive League games at Turf Moor.

Worst away sequence

Between December 7, 1901, and October 24, 1903, Burnley played 33 consecutive League games away from home without winning.

Favourite visitors?

In the last 21 League games that Aston Villa have played at Turf Moor, they haven't won once. (Their last win was 2–1 in 1936–37). Burnley haven't failed to score against Aston Villa at Turf Moor since 1919–20 (0–0). The Clarets have only failed to score twice in all the 45 Burnley v Aston Villa games played at Turf Moor. (0–2 in 1892–93 and 0–0 in 1919–20.)

Unlucky grounds?

Burnley played 20 consecutive League games away to Manchester City between 1897–98 and 1949–50 without winning one of them. (First of all at Hyde Road, later at Maine Road.) Burnley have only won once in 16 visits to Notts County for League games. They have won two in 20 League visits to Bury, 3 in 36 League visits to Sheffield United, and 7 times in 46 visits to Everton.

Lucky grounds?

Burnley have won 15 of their 34 League visits to Chelsea. They have won eight of their 20 League visits to Barnsley.

Unwelcome visitors?

Huddersfield have won eight games out of 23 League visits to Burnley. West Brom have won 18 out of 54 League visits to Burnley, whilst Newcastle have won 13 out of 41 League visits.

Highest scoring Cup run

Burnley scored 19 goals in the F.A. Cup in 1956–57. They also scored 19 goals in 1908–09 if you include the goal scored in the abandoned game with Manchester United.

Oldest player

Jerry Dawson was 38 when he made his last appearance for Burnley on Christmas Day 1928. Jack Hillman played for the first team when he was 47 in 1917–18, though only in war-time games.

Youngest player

David Thomas was 16 years and 220 days old when he made his Division One debut for Burnley (v Everton, May 13th, 1967). Tommy Lawton was slightly younger when he made his debut in 1936, but this was in Division Two.

Consecutive appearances

Jimmy Strong played in 220 consecutive League and Cup games for Burnley between August, 1946 and March, 1951.

Most League appearances

J. Dawson	522
J. Angus	438
J. McIlroy	437
T. Cummings	434
J. Adamson	425
F. Barron	399
B. Miller	379
G. Waterfield	373
W. Watson	346
J. Taylor	321
A. Blacklaw	318
G. Beel	314
H. Mather	301
B. Pilkington	300
R. Kelly	277
A. Elder	272
A. Woodruff	271
W. Bowes	268
J. Strong	264
L. Shannon	263

Leading League goalscorers

G. Beel	178
R. Pointer	118
J. McIlroy	116
L. Page	110
B. Freeman	103
A. Lochhead	101
R. Kelly	91
J. Connelly	84
W. Bowes	81
J. Robson	80
W. Irvine	78
W. Holden	75
R. Smith	74
F. Casper	69
G. Harris	69
B. Pilkington	67
J. Anderson	65
B. Cross	57
E. Hodgson	53
C. Smith	48

Record goalscorer

The highest number of goals scored in a season for Burnley was 35 by George Beel in 1927–28. Beel also has the highest aggregate of goals by any Burnley player (178). During his career at Turf Moor, he topped the Burnley goal-scorers a record six seasons.

Most players in a season

The most players to play for Burnley in the League in a season is 31 in 1936–37.

Least players in a season

The least players to play for Burnley in the League in a season is 14 in 1972–73.

Most capped player

Jimmy McIlroy gained 50 caps for Ireland while playing with Burnley. He gained four more with Stoke.

Worst Cup run

Between 1904 and 1908, Burnley played six consecutive Cup-ties without winning.

Best Cup run

Between 1913 and 1915, Burnley played 16 Cup-ties, and only lost once. (Also between 1959 and 1962, the club played 29 Cup-ties and lost only four.)

Luck of the draw

Burnley were drawn at home five times running between 1898 and 1900. Immediately afterwards, they were drawn away five times running between 1901 and 1903!

Familiar opponents

Burnley were drawn against Sunderland four times in seven seasons between 1913 and 1923.

Revenge!

The year after the 'stop the game it's snowing' match in 1909, Burnley beat Manchester United 2–0 in the F.A. Cup.

The year after Sunderland had beaten Burnley in the semi-final (1913), Burnley beat Sunderland 2–1, to go into the semi-final again.

Bolton, after being knocked out by Burnley in 1914, beat Burnley 2–1 in 1915.

Blackburn, after being knocked out by Burnley in 1959, beat Burnley 2–0 in 1960.

Goal average

Burnley finished bottom of Division Two in 1902–03 on goal average to Stockport County (0.39 against 0.53).

Burnley were relegated from Division One in 1929–30 on goal average (0.81 against 0.95 by Sheffield Utd.).

Burnley were beaten for runners-up position in Division One on goal average in 1947–48 (1.30 against 1.69 by Manchester United) and again in 1965–66 (1.68 against 2.08 by Leeds United).

Youngest referee

The youngest referee ever to control an F.A. Cup Final was Mr H. Bamlett of Gateshead, who was 32 when he took charge of the Burnley–Liverpool Final in 1914. (Mr Bamlett also refereed the famous 'stop the game it's snowing' Cup-tie in 1909.)

Penalties saved

The record number of penalties saved in a Football League match is three. W. Scott saved three for Grimsby Town against Burnley on Feb. 13, 1909. But despite his valiant efforts, Burnley still won 2–0.

Abandoned Cup-ties

Burnley have played in four abandoned Cup-ties. In 1909, against Manchester United, when Burnley were winning 1–0 (United won the replay 3–2).

In 1913, against Leeds City, when Burnley were winning 4–2. (Burnley won the replay 3–2.)

In 1956, against Bury, when it was a draw 2–2. (Burnley won the replay 1–0.)

In 1959, against Blackburn Rovers, when it was a draw 0–0. (Burnley won the replay 2–1.)

Highest League position

Champions of Division 1 in 1920–21 and 1959–60.

Lowest League position

Bottom of Division 2 out of 18 teams in 1902–03 and 19th in Division 2 in 1931–32 and 1932–33.

Most wins in a season

24 in 1959–60, 1965–66 and 1972–73.

Most draws in a season

15 in 1910–11 and 1969–70.

Most defeats in a season

22 in 1970–71.

Most goals in a season

102 in 1960–61.

Most goals against in a season

108 in 1925–26.

Least number of wins in a season

4 in 1889–90.(Lowest since 42 games is 7 in 1970–71.)

Least number of draws in a season

3 in 1888–89 and 1890–91. (Lowest since 42 games is 4 in 1953–54.)

Least number of defeats in a season

2 in 1897–98. (Lowest number since 42 games is 4 in 1972–73.)

Lowest goals for in a season

29 in 1970–71.

Lowest goals against in a season

24 in 1897–98. (Lowest since 42 games is 29 in 1946–47.)

Most points in a season

62 in 1972–73.

Least points in a season

13 in 1889–90. (Lowest since 42 games is 27 in 1970–71.)

* * *

The following played for Burnley in the years 1882–88, (from the date of the club's foundation to the beginning of the League). It is by no means a complete list, but I hope it is fairly representative of those many pioneers of football in Burnley, who played in the early years.

Some of those listed may only have played in a few games, but certainly others totalled several hundred games in the Burnley colours. Unfortunately no records were kept of player's appearances in those far-off days, and I have only been able to compile this list from newspapers of the time.

Abrahams
Arthurs
R. Beattie
A. Birley
H. Bradshaw
W. Brown
T. Bryce
Bury
Caulfield
R. B. Chase
J. Crabtree
Crawford
T. Cross
H. Culpan
Eastwood
D. Friel
Fulton
J. Gair
W. Gair
P. Gallocher
S. Hargreaves
Harper
J. W. Holden
Hunter
J. Keenan
Kennedy
A. Lang
W. R. Lathom
McConnell
R. McCrae
W. McFetteridge
A. McLintock
J. McNee
J. Marsland
L. Metcalfe
T. Midgeley
J. Murtagh
Poland
Ronaldson
Shiel
F. Slater
Strachan
F. Sugg
C. E. Sutcliffe
Taylor
G. C. Waddington
S. Waddington
H. Walton
D. Waugh
Whitehead
Whiteside
J. Wigglesworth
Woods

APPENDIX 2

LEAGUE APPEARANCES AND GOALSCORERS
(1888–89 to 1972–73 inclusive)

Minimum of 50 appearances and/or 20 goals

Player	*First Season*	*Last Season*	*Appearances*	*Goals*
Abbott, W.	1908–09	1909–10	57	16
Anderson, J.	1919–20	1923–24	121	65
Adams, E. F.	1935–36	1938–39	112	–
Attwell, R. F.	1946–47	1954–55	245	9
Aird, J.	1949–50	1954–55	132	–
Adamson, J.	1950–51	1963–64	425	17
Angus, J.	1956–57	1971–72	438	3
Bowes, W.	1890–91	1900–01	268	81
Barron, F.	1898–99	1910–11	399	13
Bannister, W.	1899–1900	1901–02	50	4
Bell, A. A.	1902–03	1908–09	101	28
Bamford, T. F.	1909–10	1914–15	137	–
Boyle, T. W.	1911–12	1921–22	210	36
Basnett, A.	1919–20	1926–27	147	5
Beel, G. W.	1922–23	1931–32	314	178
Bruton, J.	1924–25	1929–30	167	42
Brown, J.	1927–28	1934–35	228	6
Bowsher, S. J.	1928–29	1932–33	82	2
Bellis, G. A.	1932–33	1934–35	95	–
Brown, G.	1934–35	1935–36	35	24
Brocklebank, R. E.	1935–36	1938–39	121	33
Billingham, J.	1938–39	1948–49	91	35
Bray, G.	1938–39	1951–52	241	8
Brown, A.	1946–47	1948–49	88	–
Blacklaw, A.	1956–57	1966–67	318	–
Bellamy, A.	1962–63	1971–72	206	30
Crabtree, J. W.	1889–90	1894–95	74	10
Cretney, J.	1905–06	1910–11	168	6
Cross, B.	1920–21	1927–28	237	57
Conway, H.	1930–31	1933–34	81	–
Chester, T. H.	1936–37	1938–39	52	1
Chew, J.	1946–47	1953–54	226	40
Cummings, T. S.	1948–49	1962–63	434	3
Cheeseborough, A.	1951–52	1958–59	142	36
Connelly, J.	1956–57	1963–64	215	84
Coates, R.	1964–65	1970–71	215	26
Casper, F.	1967–68	–	215	69
Collins, D.	1968–69	–	81	11

Player	*First Season*	*Last Season*	*Appearances*	*Goals*
Davidson, J.	1895–96	1901–02	66	7
Dixon, A.	1901–02	1906–07	173	7
Dawson, J.	1906–07	1928–29	522	–
Devine, J.	1925–26	1929–30	114	28
Dougal, W.	1925–26	1927–28	60	2
Down, W.	1927–28	1929–30	80	–
Douglas, T.	1933–34	1934–35	55	13
Downes, P.	1934–35	1935–36	61	6
Dobson, M.	1967–68	–	177	38
Docherty, M.	1968–69	–	125	–
Espie, J.	1891–92	1895–96	96	10
Elliott, W. H.	1951–52	1952–53	74	14
Elder, A.	1959–60	1966–67	272	9
Freeman, B. C.	1910–11	1920–21	166	103
Freeman, A.	1922–23	1928–29	78	19
Forrest, A.	1927–28	1932–33	109	4
Fletcher, C. A.	1935–36	1937–38	62	22
Fletcher, P.	1970–71	–	91	26
Green, W. J.	1903–04	1908–09	147	–
Green, B. H.	1909–10	1910–11	71	28
Gray, W. P.	1953–54	1956–57	119	30
Hill, J.	1889–90	1896–97	151	39
Hillman, J.	1891–92	1901–02	175	–
Hogan, J. C.	1901–02	1904–05	93	27
Harris, J.	1910–11	1911–12	57	5
Hodgson, E.	1911–12	1914–15	121	53
Halley, G.	1912–13	1921–22	135	4
Hill, J. H.	1923–24	1928–29	184	13
Hancock, E.	1932–33	1936–37	111	24
Hetherington, T. B.	1933–34	1936–37	67	–
Hornby, R.	1934–35	1947–48	123	15
Hubbick, H.	1935–36	1936–37	59	1
Harrison, R. W.	1946–47	1949–50	62	20
Hays, C. J.	1946–47	1950–51	146	12
Holden, W.	1950–51	1955–56	187	75
Harris, G. H.	1958–59	1967–68	257	69
Irvine, W.	1962–63	1967–68	124	78
Jenkinson, W.	1898–99	1903–04	50	14
Jones, C.	1912–13	1921–22	82	–
Jenkins, E. T.	1930–31	1931–32	66	15
Jones, T. W.	1930–31	1933–34	95	24
Johnson, R. E.	1934–35	1948–49	78	–
Joyce, W.	1960–61	1963–64	70	3
James, L.	1970–71	–	81	18
Keenan, J.	1888–89	1892–93	72	–
Kelly, R. F.	1913–14	1925–26	277	91
Kindon, S.	1968–69	1971–72	102	28

Player	*First Season*	*Last Season*	*Appearances*	*Goals*
Lambie, C.	1889–90	1901–02	29	27
Lang, A.	1888–89	1893–94	123	2
Livingstone, A. L.	1892–93	1899–1900	169	3
Lockhart, G.	1900–01	1902–03	92	–
Leake, A.	1907–08	1909–10	82	2
Lindley, R.	1908–09	1919–20	138	43
Lomas, W.	1909–10	1910–11	36	21
Lindsay, J.	1914–15	1922–23	73	18
Loughran, J.	1946–47	1949–50	65	–
Lochhead, A.	1960–61	1968–69	225	101
Latcham, L.	1964–65	1970–71	149	10
Morrison, T.	1893–94	1906–07	180	27
Moffat, H.	1903–04	1910–11	201	12
Mayson, T.	1907–08	1911–12	67	15
Morley, J. B.	1908–09	1911–12	96	18
Mosscrop, E.	1912–13	1922–23	176	19
Mantle, J.	1927–28	1930–31	51	22
Miller, W. R.	1936–37	1938–39	73	18
Martindale, L.	1937–38	1950–51	69	2
Morris, W.	1938–39	1953–54	211	46
Mather, H.	1946–47	1954–55	301	–
Miller, B. G.	1955–56	1966–67	379	30
Morgan, W.	1962–63	1967–68	183	19
Merrington, D.	1964–65	1970–71	97	1
Mellor, P.	1969–70	1971–72	69	–
McFetteridge, W.	1888–89	1892–93	84	1
McLintock, T.	1893–94	1901–02	235	13
McFarlane, D.	1903–04	1907–08	122	31
McLaren, W.	1910–11	1913–14	63	–
McCluggage, A.	1925–26	1930–31	204	22
McIlroy, J.	1950–51	1962–63	437	116
McDonald, C.	1953–54	1958–59	186	–
McKay, P. W.	1954–55	1956–57	60	35
Nichol, T. H.	1890–91	1898–99	144	43
Nesbitt, W.	1911–12	1922–23	172	18
Newlands, D. H.	1954–55	1958–59	98	21
Nulty, G.	1969–70	–	78	11
O'Dowd, P.	1929–30	1931–32	65	8
O'Neil, B.	1962–63	1969–70	231	22
Place, W. Snr.	1890–91	1899–1900	143	9
Place, W. Jnr.	1894–95	1898–99	139	26
Parkin, G.	1923–24	1928–29	125	2
Page, L. A.	1925–26	1931–32	250	110
Prest, T. W.	1929–30	1934–35	79	15
Potts, H.	1946–47	1950–51	165	47
Pilkington, B.	1952–53	1960–61	300	67
Pointer, R.	1957–58	1964–65	223	118
Probert, E.	1968–69	–	62	11
Reynolds, J.	1895–96	1899–1900	109	1

Player	*First Season*	*Last Season*	*Appearances*	*Goals*
Ross, J. D.	1896–97	1898–99	51	34
Ross, H.	1899–1900	1903–04	104	3
Reid, R.	1910–11	1913–14	84	–
Roberts, W. T.	1924–25	1925–26	49	28
Richmond, G.	1932–33	1938–39	175	1
Robinson, A.	1933–34	1938–39	204	8
Rayner, F.	1934–35	1938–39	79	7
Rudman, H.	1946–47	1956–57	71	–
Robson, J.	1956–57	1964–65	203	80
Stewart, A.	1889–90	1892–93	55	10
Smith, R.	1904–05	1909–10	175	74
Smith, A.	1905–06	1908–09	105	20
Smethams, C.	1907–08	1909–10	60	4
Swift, H.	1909–10	1912–13	64	2
Smelt, L.	1919–20	1924–25	229	–
Steel, J.	1925–26	1930–31	145	5
Sommerville, G.	1926–27	1931–32	118	–
Storer, H.	1928–29	1930–31	51	5
Smith, C.	1932–33	1935–36	107	48
Scott, R. A.	1933–34	1935–36	57	–
Smith, W.	1933–34	1938–39	82	–
Strong, G. J.	1946–47	1952–53	264	–
Shannon, L.	1949–50	1958–59	263	39
Stephenson, R.	1949–50	1955–56	77	27
Seith, R.	1953–54	1959–60	211	6
Smith, D. B.	1954–55	1960–61	100	1
Smith, F.	1963–64	1969–70	84	1
Stevenson, A.	1971–72	–	59	–
Turnbull, P.	1892–93	1894–95	46	21
Taylor, J.	1894–95	1906–07	321	11
Tatham, W.	1895–96	1900–01	53	–
Toman, W.	1896–97	1898–99	63	36
Taylor, D.	1911–12	1923–24	221	6
Thorpe, L.	1913–14	1919–20	72	3
Thompson, D.	1952–53	1954–55	62	–
Talbut, J.	1958–59	1966–67	138	–
Todd, S.	1963–64	1969–70	108	1
Thomson, H.	1964–65	1968–69	117	–
Thomas, D.	1966–67	1972–73	153	19
Thomson, J. S.	1968–69	–	88	2
Walders, D.	1903–04	1905–06	96	2
Whittaker, T.	1906–07	1908–09	59	22
Watson, W.	1908–09	1924–25	346	18
Weaver, W.	1919–20	1924–25	106	16
Waterfield, G. S.	1923–24	1934–35	373	3
Willighan, T.	1929–30	1933–34	59	–
Wallace, T. H.	1933–34	1935–36	61	1
Woodruff, A.	1936–37	1951–52	271	–
Winton, G. D.	1951–52	1958–59	182	1
Waldron, C.	1967–68	–	193	10

APPENDIX 3

SUMMARY OF FOOTBALL LEAGUE RECORD

Season	P.	W.	D.	L.	Goals For	Goals Agst.	Points	Position	Division
1888–89	22	7	3	12	42	62	17	9th	One
89–90	22	4	5	13	36	65	13	11th	One
90–91	22	9	3	10	52	63	21	8th	One
91–92	26	11	4	11	49	45	26	7th	One
92–93	30	13	4	13	51	44	30	6th	One
93–94	30	15	4	11	61	51	34	5th	One
94–95	30	11	4	15	44	56	26	9th	One
95–96	30	10	7	13	48	44	27	10th	One
96–97	30	6	7	17	43	61	19	16th	One
97–98	30	20	8	2	80	24	48	1st	Two
98–99	34	15	9	10	45	47	39	3rd	One
1899–1900	34	11	5	18	34	54	27	17th	One
1900–1901	34	20	4	10	53	29	44	3rd	Two
01–02	34	10	10	14	41	45	30	9th	Two
02–03	34	6	8	20	30	77	20	18th	Two
03–04	34	15	9	10	50	55	39	5th	Two
04–05	34	12	6	16	43	52	30	11th	Two
05–06	38	15	8	15	42	53	38	9th	Two
06–07	38	17	6	15	62	47	40	7th	Two
07–08	38	20	6	12	67	50	46	7th	Two
08–09	38	13	7	18	51	58	33	14th	Two
09–10	38	14	6	18	62	61	34	14th	Two
10–11	38	13	15	10	45	45	41	8th	Two
11–12	38	22	8	8	77	41	52	3rd	Two
12–13	38	21	8	9	88	53	50	2nd	Two
13–14	38	12	12	14	61	53	36	12th	One
14–15	38	18	7	13	61	47	43	4th	One
19–20	42	21	9	12	65	59	51	2nd	One
20–21	42	23	13	6	79	36	59	1st	One
21–22	42	22	5	15	72	54	49	3rd	One
22–23	42	16	6	20	58	59	38	15th	One
23–24	42	12	12	18	55	60	36	17th	One
24–25	42	11	12	19	46	75	34	19th	One
25–26	42	13	10	19	85	108	36	20th	One
26–27	42	19	9	14	91	80	47	5th	One
27–28	42	16	7	19	82	98	39	19th	One
28–29	42	15	8	19	81	103	38	19th	One
29–30	42	14	8	20	79	97	36	21st	One

Season	P.	W.	D.	L.	Goals For	Goals Agst.	Points	Position	Division
30–31	42	17	11	14	81	77	45	8th	Two
31–32	42	13	9	20	59	87	35	19th	Two
32–33	42	11	14	17	67	79	36	19th	Two
33–34	42	18	6	18	60	72	42	13th	Two
34–35	42	16	9	17	63	73	41	12th	Two
35–36	42	12	13	17	50	59	37	15th	Two
36–37	42	16	10	16	57	61	42	13th	Two
37–38	42	17	10	15	54	54	44	6th	Two
38–39	42	15	9	18	50	56	39	14th	Two
46–47	42	22	14	6	65	29	58	2nd	Two
47–48	42	20	12	10	56	43	52	3rd	One
48–49	42	12	14	16	43	50	38	15th	One
49–50	42	16	13	13	40	40	45	10th	One
50–51	42	14	14	14	48	43	42	10th	One
51–52	42	15	10	17	56	63	40	14th	One
52–53	42	18	12	12	67	52	48	6th	One
53–54	42	21	4	17	78	67	46	7th	One
54–55	42	17	9	16	51	48	43	10th	One
55–56	42	18	8	16	64	54	44	7th	One
56–57	42	18	10	14	56	50	46	7th	One
57–58	42	21	5	16	80	74	47	6th	One
58–59	42	19	10	13	81	70	48	7th	One
59–60	42	24	7	11	85	61	55	1st	One
60–61	42	22	7	13	102	77	51	4th	One
61–62	42	21	11	10	101	67	53	2nd	One
62–63	42	22	10	10	78	57	54	3rd	One
63–64	42	17	10	15	71	64	44	9th	One
64–65	42	16	10	16	70	70	42	12th	One
65–66	42	24	7	11	79	47	55	3rd	One
66–67	42	15	9	18	66	76	39	14th	One
67–68	42	14	10	18	64	71	38	14th	One
68–69	42	15	9	18	55	82	39	14th	One
69–70	42	12	15	15	56	61	39	14th	One
70–71	42	7	13	22	29	63	27	21st	One
71–72	42	20	6	16	70	55	46	7th	Two
72–73	42	24	14	4	72	35	62	1st	Two

Totals:

Played	2,864
Won	1,161
Drawn	646
Lost	1,057
Goals For	4,535
Goals Against	4,398
Points	2,968

APPENDIX 4

INTERNATIONAL CAPS WON BY BURNLEY F.C. PLAYERS

(Up to May 1973)

For England

Angus, J.	1961 v Austria
Bannister, W.	1901 v Wales
Boyle, T. W.	1913 v Ireland
Bruton, J.	1928 v France, Belgium. 1929 v Scotland
Coates, R.	1970 v Ireland. 1971 v Greece*
Connelly, J.	1960 v Wales, Ireland, Scotland, Sweden
	1962 v Wales, Austria, Switzerland, Portugal
	1963 v Wales, France
Crabtree, J. W.	1894 v Ireland. 1895 v Ireland, Scotland
Dawson, J.	1922 v Scotland, Ireland
Elliott, W.	1952 v Italy, Austria. 1953 v Ireland, Wales, Belgium
Freeman, B.	1912 v Scotland, Wales, Ireland
Harris, G.	1966 v Poland
Hill, J. H.	1925 v Wales. 1926 v Scotland
	1927 v Scotland, Ireland, Belgium, France
	1928 v Wales, Scotland
Hillman, J.	1899 v Ireland
Kelly, R.	1920 v Scotland. 1921 v Scotland, Wales, Ireland
	1922 v Scotland, Wales. 1923 v Scotland. 1924 v Ireland
	1925 v Scotland, Wales, Ireland. 1926 v Wales
McDonald, C.	1958 v Russia (3), Brazil, Austria
	1959 v Wales, Ireland, Russia
Miller, B.	1961 v Austria
Mosscrop, E.	1914 v Scotland, Wales
Page, L.	1927 v Scotland, Wales, Belgium, Luxembourg, France
	1928 v Wales, Ireland
Pilkington	1955 v Ireland
Pointer, R.	1962 v Wales, Luxemburg, Portugal
Waterfield, G.	1927 v Wales
Watson, W.	1913 v Scotland. 1914 v Ireland
	1920 v Ireland (v Wales in a Victory Int.)
Yates, J.	1889 v Ireland
	* = Substitute

For Wales

Bowsher, S.	1929 v Ireland
James, L.	1971 v Czechoslovakia, Rumania
	1972 v Scotland, England
	1973 v England (2), Poland, Scotland, Ireland
Morris, W.	1947 v Ireland (1946 v Ireland in a Victory Int.)
	1949 v England
	1952 v Scotland, Ireland, Rest of U.K.

For Scotland

Aird, J.	1954 v Norway (2), Austria, Uruguay
Blacklaw, A.	1963 v Norway, Spain. 1966 v Poland
Morgan, W.	1968 v Ireland

For Ireland

Elder, A.	1960 v Wales
	1961 v England, Scotland, Wales, Greece, W. Germany (2)
	1962 v England, Scotland, Greece
	1963 v England, Scotland, Wales, Spain, Portugal (2)
	1964 v Wales, Uruguay
	1965 v England, Scotland, Wales, Albania, Holland (2), Switzerland (2)
	1966 v England, Scotland, Wales, Albania
	1967 v England, Scotland, Wales, Mexico
Emerson, W.	1922 v Wales
	1923 v England, Wales, Scotland
	1924 v England
Flack, H.	1929 v Scotland
Irvine, W.	1963 v Wales, Spain
	1965 v Wales, Scotland, Switz., Albania, Holland (2)
	1966 v Scotland, England, Wales, Albania
	1967 v England, Scotland, Mexico
	1968 v England, Wales
McCluggage, A.	1927 v Scotland, Wales
	1928 v England, Scotland, Wales
	1929 v England, Scotland, Wales
	1930 v Wales
	1931 v England, Wales
McIlroy, J.	1952 v England, Scotland, Wales
	1953 v England, Scotland, Wales
	1954 v England, Scotland, Wales
	1955 v England, Scotland, Wales
	1956 v England, Scotland, Wales
	1957 v England, Scotland, Wales, Portugal (2), Italy
	1958 v England, Scotland, Wales, Italy, France, Czechoslovakia (2), West Germany, Argentina
	1959 v England, Scotland, Wales, Spain
	1960 v England, Scotland, Wales
	1961 v England, Wales, West Germany (2), Greece
	1962 v England, Scotland, Greece, Holland
	1963 v England, Scotland, Poland (2)
Morrison, T.	1899 v Wales
	1900 v Wales
	1902 v England, Scotland
Todd, S.	1967 v England
	1968 v Wales
	1969 v England, Scotland, Wales
	1970 v Scotland, Russia
Willighan, T.	1933 v Wales
	1934 v Scotland

PLAYERS WINNING FOOTBALL LEAGUE XI REPRESENTATIVE HONOURS

J. W. Crabtree	1893–94 v Scottish League, Irish League
	1894–95 v Scottish League
J. Hillman	1898–99 v Scottish League
	1899–1900 v Irish League
W. Toman	1898–99 v Scottish League
W. Bannister	1900–01 v Scottish League
J. Dawson	1909–10 v Scottish League
	1910–11 v Scottish League
	1921–22 v Scottish League, Irish League
T. W. Boyle	1911–12 v Scottish League
	1912–13 v Scottish League
	1913–14 v Scottish League
H. Moffatt	1909–10 v Southern League
B. C. Freeman	1911–12 v Scottish League
	1912–13 v Irish League
	1913–14 v Irish League
E. Hodgson	1913–14 v Scottish League
E. Mosscrop	1913–14 v Scottish League
W. Watson	1913–14 v Irish League
	1914–15 v Irish League, Southern League
	1919–20 v Irish League
	1921–22 v Irish League
R. Kelly	1919–20 v Scottish League
	1920–21 v Scottish League
	1921–22 v Scottish League
	1923–24 v Scottish League, Irish League
	1924–25 v Scottish League, Irish League
J. H. Hill	1923–24 v Scottish League
	1924–25 v Scottish League
	1925–26 v Scottish League
B. Cross	1922–23 v Irish League
	1926–27 v Scottish League
J. Bruton	1928–29 v Irish League
L. Page	1929–30 v Irish League
A. Robinson	1934–35 v Irish League
	1935–36 v Irish League
F. P. Kippax	1946–47 v Scottish League, Irish League
A. Woodruff	1946–47 v Lge. of Ireland
	1947–48 v Irish League
A. Brown	1947–48 v Irish League
R. Attwell	1948–49 v Scottish League
T. Cummings	1950–51 v Irish League
W. H. Elliott	1952–53 v Scottish League, Irish League, Lge. of Ireland
C. A. McDonald	1957–58 v Scottish League
	1958–59 v Irish League, Lge. of Ireland
B. Pilkington	1958–59 v Scottish League
J. Connelly	1959–60 v Irish League, Lge. of Ireland
	1960–61 v Irish League
	1961–62 v Lge. of Ireland, Irish League, Italian League
	1962–63 v Italian League

J. Angus	1960–61 v Irish League
J. Adamson	1960–61 v Irish League
J. McIlroy	1960–61 v Irish League, Italian League
R. Pointer	1961–62 v Lge. of Ireland, Italian League
B. Miller	1961–62 v Irish League, Scottish League
G. H. Harris	1961–62 v Irish League
	1965–66 v Lge. of Ireland
B. O'Neil	1965–66 v Lge. of Ireland
R. Coates	1968–69 v Scottish League
	1969–70 v Scottish League
	1970–71 v Scottish League, Irish League
F. Casper	1968–69 v Scottish League

PLAYERS GAINING 'B' INTERNATIONAL HONOURS

For England 'B'

L. Shannon	1951–52 v France
	1953–54 v Germany
	1955–56 v Scotland
J. Adamson	1952–53 v Scotland
T. Cummings	1952–53 v Scotland
	1955–56 v Scotland, Switzerland
W. Holden	1952–53 v Scotland
B. Pilkington	1953–54 v Scotland
	1956–57 v Scotland

For Scotland 'B'

J. Aird	1952–53 v England
	1953–54 v England
G. D. Winton	1956–57 v England

For Ireland 'B'

W. Marshall	1957–58 v Rumania
	1959–60 v France
W. Wilson	1957–58 v Rumania
A. Elder	1959–60 v France

PLAYERS IN UNDER 23 INTERNATIONALS

For England

A. Cheeseborough	1956–57 v France
R. Pointer	1958–59 v Italy, and for Young England v England
	1959–60 v Hungary, East Germany, Poland, Israel
J. Angus	1958–59 v West Germany
	1959–60 v East Germany, Poland, Israel
	1960–61 v Wales, Italy, Denmark, and for Young England v England
	1961–62 v Scotland
J. Robson	1958–59 v West Germany
	1960–61 v For Young England v England
B. Miller	1959–60 v East Germany, Poland, Israel
J. Connelly	1960–61 v Italy
G. Harris	1960–61 v For Young England v England
	1961–62 v Israel
	1962–63 v Yugoslavia
J. Talbut	1963–64 v Wales, West Germany, Scotland, France, Hungary, Israel, Turkey, and for Young England v England

B. O'Neil	1965–66 v Turkey
R. Coates	1966–67 v Wales, Greece, Bulgaria, Turkey
	1968–69 v Holland (2), Portugal, Belgium
D. Thomas	1969–70 v Scotland, Bulgaria
	1970–71 v West Germany, Sweden, Wales
	1971–72 v Scotland, East Germany, Switzerland
M. Dobson	1969–70 v Bulgaria
A. West	1971–72 v Wales
A. Stevenson	1971–72 v Wales
	1972–73 v Netherlands, Scotland, Czechoslovakia
For Scotland	
A. Blacklaw	1959–60 v Wales, England
A. Lochhead	1962–63 v Wales
For Ireland	
W. Irvine	1962–63 v Wales
	1963–64 v Wales
	1964–65 v Wales
A. Elder	1963–64 v Wales
S. Todd	1964–65 v Wales
	1966–67 v Wales
	1967–68 v Wales
For Wales	
J. Parton	1971–72 v England, Scotland
L. James	1971–72 v England, Scotland
	1972–73 v England, Scotland

PLAYERS IN OTHER INTERNATIONALS

For Great Britain	
J. McIlroy	1955–56 v Rest of Europe
Charity Shield	
For F.A. XI	
J. Robson	1961 v Tottenham Hotspurs
Canadian Tour Cap	
P. O'Dowd	1931

AMATEUR INTERNATIONALS

For England	
A. A. Bell	1907 v Netherlands
	1908 v Wales, Netherlands
For Great Britain	
(Olympic Games 1948)	
F. P. Kippax	1948 v Holland, France, Yugoslavia